The Turnaround Mindset

Aligning Leadership for Student Success

The Turnaround Mindset

Aligning Leadership for Student Success

Tierney Temple Fairchild, Ph.D.
Jo Lynne DeMary, Ed.D.

Foreword by
U.S. Senator Mark R. Warner,
former Governor of Virginia

ROWMAN & LITTLEFIELD EDUCATION

A division of

ROWMAN & LITTLEFIELD PUBLISHERS, INC.
Lanham • New York • Toronto • Plymouth, UK

Published by Rowman & Littlefield Education
A division of Rowman & Littlefield Publishers, Inc.
A wholly owned subsidiary of The Rowman & Littlefield Publishing Group, Inc.
4501 Forbes Boulevard, Suite 200, Lanham, Maryland 20706
http://www.rowmaneducation.com

Estover Road, Plymouth PL6 7PY, United Kingdom

Copyright © 2011 by Tierney Temple Fairchild and Jo Lynne DeMary

All rights reserved. No part of this book may be reproduced in any form or by any electronic or mechanical means, including information storage and retrieval systems, without written permission from the publisher, except by a reviewer who may quote passages in a review.

British Library Cataloguing in Publication Information Available

Library of Congress Cataloging-in-Publication Data

Fairchild, Tierney Temple, 1967–
 The turnaround mindset : aligning leadership for student success / Tierney Temple Fairchild and Jo Lynne DeMary.
   p. cm.
 Includes index.
 Summary: "This book provides a valuable balance between what one must know and what one must do to turn around low-performing schools. The 3-E framework simplifies this complex process by focusing resources on the environment, the executive, and the execution of the turnaround plan. A set of case studies on individuals who have led successful turnarounds of schools gives life to the theoretical concepts"—Provided by publisher.
 ISBN 978-1-60709-043-4 (hardback) — ISBN 978-1-60709-044-1 (paper) — ISBN 978-1-60709-045-8 (electronic)
 1. School improvement programs—United States. 2. School improvement programs—United States—Case studies. I. DeMary, Jo Lynne, 1946– II. Title.
 LB2822.82.F35 2011
 371.2'07—dc22   2011006080

∞™ The paper used in this publication meets the minimum requirements of American National Standard for Information Sciences—Permanence of Paper for Printed Library Materials, ANSI/NISO Z39.48-1992.

Printed in the United States of America

To Greg, Naia, Cole, and Jude,
who love and inspire me.

—TTF

To Tony, my best friend and love of my life.

—JLD

Contents

Acknowledgments		ix
Foreword: U.S. Senator Mark R. Warner, Former Governor of the Commonwealth of Virginia		xi
Introduction		xiii

SECTION I ENGAGING IN TURNAROUND LEADERSHIP

Chapter 1	The National Landscape	3
Chapter 2	Approaches to Turnaround	19
Chapter 3	Understanding Turnarounds: Research Highlights	39

SECTION II A CRITICAL PATH TO SCHOOL TURNAROUNDS

Chapter 4	Approaching Turnarounds with a 2-S Model: Systems and Stakeholders	65
Chapter 5	The 3Es of School Turnarounds: Environment, Executive, and Execution	81
Chapter 6	Leveraging Management Tools	107

SECTION III TURNAROUND LEADERSHIP IN ACTION

Chapter 7	Consistency and Compassion in the Face of Chaos Ms. Aretha Eldridge-Williams at Kate Middleton Elementary School (Gretna, LA)	123

viii   Contents

Chapter 8	Systems, Structures, and a Spatula: Building a Community of Scholars Ms. Camille Wallin at P.S. 42—Claremont Community School (Bronx, NY)	143
Chapter 9	Walking in a Turnaround Leader's Shoes: Believing is Achieving Ms. J. Harrison Coleman at Fred M. Lynn Middle School (Woodbridge, VA)	163
Chapter 10	Inspiring Success through Student and Teacher Empowerment Ms. Tanya John at the High School for Violin and Dance (Bronx, NY)	181

SECTION IV POLICY ESSENTIALS FOR TURNAROUND LEADERS

| Chapter 11 | Policy Imperatives to Bring Turnarounds to Scale | 201 |

Appendixes

Appendix A	*A Nation at Risk*: Factors for Urgency	227
Appendix B	Resources on School Turnarounds	229
Appendix C	Memorandum of Understanding Sample	231
Appendix D	Turnaround Specialist Endorsement, State of Louisiana	237
Appendix E	90 Day Strategic Plan #1 and #2, Kate Middleton Elementary School	239
Appendix F	St. Helena Central High School Balanced Scorecard Sample	245
Appendx G	Communications Plan Template for Turnaround Initiative	249
Appendix H	Turnaround Readiness Sequence Template for Program Planning and Execution	251

References	253
Index	265
About the Authors	269

Acknowledgments

We would like to acknowledge the wonderful teachers, principals, and other educators we met in the course of writing this book. They were willing to tell their stories so that others might learn and benefit from their experiences. We would like to express our tremendous admiration and appreciation to the following turnaround specialists and the dedicated and knowledgeable teams of professionals supporting them in the work they do each and every day on behalf of young people: Aretha Eldridge-Williams (Jefferson Parish Public Schools, LA), Camille Wallin (New York City Public Schools, NY), J. Harrison-Coleman (Prince William Public Schools. VA), and Tanya John (New York City Public Schools, NY).

We would like to extend our thanks to Senator Mark Warner for starting this conversation in the first place and for challenging us to think differently about addressing the needs of our lowest performing schools. His leadership as Governor of Virginia gave both of us an opportunity to experience firsthand the optimism and the obstacles associated with designing and implementing a school turnaround specialist program.

Many thanks to our extremely competent research associate Jamie Deaton for his attention to detail and his valuable suggestions for improving the manuscript. We appreciate extern Sheron Carter-Gunter for lending her wealth of experience as a practitioner to our work and Daisy Lovelace and the educators who helped hone our research and give voice to the ideas in this text.

We feel fortunate to have been able to draw on our experiences with a diverse group of thought leaders committed to leadership excellence from the corporate, education, philanthropic, and policy arenas. Special thanks to our colleagues at the University of Virginia and Virginia Commonwealth University for their interest and support and to the hard-working individuals at the Virginia Department of Education and the Louisiana Department of Education who are focused on improving schools and closing gaps in student achievement. We are most appreciative to EduLead and its co-director Dr. Tom Shields who worked with us in Louisiana. We value the ideas and useful lessons provided by the Wallace Foundation and the investments it has made in turnaround development and to the many innovative entities and individuals that share our urgency for and commitment to ensuring all students have the opportunity to reach their potentials.

We'd like to thank our families who have endured what, at times, seemed to be an endless journey. Their encouragement and humor sustained us when it seemed easier to quit.

Finally, we'd like to acknowledge the thousands of young people who are the victims of our failure to teach all young people to high standards. They will continue to struggle with the challenges of poverty and discrimination each day unless we are willing to confront the issues before us.

Foreword

As an entrepreneur and venture capitalist before I was elected Governor of Virginia, it was not unusual for me to suggest that tools of the business world could be relevant in government and public education. However, it was a huge experiment for me to suggest the application of business skills and practices to address the challenge of chronically underperforming schools by creating an entirely new category of educators: an individual with the training and the tools to come into a struggling school and try to turn it around.

While the turnaround specialist is widely used in business to identify and correct problems to make faltering companies profitable, it seemed oddly strange in 2004 to welcome the first cohort of ten Virginia school leaders being trained at the University of Virginia to use business skills to turn problem schools around. At the time, there was no other university model in the nation of a graduate business school working with an education school to provide the leadership skills that could help turn schools around. Thus began the Governor's Virginia School Turnaround Specialist Program (VSTSP) taught through the Darden and Curry Schools at UVa in close collaboration with the Virginia Department of Education.

I was serious about improving schools so that Virginia's children could get the educational opportunities to which they were entitled. I was willing to propose increased compensation and school-based autonomy for these change agents who achieved results in chronically low-performing schools. As the CEO of the school, not unlike the CEO of a company, there are often unpopular and bold decisions that are required of turnaround specialists in schools. In most cases, those of us in positions of authority have to clear the way for these actions and support decisions even when it would be easier to intervene.

That is why it is exciting to find Tierney Temple Fairchild and Jo Lynne DeMary collaborating on this book about turnaround leadership. As executive director of the Darden/Curry Partnership for Leaders in Education in 2004 with a PhD from Curry and an MBA from Darden, Tierney did a masterful job of designing a model that combined business and education strategies with on-site coaching and a results-oriented credential. As the state superintendent of public instruction during my administration as Governor, Jo Lynne DeMary partnered with me on dozens of innovative educational initiatives that ultimately produced positive results on student achievement. However, her passion for and personal oversight of the VSTSP were evident.

I also salute the ten dedicated educators from all corners of Virginia who were the first participants in this Governor's initiative. These professionals studied the characteristics of high-performing organizations, analyzed their own low-performing schools, and came up with a turnaround plan to make those schools successful: ten people who were willing to take a chance on a Governor's desire to shake things up to impact student achievement.

As a U.S. Senator, I recognize that across this nation there are many examples of schools in some of our most challenging communities that are being led by courageous and highly skilled principals similar to those noted in the case studies in this book. But, sadly, there are not enough.

We need more school leadership programs that develop cadres of experts who become credentialed as Turnaround Specialists, and we need to unleash their skills and passion in service to these deserving young people through enhanced autonomy.

This book creates a common sense approach that blends research and tools from the public and private sectors and highlights leaders with a proven track record. University programs devoted to principal leadership preparation need to compare the content of their programs with the subject matter of this book. The same would hold true for foundations making heavy investments in reform, and districts and states serious about tackling student achievement in their lowest performing schools. *Turnaround Leadership* needs to be happening all across America.

U.S. Senator Mark R. Warner

Introduction

Turn on the television and you might catch an American Express commercial featuring turnaround expert Geoffrey Canada. Founder of the Harlem Children's Zone, Canada has led a transformation of one well-known but underserved neighborhood in New York City. His story, told in Paul Tough's *Whatever it Takes* (2008), chronicles his philosophies, research-based practices, and results. It's the transformation not only of schools but also of a community.

Turnaround experts in business have been around for years. In education, and public schooling in particular, these leaders are less well known, even though the urgency for their success couldn't be more pressing. Education and business entities in communities are on parallel paths, inextricably linked, and yet, only rarely are they able to leverage their assets, tools and talents effectively against some of our nation's most urgent problems.

This book approaches turnaround leadership in schools as a growing and essential subspecialty of the principalship. It draws from our research and experiences as two practitioner scholars, both having worked in academia yet finding our most rewarding experiences in direct service to public education, whether in the private or public sectors.

Our experiences are dichotomous—a forty-year education bureaucrat at the pinnacle of her career and an MBA-trained, public education reformer fresh from a decade in corporate America. Thrust together by a Governor CEO, a successful businessman intent on bringing accountability and turnaround expertise to Virginia's public schools, we found common ground in the urgency of chronic underperformance and the application of management principles to leadership development.

From these efforts, the Virginia School Turnaround Specialist Program and the University of Virginia's Darden/Curry Partnership for Leaders in

Education were borne. Microsoft's Partners in Learning program invested $3M in our vision for developing turnaround executives for public schools. The Wallace Foundation committed its resources as well, bringing the rigor and high quality of executive development afforded to business professionals not only to principals but also to district and state education leaders.

Fast forward five years and our work takes us to Louisiana, where we built on Virginia's model and, as consultants, created a blueprint for training turnaround specialist principals in a state that seems to experience more than its fair share of economic and personal hardship. We researched, reflected, visited schools, engaged stakeholders, and conferred with colleagues to hone our understanding of what makes and sustains turnarounds. Finding that critical path to turning around struggling schools is vital, and Louisiana's state leadership has embraced the promise of developing turnaround leaders with the skills necessary to do this difficult work.

This book is a stakeholder's guide to turnarounds in schools. It is our hope that leaders in all domains of public schooling—administrators, unions, education and elected officials, corporate partners, parents, community organizations and others—will find it useful. Organized as a primer on school turnarounds, it paints a picture of what turnaround leaders face and points to organizations and leaders that are making turnarounds happen. Throughout the text we leverage business principles and tools that we have seen work in turnarounds, and we don't shy away from discussing thorny issues like race and class that confound the leadership challenge.

The book is organized into four sections. Section I discusses how public educators are engaging in turnarounds. In chapter 1, we describe the national landscape for school turnarounds, including the challenges turnaround leaders face and the long history of education reform that has supported and hampered turnarounds in schools. In chapter 2, we offer a neighborhood of approaches to school turnarounds highlighting national examples of structural and human capital investments. Chapter 3 provides a brief literature review on turnarounds, drawn from management and education research.

In Section II, we outline a critical path to school turnaround. Chapter 4 presents our 2-S model for approaching school turnarounds. Here, we posit that taking a systems approach and engaging multiple stakeholders are essential underpinnings of turnaround leadership. Chapter 5 offers a 3Es framework for leading turnarounds in schools: preparing the environment, developing the executive, and focusing on execution.

In chapter 6, we discuss how leaders can leverage management tools to facilitate school turnarounds. We highlight existing tools like the 90-day plan and the balanced scorecard and discuss how they can provide transparency and accelerate improvements. We then present two new tools, the Communications Plan and the Turnaround Value Chain we developed from our own research and experience. Adapted from business concepts, these tools underscore the importance of carefully attending to the key stakeholders and essential components that drive high-quality teaching and learning.

The third section offers case studies of turnaround leaders in action. We feature four cases of turnaround specialists with compelling stories to show the possibility of turnarounds. These four leaders, two elementary, one middle, and one high school principal, offer clear examples of dramatic transformation in the face of tremendous hardship and turmoil. These cases feature leaders specially trained for their charge, underscoring that turnaround leaders embrace a set of competencies that differ from peers in higher performing environments. While the cases are school-based, they also demonstrate that turnarounds cannot be isolated at the school level; they require consideration and supports from a variety of stakeholders and policy actors.

In the final section, we turn our attention to matters of policy. Turnarounds, we argue, can never become the specialized field they need to be, one that delivers the dramatic results expected, if policy changes do not follow. The final chapter presents a set of policy imperatives we deem essential to furthering the field of turnaround leadership in schools. Scalability of the field is crucial if the dramatic gains required are to be achieved and sustained.

Given the complexity of achieving and sustaining turnaround, it is important to underscore that turnarounds simply cannot occur at scale without changing critical influences at the district and other levels. Systems and stakeholders matter. Also noteworthy is the fact that *The Turnaround Mindset* is not just for leaders of chronically underperforming or high poverty schools. Pockets of schools or students within schools in many thriving communities may benefit from turnaround leadership.

We hope the research and ideas presented in the chapters ahead are informative to many stakeholders that are currently engaged in—or seek to be involved in—turning around chronically underperforming schools. We intended to be balanced in our approach, drawing from the private and public sectors, charters and public schools, leaders at all levels. We hope our ideas will generate meaningful debate and dialogue. We intend to honor all those engaged in this difficult work, and spur on many more to join in so that we can ensure that all students have access to the talented teachers and thriving schools they deserve.

Section I

Engaging in Turnaround Leadership

Chapter 1

The National Landscape

A crisis is looming. The top management team of a large urban school district sits around the conference room table at central office headquarters. These seasoned school executives pour over mounds of data, noting the troublesome results for a number of their schools. Graduation rates hover at 56 percent while 3rd grade reading scores have marked steady improvement for the last five years. Yet, by 8th grade those gains have all but disappeared and the exodus in 9th grade is clear.

The district looks for root causes, examines demographic and socioeconomic changes, the leadership and teacher turnover. A restless community awaits news of improvement. There is some good news, but many schools are still failing large numbers of students.

Sadly, this scenario is no longer surprising to most educators. So many have been pursuing education reform for decades that some believe the system is irreparable. Others have walked away in frustration, disgust, disenfranchisement and disbelief, battle weary from political tug-of-wars that seem oddly adult- rather than student-centered. New, fresh eyes come in, yet few stay long enough to see a demonstrable or sustainable impact.

Fortunately, many continue to dig in. They remain committed to seeking new strategies and ideas to meet the needs of their communities. They are undeterred by changing winds of politics, economic uncertainty, or changing demographics of their schools. They focus on equity and pursue excellence for all students. They connect school with community, teacher with student, school district and state, administrator with policymaker, practitioner and researcher, all in the name of improved student learning.

Yet, this crisis has been simmering—even boiling—for decades. Like the proverbial frog that slowly dies in the simmering pot, this nation can't "jump out" unscathed by the scars of failed efforts to educate all children and challenge them at high levels. Recent history points to the complexity of the problems and the demand for new strategies; and it underscores the urgency of improvement.

SCHOOL TURNAROUNDS: A MORAL IMPERATIVE

All, regardless of race or class or economic status, are entitled to a fair chance and to the tools for developing their individual powers of mind and spirit to the utmost. This promise means that all children by virtue of their own efforts, competently guided, can hope to attain the mature and informed judgment needed to secure gainful employment, and to manage their own lives, thereby serving not only their own interests but also the progress of society itself.

—*Nation at Risk*, 1983

The "crisis" in public education is not a new topic of conversation in the United States. In 1957, the launch of Russian rocket Sputnik nearly brought U.S. public education to its knees as educators across the nation faced the grim reality that American technological preeminence and scientific acumen were being eclipsed by a Cold War threat. The United States was on the defensive and the education of its youth, especially math and science preparation, was under the microscope.

Few indicators could pinpoint the exact problems. The National Assessment of Educational Progress (NAEP) and the Trends in International Mathematics and Science Study (TIMMS)[1] were years, even decades away. At this time, most nationally reported data on schools focused on the cost of education, including "input" variables like per-pupil expenditures, attendance, and teacher salaries. It wasn't until U.S. Commissioner of Education Francis Keppel (1962–1965) spearheaded a focus on assessing educational outputs (i.e., student learning) that the federal government and legislators pursued a better way to gauge the progress being made in U.S. education.[2]

International competitiveness was at stake as the Soviet Union, as it was known then, successfully launched and orbited a satellite the size of a beach ball around the earth. Just a few years later, President Kennedy challenged Americans to put a man on the moon. The "Space Race" had begun.

Yet, this educational angst went well beyond science classrooms in those years. A different "race" was making the news. Three years earlier, a landmark Supreme Court ruling had shaken some schools across the country to the core. *Brown v. Board of Education* (1954) exposed inequalities in the "separate but equal" system that the *Plessy v. Fergusen* (1896) decision set up sixty years earlier. The *Brown* decision had effectively ended *de jure* segregation in the nation's schools and universities.

The Civil Rights Movement ushered in a turbulent era that struck at the heart of public education and its mission of providing a free and appropriate education to all students. Race riots destroyed urban centers in the north and south. Parents who grew up in segregated America, on the back of the bus, at "colored" water fountains, and in separate schools had persevered to see the dawn of a new day, one that changed opportunities for their children.

Integration stood on strong legal footing but shaky and highly charged emotional ground. The Massive Resistance Movement in Virginia, for instance, led by Senator Harry S. Byrd, Sr., went so far as to close public schools and educate white students in homes and churches to avoid having white children and black children attend school together.

The fabric of what many people knew and expected for their children was being torn apart. The same year Sputnik threatened America's military dominance, a small group of African American parents in Little Rock, Arkansas needed military protection for their children enrolled at Little Rock Central High School. On September 4, 1957, the "Little Rock Nine," as they came to be known, were prevented from entering their school. Twenty days later President Eisenhower intervened over Governor Orval Faubus' resistance, ordering the 101st Airborne Division of the United States Army to the capital city to ensure the students' safety.

The students successfully entered the school on September 25th, but inside they were taunted, teased, and threatened. David Halberstam recounts this struggle in his 1993 book *The Fifties*.[3] He writes, "The mob was no longer a problem, but inside the school there was a systematic and extremely well organized assault upon the nine children by high-school-age segregationists. They not only harassed the black children but, more effectively, any white child who was courteous or friendly to them" (p. 688).

Halberstam goes on to describe how the black students were treated.

> The nine students were in for a very hard and ugly year. There was a relentless assault upon them—kicking, tripping, hitting them from behind, harassing them with verbal epithets as they walked down the hall, pouring hot soup on them in the cafeteria. Their lockers were broken into regularly, their books stolen. The school administrators knew who the ringleaders were but found them boastfully proud. (p. 688)

During those years and throughout the 1960s and 1970s, racial tensions ran deep in many schools, not only those in the South. Desegregation orders in Boston, among other cities, led to racial riots and white flight to the suburbs.

Property tax revenues and consumer spending fled with these residents, leaving the urban blight and its more diverse and less affluent populations behind.

During this same period, Americans were fighting in Vietnam, a war that claimed the lives of nearly 60,000 U.S. citizens, most of whom were under 22 years old and enlisted men.[4] Those in college and graduate school could take a deferment. The country was uneasy with the changes at home and the challenges abroad. Leaders died. There was a pervasive distrust of government, for on top of racial tensions and protests over the Vietnam War President Richard Nixon had resigned in disgrace over the Watergate tapings. The economy spiraled downward in the mid-1970s and while poverty rates dropped to the lowest recorded rate of 11.1 percent (and have since stayed below 15 percent), millions of children and families—disproportionately of color—still faced economic and education challenges.[5]

Given the social, economic, and military crises with which Americans wrestled during this period, it's not surprising that educational progress suffered. In 1983, the now famous *A Nation at Risk* report, commissioned by President Ronald Reagan, delivered a scathing review of the state of public education. The commission cited a number of reasons for the urgency for action. These factors included international comparisons of achievement; rates of functional illiteracy among adults; high school achievement; achievement of gifted students compared to tested abilities; declines in Scholastic Aptitude Test (SAT) scores; decreasing levels of science achievement; and the increasing need for remediation coursework. (For a more complete listing, see Appendix A.)[6]

Driven in large part by economic urgency, *A Nation at Risk* became a touch point for education reform. The report cited the increasing loss of manufacturing jobs; the growing influence of computers in our daily lives; and the fact that technology was changing the way people did their jobs across a variety of occupations from health care to construction. Again, international competitiveness was at stake.

More than twenty-five years after *A Nation at Risk* shattered the Lake Woebegone–like belief that all American children and their schools are above average, the United States continues to confront chronic underperformance in an alarming number of schools. The story is not new, and, if the past is any predictor of the future, intended reforms and innovations may also spur unintended consequences, some which accelerate performance, some which surface new challenges. As this brief history lesson underscores, unpredictable forces in the national and global environment and political economy may hasten, delay, or impede educational progress as well as mitigate reform efforts.

Gains have been made, but it is difficult to imagine reaching the No Child Left Behind (NCLB) law's 2014 goal of 100 percent proficiency. Examining the Nation's Report Card—results from the National Assessment of

Education Progress (NAEP)—it is clear that increases in achievement have occurred for different demographic groups.

The National Assessment of Educational Progress (NAEP), the nation's "yardstick" on how students are fairing in public, private, and parochial schools across the nation, gives educators, legislators, policymakers, parents and other stakeholders a picture of how well states are educating their students. It offers the only consistent measure to evaluate how well students are doing in schools across the nation. The NAEP Long-Term Trend (LTT) Assessment in reading was first administered in 1971 and for mathematics in 1973. It is given every four years to a sample of 9-, 13-, and 17-year-olds to represent the nation and provides results to give a picture of how performance has changed in the United States over time.[7]

In 2008, the most recent assessment for instance, all three age groups tested showed significant gains since 2004 for reading.[8] Looking back to 1971, students have made 12-point and 4-point gains in reading scores in the 9- and 13-year-old age groups, respectively. Yet, 17-year-olds' scores were not significantly different than those in 1971 (Rampey, Dion, and Donahue, 2009).

Similarly, mathematics scores showed significant gains in the younger two age groups in 2004 but no significant changes at the 17-year-old level. Comparing 2008 to 1973, the first year of available data, average scores were up 24 and 15 points, respectively, for 9- and 13-year-olds. Again, there was no significant change in the 17-year-old scores.

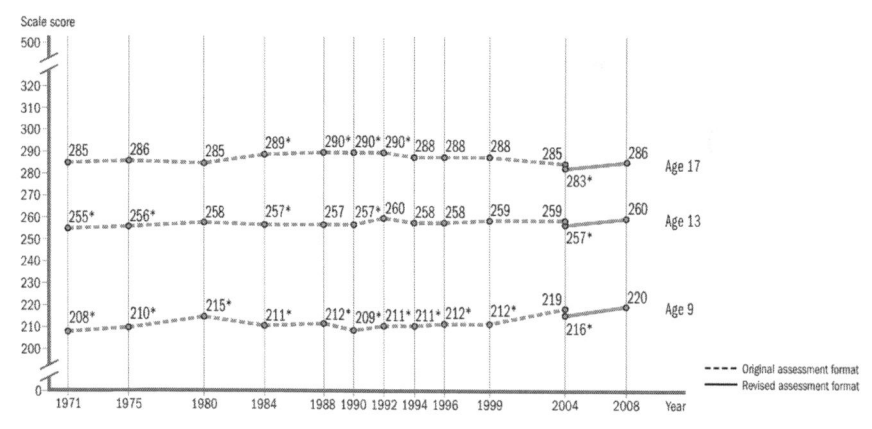

Figure 1.1. NAEP trends—reading. Trend in NAEP reading average scores for 9-, 13-, and 17-year-old students.
*Significantly different (p<.05) from 2008.
Source: U.S. Department of Education, Institute of Education Sciences, National Center for Education Statistics, National Assessment of Educational Progress (NAEP), various years, 1971–2008 Long-Term Trend Reading Assessments.

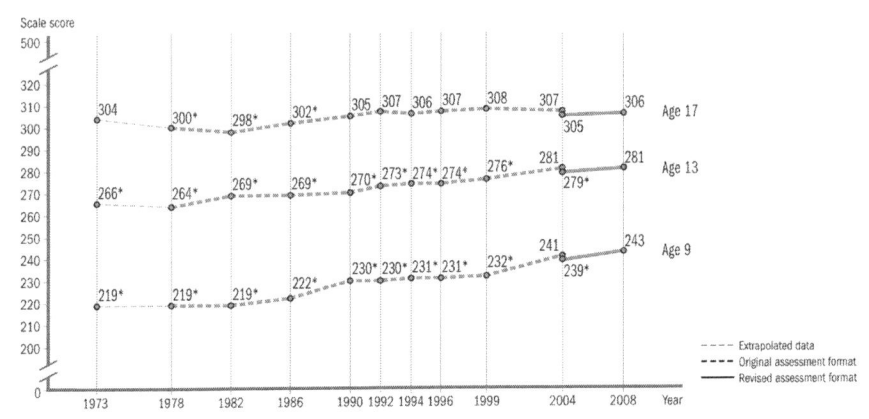

Figure 1.2. NAEP trends—mathematics. Trend in NAEP mathematics average scores for 9-, 13-, and 17-year-old students.
*Significantly different (p<.05) from 2008.
Source: U.S. Department of Education, Institute of Education Sciences, National Center for Education Statistics, National Assessment of Educational Progress (NAEP), various years, 1973–2008 Long-Term Trend Reading Assessments.

Achievement gaps, especially in reading and mathematics, remain a troubling fixture in national scores. NAEP scores, for instance, show no significant narrowing between 2004 and 2008 for either subject, despite some significant improvements since the 1970s.[9] Black students, for instance, have made greater gains in reading in all three age groups (34, 25, and 28 points, respectively) than white peers that posted gains of 14, 7, and 4, respectively. Likewise, a larger percentage of 17-year-olds in 2008 reported taking advanced mathematics courses, including calculus, pre-calculus, and trigonometry, than in 1978.

Examining what looks like a relatively flat if slightly positive trend line leads to a few burning questions for those employing turnaround strategies in schools. Why haven't 17-year-olds showed significant improvements since the early 1970s? What would it take for gaps to close precipitously and dramatically? And just what kind of progress might our trend lines show if the current focus on turnarounds is successful?

Even as progress toward educating all students at high levels seems unacceptably slow, some technological advances have facilitated the tracking and use of student achievement data to improve instruction. Online technology offers innumerable ways of monitoring performance, and while it is not always easy to compare schools with similar data because of differing state accountability systems, sources like the Institute of Education Sciences and its National Center for Educational Statistics offer evidenced-based practices and longitudinal data across subgroups to create transparency that is accessible to the public. The key is finding apples-to-apples comparisons, and knowing what is being measured and where to find it.

In the 1980s, personal computers were barely reaching the mass market, and mainframes still processed achievement data that took months to analyze and assemble. A principal's or superintendent's ability to use the data was at best cumbersome and certainly not timely. States didn't have standards by which to measure "what students know and are able to do." Teachers and principals generally were rated as either satisfactory or unsatisfactory under the watchful eye of unions. Unless visible, the need for turnaround may not have been evident for years.

Fortunately, even though far too many schools continue to under-serve their students, important questions can be better answered with more fluid and nimble technology that has changed the way data can be analyzed and reported. Growth testing, for instance, allows students to be regularly tested on their skills and knowledge to see what individual growth has occurred across content strands that meet state education standards. Armed with these and other interim data, savvy teachers can challenge, remediate, or group students to optimize learning and growth.

Technology and data collection also have helped make the dropout crisis more transparent. Ten years ago, for instance, few schools had a handle on what might be called the "enrollment gap" between the students that come to the school in 9th grade and those that graduate in 12th. Now, schools calculate dropout rates in multiple ways,—"event dropout rates," "status dropout rates," and "cohort drop out rates"—in an effort to be more accurate and consistent. The cohort dropout rate is considered the most accurate. A recent national analysis of longitudinal data found that at least 20 percent of 8th graders dropped out at some point during their high school career.[10]

According to the 2009 Graduation Counts survey, 22 states calculate and publicly report a dropout rate, with most using the cohort dropout rate. Because it is based on longitudinal data, the cohort rate is the most accurate means of characterizing the dropout problem. Unfortunately, many states cannot report a cohort dropout rate because they do not yet have adequate longitudinal data systems.[11]

We now know, however, that a number of high schools—serving a disproportionate number of students of color and students in poverty—have been labeled "drop out factories."[12] This designation refers to approximately 2,000 high schools or technical schools where no more than 60 percent of the freshman students make it to their senior year. District leaders may have missed the data, ignored it, or simply failed to track students leaving school between 9th and 10th grades (upwards of 50 percent at some schools), presumably because it was not a required measure.

Similarly, reading levels of 9th graders may also not have been measured, resulting in a lack of understanding that a host of students may have been reading not just below grade level but at levels they should have mastered in elementary school. One conclusion that may be drawn from what appears to be educational neglect is that it is difficult to know what to fix if you don't measure it.

Today, data warehouses, the Internet, sophisticated testing programs, growth measures, state standards, and numerous foundations and associations tracking data have made information more publicly accessible and readily usable to improve instruction. While too many schools and parents still live on the other side of the "digital divide,"[13] making access more challenging, information access and the speed of technology only promises to improve over time. Some skill is still required to gain access to the data—to know where to look for it, how to interpret it, and, at the classroom or building level, how to use it to strengthen instructional practices. The amount, availability, and relevance of data is exponentially different from twenty-five years ago (as will be the case twenty-five years from now).

With such access and analysis, the ability at least to diagnose the need for turnaround should be much more rapid. Many independent think tanks now publish reports that offer detailed analysis of these data, and the Council for Chief State School Officers houses a free national searchable database[14] by which parents and the larger community can easily benchmark their schools against like others. Whereas before we needed to commission a report to surface signs of educational distress, today schools needing turnaround leaders can be readily identified by any interested stakeholder.

State databases track and mine data such that parents can readily access data about their child's school. Even some school and district websites incorporate a level of transparency and easy-to-read trend data on student performance data and other indicators like discipline, and student and teacher attendance. Each city school's website in Philadelphia, for instance, displays colorful charts that show performance trends that clearly illustrate progress, stagnation, or decline.

When examined in isolation, the current state of education is especially bleak for only certain Americans.

> Nationwide, 7,000 students drop out every day and only about 70 percent of students graduate from high school with a regular high school diploma. Two thousand high schools in the U.S. produce more than half of all dropouts and a recent study suggests that in the 50 largest cities, only 53 percent of students graduate on time. Research shows that poor and minority children attend these so-called "dropout factories"—the 2,000 schools that produce more than 50 percent of our nation's dropouts—at significantly higher rates. (Committee on Education and Labor Press Release, May 12, 2009.)[15]

Yet, the disproportional impact on poor and minority families has far-reaching economic consequences. Edward E. Gordon, writing for the Association for Career and Technical Education, noted the following in September 2009.

Between 2010 and 2020 it is estimated that the United States will lack the qualified talent to fill anywhere from 12 to 24 million essential jobs throughout our economy. These same talent shortages are beginning to appear around the world. Soon 75 percent of all U.S. jobs will demand far higher entry-level qualifications, *i.e.*, a good liberal arts education plus postsecondary career-specific technical skills. (Gordon, p. 29)[16]

Many sources of data—achievement gaps, dropout rates, college completion to name a few—indicate the need for dramatic change. In the 2009–2010 school year, 5,017 schools were placed in the No Child Left Behind (NCLB) category of "restructuring," which requires schools to choose among various intervention options directed toward comprehensive change. This number has more than doubled from 2008, and nearly two thousand more schools in the "corrective action" stage of NCLB are at risk of being put into restructuring in 2011 if improvements are not made.[17] Performance pressure can be felt from the student's to the superintendent's desks. However, many states and districts continue to pursue programmatic versus structural improvements (Mead, 2007).

With the number of schools in restructuring on the rise and an administration eager to address the bottom 5 percent, a growing number of states and major cities are making policy and program changes to assist these underperforming schools. At the same time, the 2009 American Recovery and Reinvestment Act (ARRA) cites "turnaround" as one of several intervention strategies available to the estimated 5,000 schools in distress. "When a school continues to perform in the bottom five percent of the state and isn't showing signs of growth or has graduation rates below 60 percent, something dramatic needs to be done," Secretary Duncan said in announcing these grants.[18]

The case for turnaround is especially strong in light of achievement gaps between groups and considering the economic impact on society. Management consulting giant McKinsey & Company's Social Sector Office (2009) analyzed achievement data across different groups and found significant international, income, race, and system gaps.[19] Notable findings include:

- Seventeen countries have higher test scores and lower income-based inequality than the United States.
- Neighboring states like Oklahoma and Arkansas, or Maryland and Delaware with similar overall test scores on the National Assessment of Educational Progress (NAEP) can have large black-white achievement gap differences.
- Black and Latino students are noticeably absent from "advanced" level achievement, forming a "top gap" such that less than 3 percent of black and

Latino students score in the advanced level in reading and math, a percentage that erodes to 1 percent by 12th grade.
- Students from low socioeconomic backgrounds start behind their well-resourced peers, and that gap continues through college.
- Poor white students in Alabama (the lowest-performing state for low-SES whites) still outperform poor black students in Texas (the highest-performing state for low-income blacks).
- Variations between states and between schools exists but there is actually more variation *within* schools, which speaks to the influence of quality teaching.
- Districts with similar demographics, like poverty levels and racial composition, can consistently produce different levels of achievement and dropout rates.

Unraveling achievement gaps requires not only a nuanced understanding of data but also an appreciation for the cultural milieu, political environments, racial and economic histories, as well as the stereotypes and implicit biases that may underpin the results. On the one hand, problems that have festered for years may not be easily—or readily—tackled. On the other hand, scores of programs, interventions, and resources may have been poured into a school or district with limited success.

And yet, the McKinsey report concludes, "The wide variation in performance among schools serving similar students suggests that these gaps can be closed. Race and poverty are not destiny" (p. 6). Armed with these data, states, districts, and individual schools can begin to make choices for their students. They can examine the potential causes of the gaps and benchmark similar districts that outperform them. They can raise expectations and adapt and implement strategies to change current performance.

The bottom line is student achievement. That is the immediate goal. The long-range goal, however, is a more active and engaged citizenry, one that innovates and solves local and global problems. In a democracy embracing free market capitalism, the costs of not solving these problems quickly are dear. McKinsey posited, "These educational gaps impose on the United States the economic equivalent of a permanent national recession" (p. 5). Trillions of dollars are lost when capable minds are underutilized. Productivity and, as McKinsey estimated, the nation's GDP (gross domestic product), will improve as gaps are closed.

If ever there were a time to employ turnaround strategies in schools, this era may be it. With billions of dollars being infused through competitive processes, schools have many more tools available to address chronic underperformance. Turnaround leadership is not only essential in education today; it is a moral imperative.

THE SERIOUS BUSINESS OF TURNAROUNDS

Urgency. Triage. Alignment.
Teamwork. Commitment. Expectations. Analysis.
Resilience. Results.

Turnarounds are serious business. Consider the mom 'n pop shop that failed on the corner, the corporation that filed for bankruptcy, or the company that was taken over or let go in a "fire sale." Now reflect on the neighborhood elementary school in physical and academic disrepair or the high school that closed after decades of failing its students, some of whom now have children of their own who would have attended that same school.

It is not difficult to see how challenging reversing a decline can be. It is not about one person and cannot be fixed overnight. It is about leadership, courage, and tenacity, and it must be done with a sense of urgency and strategic actions that demonstrate that failure is not an option.

Turnarounds require focus. Leaders charged with reversing chronic underperformance must be able to strategically assess the situation and hone in on the "quick wins" that demonstrate all is not lost. They must carefully choose where to place effort and drive toward a vision for improvement. They find a skilled and willing few and build out a new culture. Turnaround leaders resuscitate.

Chronic underperformance can grow like a cancer, attacking the vital organs of an organization and demoralizing its employees, sapping the confidence of internal and external stakeholders. Failure can spread quickly to interconnected domains, partners, or related industries. Understanding causation is essential to stop the bleeding, inform chosen remedies, and avoid past mistakes. There are the policies and practices that led to the decline, and then there is the psychology associated with the failure, the demoralization that saps energy, drains expectations, and extinguishes leadership. Devolving into blame may only serve to fan the downward spiral.

Many schools in need of turnaround have experienced slow or spiraling declines, entrenched stagnation, or prolonged underperformance. They may be clustered in large urban districts where entire school populations are underserved. These districts may struggle to meet the basic needs of most students and minimum standards for achievement. Archaic systems of education, large bureaucracies, and competing interests of constituencies challenge many.

Other school districts contend with contextual hardships, like those found on an Indian reservation or in a rural community, with high poverty, teacher turnover, and unemployment rates choking growth. Still others may be less obvious, essentially hiding in districts that serve most students well but suffer from staggering economic and racial achievement gaps that separate well-resourced achievers from their less affluent and informed peers.

Turnarounds are messy. They require the skillful detangling of interests, expectations, and offerings to get to the core of what students are learning. And yet, in addition to aligning curriculum, rejuvenating staff, engaging students and parents, and raising expectations, some leaders must literally clean up their schools. The job can be a physical one, requiring a strong constitution to deal with the stench accompanying years of neglect. Clogged toilets, noisy pipes, flooded classrooms, broken windows, filthy floors, moldy books, rusty and useless equipment, and rodent infestations are just some of the realities principals may find. The state of disrepair can overwhelm. Considering that these are places of learning is both heartbreaking and depressing.

What keeps turnaround leaders from walking away? Students. Students lie at the heart of turnarounds in schools. They deserve more—much more. Some may be causing unrest, lack focus, and act as if they don't care. Some have learned not to care or are imprisoned by the expectation of failure. They seem to be the problem, and their families don't appear concerned.

Turnaround leaders know differently. They know that their students' actions are only symptoms of the problems. They know not to blame or write off all because of the actions of a disruptive few (or more than a few). They keep their eye on a future state where their students can learn in a safe, supportive, physically appealing environment where committed, caring, competent teachers set high expectations for them and where students can see a purpose to their education.

Turnaround as a strategy applied to education is still relatively new. Taking media coverage as one indication of emerging trends, *Education Week*'s archives (as of May 2010) show 49 articles mentioning "school turnaround" since 1981 (the year data became available). All except one of these articles were published in the last decade and over 90 percent (94 percent) appeared since 2005. Confirming how widespread the term has become, the large majority (more than 70 percent) of these articles were written since 2009 when the Obama Administration made turning around underperforming schools one of its four priorities for education.[20]

Many educators may rightly be suspicious of what sounds like another business solution being put forth as a potential panacea for chronic school underperformance. In an industry riddled with program fads, overwhelmed by legal do's and don'ts, governed by politics, subject to FOIA (Freedom of Information Act), constrained by unions, and constantly pursued by companies clamoring for a piece of the 15,000-school-district market share pie, it's no wonder that educators would question whether applying turnaround leadership to schools could actually work. Fortunately, while statistical research is scarce, there are a growing number of examples of how turnaround leaders are reversing the decline and stagnation, restoring rigor, and instilling hope in places—and in students—that have heretofore been written off.

Turnarounds are tough business. They are not for the faint-hearted, the indecisive, or pleasing types. In the business sector they are called "operators," conjuring clandestine images of principals moving with purpose to fix the machinery of schools. These operators bring the tools, tactics, and influence that get the job done. They use data, eliminate crises, communicate empathetically, and suit up to drive toward results.

By definition, turnarounds require accountability. They are bound by dismal performance on one end and dramatic gains on the other and must be accomplished with notable speed to justify the term. While culture, community, and communication are important, the bottom line is student achievement.

Turnarounds demand urgency. Swift decision-making is essential. A languishing school did not get that way overnight, and while it won't be fixed overnight either, quick and dramatic action is crucial. Turnarounds are not just school improvement repackaged; they require more than incremental, steady action. Like in a medical situation, schools with chronic underperformance must be "triaged," prioritized, and fixed with swift, decisive, and informed measures that lead to accelerated improvements to avoid more "casualties" like dropouts or over-aged students left behind.

The consequences of inaction are stark. One only has to look at prison rates or graduation rates to see that children's lives are indeed at stake. For instance, in 2009, Northeastern University published the study *The Consequences of Dropping Out of High School.* The study reports,

> During the 2006–2007 time period, 1.4 percent of the nation's 16–24 year olds (men and women combined) were institutionalized of whom nearly 93 percent were residing in correctional facilities (jails, prisons, juvenile detention centers). Only 1 in 1,000 bachelor degree holders were institutionalized versus .7 percent of out-of-school adults who completed 1–3 years of post-secondary schooling, 1.0 percent of high school graduates, and 6.3 percent of high school dropouts lacking a GED certificate. The incidence of institutionalization problems among young high school dropouts was more than 63 times higher than among young four-year college graduates (p. 9).[21]

The cost of inaction is tangible. Drawing from the 2006 and 2007 American Community Surveys the study reports, "Young female dropouts were six times as likely to have given birth as their peers who were college students or four-year college graduates" (pp. 5–6). For young black male dropouts, 23 of every 100 were institutionalized, compared to only six to seven of every

100 Asian, Hispanic and white males. Only one out of every 500 men who held a bachelor's degree or higher was institutionalized.

Dropouts have harder times getting work before incarceration, and with limited skills as they re-enter the workforce they often have higher recidivism rates after being released. With 37 percent of high school dropouts in poor or near poor families, it is not surprising that over the course of their lifetimes, they offer a negative net fiscal contribution to society versus the $287,000 positive contribution of their high school graduate peers. (Sum, Khatiwada, McLaughlin. & Palma, 2009, p. 15).

Turnaround leaders know that expectations matter. Leaders must be confident that change is not only possible but also vital and sustainable. They must have an unwavering belief in the potential of all children to succeed in school and know deeply that the school can facilitate that success. After *A Nation at Risk* was published in 1983 the notion that "all children can learn" became a popular phrase in education nomenclature. The "No Child Left Behind" law attempted to put teeth into the expectation that schools educate *every* child. Phrases like these, however, can wear thin over the years, especially when educators must tackle the myriad of problems facing chronically underperforming schools or groups of students experiencing academic distress.

Stereotypes, including implicit ones, are woven into the fabric of schools' cultures. Subtle and not so subtle indications of who can and cannot achieve, evidenced in achievement gaps between groups, make the challenge of turnaround not only urgent but also crucial to the health of our economy and fulfillment of our democracy. Underserved students may have learned not to count on their teachers; parents may expect little because they are constantly confronted with roadblocks to their own success; burned out and cynical faculty may relay seemingly harmless yet bias-laden excuses for underperformance, however unintentional, resulting in the perpetuation of low expectations.

Turnarounds require money. Salvaging old buildings, upgrading technology, ensuring students have textbooks and other essential tools, paying teachers and offering incentives for performance, training principals and their teams to do these tough jobs and rewarding them for success—all of these efforts require funding, some of which is well beyond standard per pupil allocations.

Not everything is about new money though. Realigning resources, eliminating ineffective programs, unburdening schools from intervention overload, and streamlining local, state, and federal requirements can free up significant human and financial capital that then can be repurposed toward turnaround.

Turnaround leaders have both the sense to do what is right and the skill to do it well. They call out the elephant in the room and have the difficult conversations to alter cultures laden with implicit assumptions that justify underperformance. They can motivate a faculty that may have been demoralized for years and re-engage a disenfranchised community. They know what success looks like and can get there quickly by combining instructional strategies with behavioral and emotional support. They know that turning around student performance means turning around people's attitudes and offering them a new "world view."

Passion and commitment ground the work of turnarounds. Leaders think seriously and feel deeply, led by their heads and moved to action by their hearts. Burdens of dysfunction, even death, surround them and yet even when emotionally drained, they always go back for more. They know people expect them to persevere, or just provide words of encouragement. They anchor change.

Turnaround leaders rejuvenate and, when most successful, institutionalize new thinking, processes, actions and achievement so that the turnaround becomes transparent, transformational, and ultimately sustainable.

Turnaround leaders can be found in all aspects of the school community. Turnaround leadership is a mindset that is not reserved for the principalship. It must include teachers, district and state administrators, union representatives, parents, and other key stakeholders.

A turnaround mindset is an attitude followed by actions that lead to durable changes that benefit students. If this mindset cannot be embraced by a critical mass of district administrators then "lead partners" (MERI 2007) should be engaged, creating a turnaround unit that operates alongside or within a state or district to ensure that bureaucratic obstacles are removed and conditions facilitate success. Turnarounds require systems to change so that success can be sustainable.

NOTES

1. NAEP, the National Assessment of Educational Progress, began in 1969 and TIMMS, the Trends in International Mathematics and Science Study, were first administered in 1995.

2. Lehman, I.J. (2004). "The genesis of NAEP." In L.V. Jones and I. Olkin (Eds.), *The nation's report card: Evolution and perspectives* (pp. 25–92). Bloomington, IN: Phi Delta Kappa Educational Foundation.

3. Halberstam, D. (1993). *The fifties.* New York: Villard Books.

4. http://www.archives.gov/research/vietnam-war/casualty-statistics.html, Accessed 9-17-09.

5. http://www.census.gov/prod/2006pubs/p60-231.pdf p. 20. Accessed 9-17-09.

6. http://www2.ed.gov/pubs/NatAtRisk/index.html. Accessed 9-19-10.

7. http://nces.ed.gov/nationsreportcard/about/#overview Accessed 11-4-10.

8. Rampey, B.D., Dion, G.S., and Donahue, P.L. (2009). *NAEP 2008 Trends in Academic Progress* (NCES 2009-479). National Center for Education Statistics, Institute of Education Sciences, U.S. Department of Education, Washington, D.C.

9. Ibid.

10. An *event dropout rate* is the proportion of students who leave school each year without completing a high school program. The national event dropout rate was 3.8 percent in 2006 for students ages 15 to 24 in grades 10 to 12. A *status dropout rate* measures the proportion of a population that has dropped out of school, regardless of when they last attended school. The national status dropout rate was 9.3 percent in 2006 among individuals ages 16 to 24. A *cohort dropout rate* measures the proportion of students in a defined cohort who left school in a defined period of time. National Governor's Association Center for Best Practices (2009), *Achieving graduation for all: A guide to dropout prevention and recovery.* Washington, D.C.: Daniel Princiotta and Ryan Reyna. p. 11.

11. National Governor's Association Center for Best Practices. (2008). *Implementing graduation counts: State progress to date, 2008.* Washington, D.C.

12. Everyone Graduates Center, Johns Hopkins University. (2007). *State summary table: Promoting power.* Baltimore, MD: Johns Hopkins University, Everyone Graduates Center.

13. According to Fairlie (2005), "The Digital Divide is large and does not appear to be disappearing soon. Blacks and Latinos are much less likely to have access to home computers than are white, non-Latinos (50.6 and 48.7 percent compared to 74.6 percent). They are also less likely to have Internet access at home (40.5 and 38.1 percent compared to 67.3 percent)" (p. 2). Fairlie, R.W. (2005). Are we really a nation online? Racial and ethnic disparities in access to technology and their consequences. *Report for the Leadership Conference on Civil Rights Education Fund.* Washington, D.C.

14. See http://www.schoolmatters.com/.

15. Committee on Education and Labor (2009, May 12). "High school dropout crisis threatens U.S. economic growth and competiveness, witnesses tell house panel." Press Release. http://edlabor.house.gov/newsroom/2009/05/high-school-dropout-crisis-thr.shtml. Accessed 5-10-10.

16. Gordon, E.E. (2009, September). 'The future of jobs and careers." *Techniques.* ACTE Online. http://www.acteonline.org/techniques.aspx. Accessed 11-10-10.

17. Kutash, J. Nico, E. Gorin, E. Tallant, K., and Rahmatullah, S. (2010). *School turnarounds: A brief overview of the landscape and key issues.* Boston: FSG Social Impact Advisors. http://www.galeaders.org/site/documents/education_turnaround_brief.pdf. Accessed 9-19-10.

18. Source: http://www.ed.gov/blog/2010/04/support-for-turning-around-low-performing-schools. Accessed 5-10-10.

19. McKinsey & Company, Social Sector Office (2009, April). *The economic impact of the achievement gap in America's schools.*

20. This analysis was performed using *Education Week* online archives (5-3-10). Articles also include printed corrections, letters to the editor, etc.; turnaround as Obama priority, as seen in AARA, among other policy initiatives.

21. Sum, A., Khatiwada, I., McLaughlin, J. and Palma, S. (2009). *The consequences of dropping out of high school: Joblessness and jailing for high school dropouts and the high cost for taxpayers.* Boston: Northeastern University. http://www.clms.neu.edu/publication/documents/The_Consequences_of_Dropping_Out_of_High_School.pdf. Accessed 9-19-10.

Chapter 2

Approaches to Turnaround

TURNAROUNDS UP CLOSE

In a large urban district, a 1,000-student high school enters its sixth year of "corrective action" under the No Child Left Behind law. The building, which spans a city block, harkens back to another era with signs etched above the doors on either end denoting entrances for "boys" and "girls."

The student body, largely African American and economically disadvantaged, is one in which 70 percent of students are performing below basic reading levels on state tests. Just 22 percent pass basic standards set for math. In 11th grade, only 11 percent of students (versus a nearly 40 percent district average) pass reading tests. Reports of serious incidents have been cut in half in recent years, but average daily student attendance rates, a measure of how many students come to school over the school year, have yet to break 80 percent when high-performing schools regularly top 90 percent.

Drive ten blocks east and you arrive on the campus of a prestigious university with studious "twenty-somethings" preparing for careers in medicine, law, business, and the arts. Ten blocks further west puts you in the middle of what looks like a war zone, with burned-out buildings, scores of graffiti-strewn edifices, and weary-faced residents. The school is one of many in this district trying to serve a diverse and increasingly needy population of students.

Across the country a rural district with low socioeconomics suffers equally. The superintendent and his much smaller executive team weigh reams of data, following trends and looking for clues that can rebuild confidence and motivate high performance. They find that despite numerous interventions, Title I infusions, and a stable albeit low-income community, third grade reading scores have stagnated at 75 percent proficiency and eighth grade math has reached only 65 percent. By high school, students are dropping out in droves and of those that do graduate only 23 percent are college bound. Many teachers are nearing retirement and new ones will be hard to recruit to this remote area. The community itself is in need of a turnaround, but the schools suffer disproportionately as they struggle to provide hope to the students inside.

In a suburban school district across the state, a "principal chat" is underway with the parents of an elementary school in a university community. At this school, a crisis has been simmering for years. A staggering achievement gap is noticeable to those that look, but overall this well-integrated school is doing fine, the high achievement of one group masking the low achievement of another. The urgency for change eludes many.

Overall pass rates reach over 75 percent, yet only 63 percent of the African American students (and just 58 percent of economically disadvantaged students) versus 98 percent of the white students pass the third grade reading test. In math, a nearly 30-point gap remains between white and black students (40 percent of the student body). This is improvement, for just four years ago only a quarter of black students were passing the third grade reading tests.

The community is vibrant but suffers from its "town and gown" reputation and deep scars from its racial history. The school is prized by many but the data reveal a bifurcated system—the well-resourced students of faculty, largely white, and the under-resourced students, mostly of color, many of whose parents and guardians support the university, cleaning dormitories, cooking food, and maintaining grounds. To tackle the performance gap, this school, too, needs a turnaround strategy.

Drive for a day and you arrive at a mostly black high school in this Southern state. It's on the "other" side of town from the district offices and the other, mostly white high schools in this community. Students hustle to class as the principal gives a tour to a group of state auditors, his ninth in one year. They are evaluated on nearly 200 indicators, the results of which are distilled into a three-year plan for improvement, handed to him for implementation. He relies on one assistant principal to lead instructional changes; his other assistant principal is out on leave from some combination of mental exhaustion, burnout, and personal challenges.

Some people in this city never make it over to his side of town. This principal grew up in the community and seems to know everyone. He not only brings successful alumni back to the school to talk with students, he also relies on those who dropped out or had trouble with the law to make actions and their consequences "real" to his students, many of whom are being raised by grandparents.

His student body is nearly 90 percent African American while the district averages just under 50 percent. Three quarters of his students qualify for free or reduced-priced lunch. His teaching staff reflects the same racial composition as his student body and yet a desegregation order restricts him from hiring additional teachers of color, no matter their talents. His school must be racially balanced, at least at the staff level.

The principal is well positioned to guide parents (or grandparents) and students to overcome years of dismal performance and a culture of failure, as long as he's able to stay above the fray in the district and avoid cooptation by those who fear change. He has a turnaround strategy, but only time will tell whether he can overcome district and other obstacles and implement it effectively.

While many may assume that chronically underperforming schools reside only in urban centers, schools in need of turnaround can be found in rural and suburban communities as well. For a student or group of students underserved by a school or district, the need for leaders of their schools to employ turnaround strategies—and a turnaround mindset—could not be greater.

Scores of interventions have been tried. Fads like "new math" and "whole language" have gone by the wayside or have morphed into more relevant, research-based initiatives like "response to intervention" and balanced literacy. More interventions are tried, but they are not the answer. What is needed is a cohesive, data-driven strategy fueled by the urgency demanded by the direness of the situation. Enter turnaround.

THE GROWING DEMAND FOR TURNAROUND

With the heightened expectations required as a result of the No Child Left Behind (NCLB) law and, most recently, the American Recovery and Reinvestment Act and ever-increasing sanctions for continually underperforming schools, the challenges for school, district, and state leaders mount quickly when student performance falls short of targets.

The focus on intensive support, effective interventions, and improved achievement in schools that need it the most represents a policy resolution to address the long-standing failure of many schools serving poor and minority children. Consequently, the need also increases for turnarounds that respond successfully to increasingly rigorous state accountability systems and NCLB-required interventions.

In *Considering School Turnarounds: Market Research and Analysis,* a report developed for NewSchools Venture Fund, Mass Insight Education & Research Institute (April 2007)[1] described its market analysis of the climate for school restructuring by charter or school management organizations in six urban school districts across the country. These districts comprised 2.7 million students, with 75 percent from low-income families. In 2005–2006, 250 schools in these districts were already in restructuring (e.g., creating a charter, replacing staff, turning over management to a third-party management organization), another 250 were preparing to enter restructuring, and another 600 were in "corrective action," the status that precedes restructuring. The national urban landscape these six districts represented in microcosm indicated an immediate need for organizations and solutions that would meet the growing demand for leadership in turnaround environments.

A 2010 report by FSG Social Impact Advisors confirms the unfortunate but growing demand for turnaround.[2] By 2009–2010, more than 5,000 schools entered restructuring, with nearly 2,000 in "corrective action." At this time, however, only a limited number of providers are positioned to offer support to these schools. Chief among the concerns of those working in or planning to enter the turnaround arena is the availability of the autonomy and flexibility needed to change school environments and cultures and, in so doing, achieve and sustain educational success.

While educators have been confronting chronic underperformance in schools for decades, applying the practices and principles of turnaround leadership in schools is relatively new. The U.S. Department of Education suggested in 2009 that at least 5,000 schools are in need of turnaround[3] and there are at least four different research-based approaches to getting there. These include:

- *The turnaround model.* Signaling dramatic change, this model requires the superintendent to replace the principal and at least 50 percent of the staff. Moreover, the principal must operate within a new governance structure, such as reporting directly to the superintendent or to a new "turnaround office" or entering into a multi-year contract that exchanges augmented flexibility for increased accountability. The principal would be a "turnaround leader" presumably with the skills and proven track record to address the chronic underperformance swiftly and successfully. The turnaround model requires leaders to employ strategies that increase instructional time, offer job-embedded professional development, use data to inform decisions, and differentiate instruction and provide social and community supports for students.
- *The restart model.* In this model, the school operates under new management, either by a charter management organization (CMO) or an education management organization (EMO). In this scenario, the turnkey operations of the school are effectively outsourced to the CMO and EMO, though

students in the former school must have the opportunity to attend the newly reopened school.
- *School closure.* Under this option, a district has the option of closing a chronically underperforming school, in which case students then enroll in other, higher-achieving schools in the district.
- *Transformation model.* Four areas of transformation underlie this model. They include (a) developing effective teachers and school leaders; (b) implementing comprehensive instructional reforms; (c) extending learning time and creating "community-oriented" schools; and (d) providing operating flexibility and sustained support.[4]

Through the America Recovery and Reinvestment Act (ARRA), principals, superintendents, and school boards faced with the challenges of chronic underperformance have new options and resources by which to focus their pursuit of the renewal of their lowest-performing schools. While grounded research is still scarce in this nascent field and some education researchers may prefer to wait for proven strategies, the federal legislation indicates urgency for action.

The American Education Research Association, in their comments about the Race to the Top funds, noted, "There has been much less research about the turnaround strategies identified in the proposed regulations than about charter schools, and, consequently, even less is known about conditions required for their success."[5]

Yet, while specific turnaround research-based strategies may not yet be available, other education thought leaders posit that there are a number of promising models to inform practice in chronically underperforming schools. As Grover J. "Russ" Whitehurst at the Brookings Institution notes, sometimes policy must be in front of proven practice.[6] As educators and related stakeholders employ turnaround strategies to improve schools, they have a number of models with promising results on which to draw.

While the term "turnaround" has only recently found its way into common education parlance, strategies related to what now may be called "turnaround leadership" have been pursued for years. From innovative leadership programs focused on underserved urban schools to charter school organizations offering turnkey solutions to state and federal "takeover" or reconstitution, the selection of approaches to turnaround is more extensive than one might think. To be sure, not all approaches are yielding results.

The brief typology that follows examines a set of approaches that have gained national attention in the last five years. Organized into structural approaches and human capital investments, some fall within the public and higher education arenas, and some are innovations outside these domains.

While not an exhaustive list, these approaches demonstrate the types of options and strategies that leadership and stakeholders can apply and learn from.

STRUCTURAL APPROACHES TO TURNAROUND

Some initiatives engaging in what is now referred to as turnaround work lead with structural change to address chronic achievement deficits. Approaches to underperformance in this neighborhood may include school takeover, designated areas or zones within school districts or states, and charterization.

Louisiana's Recovery School District

In Louisiana, the State Board of Education and Secondary Education (BESE) governs the Recovery School District (RSD), created in 2003 by the Louisiana legislature to turn underperforming public schools into successful centers of learning. Schools failing to meet minimum academic progress goals for four years may be placed into the RSD or must enter into a binding Memorandum of Understanding with the state that outlines the necessary actions needed for the school district to avoid being placed in the RSD. Louisiana's RSD includes schools in parishes such as East Baton Rouge and Caddo, although New Orleans is arguably the most well known, and by far the largest set of schools in the Recovery School District.[7]

The RSD in New Orleans took a systemic approach to addressing underperformance. Following Hurricane Katrina, in the November 2005 Special Session of the Louisiana Legislature, the definition of a "failed school" was expanded to include any school that scored below the state average and that was part of a school district deemed to be in "academic crisis." As a result, 107 Orleans Parish schools were allowed to come under the authority of the RSD and its role of turning around struggling schools.

This was seen as an important opportunity for New Orleans, whose poor academic performance was well documented and included a 50-point achievement gap between African American and Caucasian students, low high school graduation rates, high poverty rates among the students, high illiteracy rates among the general population, poorly maintained facilities, and ineffective governance and fiscal mismanagement of the schools.[8] Working with a portfolio of direct-run and public charter schools,[9] RSD-NOLA (New Orleans) has broken away from the traditional notion of a public school system and is operating as a majority charter school district. Assessment index data for its 32 public charters and 29 direct-run schools for 2007–2009 show a range of progress in the schools, with both charters and direct-run elementary schools posting some of the most and least promising growth.[10]

In any state takeover, one challenge is to define when and how the district (in this case the parish) will regain local control. Considerations around the stability of local governance, the sustainability of gains in student achievement, and change in extra support or resources that may have been employed are substantial. Louisiana's RSD is just completing its first five-year cycle and State Superintendent Paul Pastorek, BESE, and local leadership must together decide how to fulfill their commitment to these schools and the parents in the community, a transition that requires careful planning in order to further academic achievement.[11]

The creation of a Recovery School District is similar to the type of "Turnaround Zone" that Mass Insight (MERI, 2007) defined, whereby schools are designated Zone schools and the conditions necessary to support turnaround are employed. Mass Insight advocates that districts and even states create separate units so that the enabling conditions for turnaround can be established. In these cases, there is recognition of some level of system failure, that "business as usual" no longer works and that turnarounds can be more effectively engineered, sustained, and scaled by setting apart the district or a set of schools from better-performing peers. Such a clustering of schools is not necessarily new. What is new is creating charter management-like organizations to operate these schools for the district.

Harlem Children's Zone

The Harlem Children's Zone has gained national attention for its systemic approach to turnaround. Led by visionary Geoffrey Canada and detailed in Paul Tough's 2008 book *Whatever It Takes*, the culmination of a five-year study of Canada's work, the Harlem Children's Zone (HCZ) focuses on addressing all the needs of poor families in what grew from a 24-block area in 1997 to 100 blocks in 2007. Pulling together a set of programs—after-school, truancy, health services, and education—the zone includes schools like the Promise Academy public charters, supplementing them with after-school and in-school support, while offering a more comprehensive set of programs to strengthen families from Baby College parenting workshops to the Harlem Gems preschool program.

Canada's organization started with the end in mind, focusing on stopping the cycle of urban poverty and providing opportunities for children to successfully graduate from high school and college and enjoy a middle-class life. HCZ's 10-year business plan begins with the principles of a "critical mass" of engaged adults and families in the community and "early and progressive intervention" in the development of children.[12] These tenets drive the work of the HCZ, which includes clear boundaries of the zone, goals for community participation, a "shopping mall" of social services to support families and youth, alignment of programs to meet the critical needs of HCZ children, and a sophisticated evaluation team to monitor and track results.

Among its accomplishments, the HCZ boasts that 100 percent of Promise Academy I and II third-grade students met or exceeded grade level expectations on the math exam, outperforming New York State, New York City, District 5, and black and white student peers. Similarly, 93 percent of Promise I Academy third graders tested at or above grade level in English and Language Arts. At the Promise Academy high school, 93 percent of ninth grade students passed the statewide Algebra Regents exam.[13]

With these and many other impressive results, the Harlem Children's Zone has fast become a model for turnaround leadership not only for schools but also for impoverished communities. Canada's work has led to the federal Neighborhood Promise Grant program, which recently awarded it first $500,000 seed grants to 21 communities. Its best practices have been studied by notable academics like Harvard's Roland Fryer, who is working with New York City to achieve similar results in a set of public schools.[14]

Charter Schools

Charter schools, particularly those that target underserved populations, are another approach to turnaround. They began in 1991, with a law in Minnesota under a cloud of controversy around privatization of schools, and now flourish in many communities, including the Harlem Children's Zone. Today, more than 1.5 million children attend one of the nearly 5,000 charter schools in thirty-nine states plus the District of Columbia.[15] The Education Commission of the States defines charters schools as follows:

> Charter schools are semi-autonomous public schools, founded by educators, parents, community groups or private organizations that operate under a written contract with a state, district or other entity. This contract, or charter, details how the school will be organized and managed, what students will be taught and expected to achieve, and how success will be measured. Many charter schools enjoy freedom from rules and regulations affecting other public schools, as long as they continue to meet the terms of their charters. Charter schools can be closed for failing to satisfy these terms.[16]

State statutes vary, though most charters are granted by local school boards or the state board of education. Some view charter schools as the research and development arm of public schools; others see them as a competitive force in the education space. Performance can vary dramatically, from charters in New York City showing stronger growth than peer public schools[17] and charter management organizations (CMOs) like KIPP and Achievement First showing some dramatic gains in student achievement, to "mom and pop" charters that are not meeting expectations set forth in their contracts.

Knowledge Is Power Program: KIPP

Within the collection of charter schools, a number of approaches have gained national attention and may offer insights for turnaround leaders in public settings. One of the most impressive and successful school approaches to educating children from low socioeconomic backgrounds is the Knowledge Is Power Program (KIPP). Founded by two Teach for America corps members assigned to the inner-city public schools of Houston, KIPP requires almost 60 percent more time in school for their students through an extended day and an extended year. KIPP bases its program on five operating principles they call the Five Pillars, which include high expectations, choice and commitment, more time, power to lead, and focus on results.[18]

The students who attend this 16-year-old national network of 82 charter schools in 19 states consistently score well on statewide tests. Eighty-five percent of the students who graduate from school go on to college with an 80 percent graduation rate. This post-secondary graduation rate is impressive compared to the national average of 57 percent for four-year institutions.[19] Much of their success in college can be attributed to the fact that 90 percent of KIPP students get scholarships to private or parochial high schools.[20] With strong results, a committed "no excuses" culture, and measured growth, KIPP received a $50 million Investing in Innovation (i3) Scale Up grant from the U.S. Department of Education in September 2010 (secured with $10 million in matching funds), allowing it to double in size over the next 10 years and share best practices for leadership development and training.[21]

Green Dot Public Schools

Located in some of the highest-need areas of Los Angeles, Green Dot Public Schools has opened 18 charter high schools to address a level of education that has consistently resisted change. The parents of students attending these schools are required to be involved in their young person's education through volunteering (at least 35 hours annually). The state assessment scores of students attending Green Dot schools are nearly 19 percent greater than those of their peers at regular public schools throughout Los Angeles. With an 81 percent graduation rate, Green Dot schools considerably outperform their regular peer schools at 51 percent.[22]

Green Dot schools must abide by Six Tenets of High-Performing Schools, which include small, safe, personalized schools (not more than 560 students); high expectations for all students through a rigorous college-prep curriculum; local control, with extensive professional development and accountability; parent participation; funding maximized to the classroom; and schools open until 5:00 p.m. to provide safe and enriching activities and community and neighborhood ownership of the school.[23]

Green Dot's transformation of Locke High School demonstrates its approach is working. Green Dot took over Locke from the Los Angeles Unified School District (LAUSD) in the 2008–2009 school year after more than 50 percent of tenured teachers signed a petition for Green Dot to assume its governance. With a combination of interventions, small-school approaches, new principals and teachers aligned with the educational mission, a focus on cleanliness and safety, and an integrated alternative education program, Locke students showed dramatic improvements in not only test scores but also retention rates. After two years, 800 more students, or 73 percent of the freshman class, remained as compared to the two-year LAUSD cohort average of only 43–44 percent.[24]

Achievement First

A small network of charter schools, Achievement First runs seventeen public charter schools in Connecticut (New Haven, Bridgeport, Hartford) and New York (Brooklyn). These seventeen college preparatory academies serving 4,500 K-12 students are focused on high levels of achievement, college graduation, and community leadership. Founders came together in 1998 to form their flagship Amistad Academy, a public charter school in New Haven, Connecticut. Amistad Academy, which serves urban students selected through a blind lottery (78 percent free and reduced lunch; 98 percent African American and Hispanic), became a proof point for the notion that urban students could achieve at levels similar to their more affluent suburban peers. Achievement First became the network of schools built on Amistad Academy's best practices.[25]

With a laser-like focus on improvement, the New York students who have attended Achievement First schools the longest demonstrate 93 percent proficiency in English Language Arts and 99 percent proficiency in math on the New York state tests. This is coupled with Achievement First Hartford Academy's fifth grade students demonstrating the greatest fourth grade performance gains of any Hartford public school. Longer school days plus tutoring before and after school and a mandatory three-week Summer Academy add up to an additional year of school over the course of thirteen years.[26]

One of the hallmarks of Achievement First's approach is developing a data-driven culture where teachers embrace student data to improve instruction. Teachers in Achievement First schools use consistent scope and sequence of instruction and regularly check in on student learning through interim assessments modeled on those used successfully at the Amistad Academy. Teachers and administrators spend hours on these assessments, administering, analyzing, and planning for instruction. As important, they are trained in how to use and discuss the data most effectively so that instruction is enhanced and students benefit.[27]

These are just a few examples of the ways in which organizations are addressing struggling school performance from a structural framework. With more public charter school networks available to communities, closing schools has become a more frequent option for districts and communities with schools that have chronically failed to meet students' academic needs. The high-performing charters described above, like peers such as Aspire Public Schools, Mastery Charter Schools, Yes Prep Public Schools, and LEARN Charter School Network, are among an elite set of school organizations that have been able to demonstrate results, are focusing on scaling up, and are contributing to the growing turnaround sector.

HUMAN CAPITAL INVESTMENTS

Another set of approaches to turning around low-performing schools involves investments in the human capital assets of a school. Sometimes these investments occur in addition to pursuing structural changes in contracts, school design, and organization, as with NewSchools Venture Fund's investment in the Academy for Urban School Leadership (AUSL). Many of the more successful charter management organizations, like those discussed above, couple their structural change with leadership development focused on a particular set of guiding principles and competencies. In other cases, states and districts have pursued principal development programs that offer turnaround leaders a set of skills that differentiate the hard work of turnaround from other principal experiences.

New Leaders for New Schools and the New York City Leadership Academy, two principal development and placement organizations, are notable approaches in this neighborhood. Each organization focuses on developing principals who can demonstrably change student outcomes in urban schools. The following profiles highlight these nonprofit approaches.

New York City Leadership Academy

The New York City Leadership Academy, created in 2003, has served as a centerpiece of Mayor Bloomberg's efforts to reform the city's most chronically low-performing schools. Operating as an independent nonprofit, the Academy offers a comprehensive set of leadership development programs and support services aligned with NYC Department of Education initiatives. Programs broach theory, research, and practice in the context of authentic school experiences.

The three-phase flagship leadership development program, the Aspiring Principals Program (APP), for instance, begins with a six-week "boot camp" summer simulation followed by a 10-month school residency with an experienced mentor principal. The second summer is a planning opportunity with coaching support as the participants transition into new leadership roles. Once leaders are in these challenging positions, the Academy provides ongoing standards-based coaching during the first year to facilitate ongoing reflection and continuous improvement.[28]

With over 400 graduates, most of whom have become principals, the Leadership Academy graduates are now responsible for 15 percent of New York City schools. An evaluation completed by researchers at New York University (Corcoran, Schwartz & Weinstein, 2009) found that elementary and middle schools led by APP principals had, after their first three years, comparable or better growth trends than comparison schools. English test scores at elementary and middle schools increased at a faster pace than those of more traditionally trained new principals. The rate of math gains was similar to citywide averages. APP principals also were more likely to be placed in lower-performing schools and schools with a higher proportion of African American students.

This organizational development provider for the New York City schools is building leaders that fill a labor market shortage and can address some of the most challenging circumstances plaguing underperforming schools. The program is one of the few that has shown a program effect in addition to achievement results.

The Leadership Academy's programs now extend beyond New York City to a number of states and districts interested in utilizing and adapting the Leadership Academy's well-researched tools, practices, and programs to improve student achievement. The New York City Leadership Academy supports the customization of its approach to states and districts seeking to align leadership development with student achievement. Over a thousand visitors have come to see the Academy's work firsthand. Coaching standards, the School Leadership Performance Standards Matrix, and the Performance Planning Worksheet, which is being utilized in 243 sites and 19 colleges and universities, are just a few of the tools that hundreds of districts and a number of universities are employing.[29]

New Leaders for New Schools

New Leaders for New Schools, founded in 2000, targets first-time principals and provides an intensive four-week training institute focused on instructional and organizational leadership skills by tapping the expertise of national leaders and outstanding educators. This rigorous institute is followed by a year-long, full-time assignment as a paid resident working alongside a mentor principal. The academic core, Foundations, continues through projects and two weeklong intensives through the mentor year. New Leaders hone leadership competencies, creat a leadership development plan, and acquire tools and skills from their Urban Education Framework™ to apply when assigned their own school.[30] A RAND evaluation is underway and preliminary results point to a positive impact on three-year principals on student achievement (Martorell, Heaton, Gates and Hamilton, 2010), a finding those engaged in change can appreciate. The RAND working paper (final report due in 2014) notes, "These results are consistent with the organization's theory of action which stipulates that the full benefit of the training and program support is only realized after several years, by which time a principal will have had time to institute changes and reforms to a school" (p. 23).

New Leaders for New Schools is committed to recruiting and developing talented educators that can lead schools to exceptional results. Through a rigorous selection process yielding a selectivity rate of less than 7 percent, New Leaders is focused on finding leaders that demonstrate "an unyielding belief and sense of urgency to ensure all students achieve academically at high levels; a relentless drive to lead an excellent urban public school; instructional expertise in a K-12 classroom; exceptional leadership skills; and the ability to achieve in the face of obstacles."[31] In nine years, New Leaders for New Schools has trained and supported over 640 New Leaders across 12 urban centers, more than 60 percent of whom are African American or Latino.[32]

New Leaders work extends beyond the training and placement of principals. The Effective Practices Incentive Community (EPIC) provides incentives to teachers and principals to both achieve results and share their best practices. Developed in 2006 and funded by the U.S. Department of Education's Teacher Incentive fund, school district and charter school partners, and private philanthropic funders, EPIC focuses on furthering value-added models for analyzing student achievement, recognizing and rewarding school leaders and educators making high gains in their schools, and cataloging their success through comprehensive case studies that are shared through the online EPIC Knowledge System, available to EPIC partners and the New Leaders Community.[33]

Through this and other targeted initiatives, New Leaders for New Schools, like the NYC Leadership Academy, is developing and scaling human capital assets that can transform schools. These are just two examples of nonprofit organizations gaining influence and traction toward changing the way educators develop leaders to support high-need schools. These innovators' work involves different approaches, yet both extend well beyond the school itself, building partnerships with complementary high-impact organizations, states, cities, associations, and universities that share their drive, urgency, and systems orientation about how leadership development accelerates student achievement.

University of Virginia Darden/Curry Partnership

States, districts and universities have also weighed in on the side of human capital investments, leveraging faculty expertise with state and local resources that can build leadership capacity to address chronic underperformance. The University of Virginia's School Turnaround Specialist Program (UVA-STSP), for instance, launched in 2004 when then Governor Mark Warner sought to develop a cadre of principals specially trained to lead turnarounds in Virginia's underperforming schools as an effort to serve Virginia's most needy communities.

The University of Virginia's (UVa's) Darden/Curry Partnership for Leaders in Education, then a newly founded collaboration between the University of Virginia's Darden Graduate School of Business and the Curry School of Education to provide innovative executive development solutions for K-12 administrators and stakeholders, was awarded the contract to design and deliver Virginia's School Turnaround Specialist Program. The program was largely funded by the General Assembly, the Commonwealth of Virginia's legislative body, with additional support from the Wallace Foundation. The four major components of that program were:

- selection of experienced principals to lead turnaround initiatives;
- design and delivery of a case-driven executive education program, combining the best practices and strategies from business turnarounds with education research focused on school improvement and leading change;
- creation of a network among principals offering coaching resources and peer support; and
- implementation of a performance-based credential in turnaround leadership awarded to those principals meeting a set of agreed-upon targets tied to state accreditation and NCLB.

Through a grant from the Microsoft Partners in Learning Program, the Darden/Curry Partnership at UVa researched and designed a program with national reach. According to the University of Virginia School Turnaround Annual Report (2004–2008),[34] a majority of the schools engaged in turnaround under the leadership of a UVA-STSP-trained principal (in the first three cohorts) demonstrated gains in student achievement. Upon completion of the two-year program, for instance, approximately 60 percent of schools demonstrated at least a 10 percent boost in reading proficiency while 53 percent demonstrated at least a 10 percent boost in math proficiency.

Among the findings of research on the program conducted by education policy and management consulting firm Public Impact, 16 of the 25 schools for which they were able to identify meaningful comparisons exceeded student learning gains in comparable schools. Turnaround initiatives in

UVA-STSP-led schools appear to be having a greater impact upon student performance in reading than in mathematics. Schools led by UVA-STSP principals demonstrated Adequate Yearly Progress (AYP) at a greater rate than their peers in comparable schools.[35] UVa continues to hone its turnaround program, working at the state level in Texas and with clusters of schools in cities like Cincinnati.

Louisiana recently launched its own state version of turnaround leadership, complete with the nation's first turnaround leadership endorsement. Louisiana's regional provider approach engages selected universities in offering credit courses and following a standard curriculum to prepare and support turnaround specialist leaders. Notable in both the University of Virginia and Louisiana approaches is the inclusion of district administrators and a school leadership team in the executive program for the purpose of developing a team of critical stakeholders to accelerate performance and sustain results.

Since Virginia's inaugural program in 2004, the field of turnarounds in education has expanded greatly. The state of Arizona, for instance, used the Virginia model as a basis for the design of its development program, which offers training to a cadre of "turnaround professionals" drawn from all levels of school personnel, including teachers, principals, and central office administrators.

Similarly, Tennessee established a group of retired exemplary educators called STAT (System Targeted Assistance Team) that works in schools and districts in "corrective action" to analyze data, observe classrooms, and provide insights to assist school leaders (Sarrio, 2007). New Mexico, Georgia, Indiana, Delaware, Kentucky, and Ohio are among the states that have participated in the Wallace Foundation's Executive Leadership Program, offered by Harvard University and the University of Virginia, which focused on states and districts to strengthen their leadership capacity and develop policies that can accelerate student achievement.

Few others have engaged in statewide programs, though efforts have been made in large urban districts to focus resources on the schools most in need. The Chicago and Philadelphia school districts, for instance, have participated in the national program at the University of Virginia and employ other turnaround models, including AUSL (Academy for Urban School Leadership) in Chicago and Mastery Charter Schools in Philadelphia. These models focus on developing leaders (teachers, school managers) who work in underperforming schools with various supports (Chicago) and creating charters to replace some of the most high-need middle and high schools (Philadelphia).

The AUSL turnaround model is built on specially trained AUSL teachers who have gone through a rigorous one-year residency program before being placed as a teacher in a AUSL-managed turnaround school. It was not until a sufficient number of training academies were established that AUSL opened its first turnaround school in 2006. As of 2010 there are 12 turnaround schools and six training academies.

Chicago Public Schools assigns to AUSL some of its lowest-performing schools with significant achievement gaps compared to other schools. Through goal setting, shared responsibility for learning, and engaged and personalized instruction of a rigorous, college prep curriculum, significant improvement in student achievement is being realized.[36]

Human capital investments lay at the heart of the charter and public schools that successfully achieved turnaround. Some criticize charters for greater selection through lotteries, since students can enter only if they have parental consent. What is most important in either environment is that underserved students are benefitting from high quality teaching and leadership that understands how to foster and support academic achievement.

AUSL and KIPP might best be termed a combination of "hybrid" approaches to turnaround, wherein organizations can create structural change (e.g., charter schools, turnaround zones, and partners) that, combined with investments in human capital, form a powerful combination of forces and strategies that facilitate turnaround. Moreover, these nontraditional approaches often connect to other entities like Teach for America that have a track record of providing quality teachers ready to teach in urban and rural high-poverty schools where traditionally certified teachers may not be available.

This typology offers a framework for understanding current turnaround models. Whether leading with structural change or human capital asset development, the approaches outlined here offer insight into the evolving field of school turnarounds. No two approaches are identical and, with the possible exception of the NYC Leadership Academy, which has shown both improvements in academic achievement and a program effect, none of the programs and approaches here has compiled the longitudinal data necessary to show statistically valid results. Despite the lack of evidence, these approaches have promising results that can inform current and future turnaround models.

What is evident in this typology is that these initiatives target principal leadership and recognize there are nuances to leading schools in distress that require new competencies. Some districts own this effort, as with the New York City Leadership Academy, while others outsource this training to places like University of Virginia. Most successful charters, like KIPP and Achievement First, train their own principals, just as the Broad Center trains future urban superintendents. Venture capital like NewSchools Venture Fund and the Chicago Public Education Fund are also investing in turnaround models and supports. At the state level, the Wallace Foundation and Mass Insight in particular are investing in building leadership capacity in state departments of education and in school districts to accelerate student performance.

More and more, districts are supporting a portfolio of approaches. Chicago, for instance, hosts a number of charter schools and New Leaders for New Schools, has participated in the UVa School Turnaround Specialist Program, has worked with NewSchools Venture Fund to develop the AUSL, and works closely with a number of foundations as well as the Chicago Public Education Fund.

Rather than invest in one approach, districts are leveraging strategies that support charter schools with those that can assist their public schools, defining leadership competencies that drive principal success as well as those that define teacher quality, and embracing incentive programs like the Teacher Assistance Program (TAP) that helps link teacher effectiveness with performance incentives. More and more districts and states are bridging fields and eliminating silos between operations and instruction. They are replacing competitive forces with collaborative efforts to accelerate turnaround and scale success.

To do this most effectively, however, stakeholders including educators, administrators, unions, companies, foundations, and boards may benefit from an understanding of the historical tension between business and education and the relevant literature that informs turnaround as an emerging subspecialty of principalship.

NOTES

1. Mass Insight Education & Research Institute. (2007, March). *Considering school turnarounds: Market research and analysis.* Boston, MA. Prepared for NewSchools Venture Fund. The six districts included Chicago, the District of Columbia, Los Angeles, New York City, Oakland, and Philadelphia.

2. Kutash, J., Nico, E., Gorin, E., Tallant, K., and Rahmatullah, S. (2010). *School turnarounds: A brief overview of the landscape and key issues.* Boston: FSG Social Impact Advisors.

3. http://www.ed.gov/blog/2010/03/whats-possible-turning-around-americas-lowest-achieving-schools/. Accessed 11-3-10.

4. U.S. Department of Education Office of Elementary and Secondary Education. (2010, June). *Guidance on school improvement grants: Under section 1003(g) of the Elementary and Secondary Education Act of 1965.* http://www2.ed.gov/programs/sif/sigguidance05242010.pdf. Accessed 11-4-10.

5. Viadero, D. (2009, October 2). "Race to the top said to lack key science." *Education Week.*

6. Ibid.

7. http://www.rsdla.net/InfoGlance/FAQs.aspx. Accessed 10-6-09.

8. *Recovery School District legislatively required plan.* June 7, 2006. http://www.louisianaschools.net/lde/uploads/8932.doc. Accessed 9-20-10.

9. Type 5 Public Charter Schools are authorized by BESE and overseen by the RSD. Source: *Recovery School District legislatively required plan*. June 7, 2006.

10. State of Louisiana Department of Education. *Recovery School District 2007–2009 Assessment Index Data*. Sorted by growth, shows the top seven elementary schools posting more than 30 points growth (five charters, two direct-run); four elementary schools showed negative growth (one charter, three direct-run); growth in 10 high schools ranged from 4 to 24 points.

11. Chang, C. (2010, September 14). "Pastorek presents plan for eventual return of New Orleans schools; read the plan." *The Times-Picayune*. http://www.nola.com/education/index.ssf/2010/09/pastorek_present_plan_for_retu.html. Accessed 10-2-10.

12. Harlem Children's Zone, Inc. (HCZ) *Growth Plan FY 2001–FY 2009*, updated Fall 2003. http://www.hcz.org/images/stories/pdfs/business_plan.pdf. Accessed 9-22-10.

13. http://www.hcz.org/our-results/by-the-numbers. Accessed 9-22-10.

14. Brooks, D. (2009, May 7). "The Harlem miracle." *The New York Times*. http://www.nytimes.com/2009/05/08/opinion/08brooks.html. Accessed 10-3-10.

15. http://www.publiccharters.org/aboutschools/benefits. Accessed 11-3-10.

16. Education Commission of the States. (2010). "Charter schools." http://www.ecs.org/html/issue.asp?issueID=20. Accessed 11-15-10.

17. http://www.edreform.com. Accessed 6-25-10.

18. http://www.kipp.org/about-kipp/five-pillars. Accessed 9-22-10.

19. Approximately 57 percent of full-time, first-time bachelor's or equivalent degree seekers in 2002 attending four-year institutions completed a bachelor's or equivalent degree at the institution where they began their studies within six years. Knapp, L.G., Kelly-Reid, J.E., Ginder, S.A. *Enrollment in postsecondary institutions, Fall 2008; Graduation rates, 2002 & 2005 cohorts; and Financial statistics, fiscal year 2008*. http://nces.ed.gov/pubs2010/2010152rev.pdf. National Center for Education Statistics. Accessed 11-3-10.

20. http://kipp.org. Accessed 6-26-10.

21. http://www.kipp.org/news/kipp-secures-10-million-in-matching-funds-for-federal-grant. Accessed 9-22-10.

22. http://www.greendot.org/news/article/green_dot_helping_schools_make_grade. Accessed 6-26-10.

23. http://www.greendot.org/about_us/school_model. Accessed 9-17-10.

24. http://www.greendot.org/green_dot039s_transformation_of_locke_high_school_yields_impressive_retention_and_enrollment_rates. Accessed 9-17-10.

25. http://www.achievementfirst.org/about-us/history/. Accessed 9-20-10.

26. http://achievementfirst.org/. Accessed 6-26-10.

27. Petersen, J. (2007). The brave new world of data-informed instruction. *Education Next*. Winter.

28. http://www.nycleadershipacademy.org/overview/overview. Accessed 11-4-10.

29. http://www.nycleadershipacademy.org/knowledge/our-work. Accessed 11-3-10.

30. http://www.nlns.org/Foundations.jsp. Accessed 6-27-10.

31. http://www.nlns.org/Program.jsp. Accessed 9-23-10.

32. http://www.nlns.org/Results.jsp. Accessed 9-23-10.
33. http://www.nlns.org/epic.jsp#epicknowledge. Accessed 11-4-10.
34. University of Virginia School Turnaround Specialist Program. (2010, March 15). *Annual Report excerpts (2004–2008)*. http://www.darden.virginia.edu/web/uploadedFiles/Darden/Darden_Curry_PLE/UVA_School_Turnaround/UVASTSPAnnualReport2008_Excerpts.pdf. Accessed 11-3-10.
35. Ibid.
36. http://ausl-chicago.org/about.html/. Accessed 6-26-10.

Chapter 3

Understanding Turnarounds
Research Highlights

Turnarounds are fast becoming the next business adaptation in the education sector. To advocates, turnarounds offer a refinement of the principalship, allowing for a differentiation between the leadership skills and work required to successfully run healthy schools and those needed to ameliorate conditions impeding troubled ones. Turnarounds in education are necessary because of the stark reality that, despite many efforts and reforms, too many schools are not serving students well. There is no time to waste, and leaders skilled in turnarounds are able to help.

Turnaround may have its roots in the private sector, but the application is an approach that some educators have been using for years. It's a strategy, not a prescribed solution, that, if successful, by definition will produce dramatic results. Turnarounds vary by context, as is evident from the many approaches presented in the previous chapter. Yet, as will be apparent from the case studies presented in later chapters, there are consistent methods, frameworks, and belief systems that guide turnaround leaders through this arduous yet exhilarating work.

Some healthy skepticism may accompany the pursuit of turnaround as an education strategy, especially for those who may have seen other business adaptations in the public sector come and go. For some, turnarounds conjure up the legacies of "Chainsaw Al" Dunlap or "Neutron Jack" Welch, shedding jobs and streamlining product lines to improve results. Others may view the recent financial crisis as a convenient cautionary tale about how much trust to put in business practices.

Why should educators, parents, or politicians believe turnaround strategies could work in schools when plenty of "white knights" have brought funding, programs, and technology to schools in need for decades, and chronic underperformance remains? Leaders across the country are employing turnaround strategies with success. That is the first piece of evidence.[1]

As the field of turnarounds gains traction, it is ever important to understand both the context for turnarounds in education and the insights from existing literature. Building an arsenal of knowledge around turnarounds as an education strategy should offer stakeholders engaging in this work a foundation on which to build and support this field. The remainder of this chapter will offer insights into the history of business-education interactions as they relate to turnaround; it will highlight the existing research on turnarounds and attend to the less discussed issues of race and poverty as they impact struggling schools and this emerging field.

BUSINESS/EDUCATION INTERACTIONS

As turnaround takes hold as a viable education reform strategy and receives support and funding from the government and philanthropic sectors, a brief discussion of the history of business-education interaction may offer insights to those pursuing this work in schools. Educators are no strangers to private sector influences and reforms. For decades, teachers and administrators have benefited from small grants to large influxes of dollars from the philanthropic arms of private corporations and well-endowed foundations. In the past, many of these supplements came with few strings attached. Instead of specific outcomes, many relied on the goodwill generated by a handy check (and photo opportunity) for an enrichment program that exceeded the resource-constrained budget of a school district.

Most educators would welcome such hands-off involvement for a holiday party here, an after-school music or technology program there, with some reading volunteers or "study buddies" added in for good measure. Teachers and principals might amass a large handful of such projects for their school in any given year, filling as many unmet needs as they could for their students. Such efforts often required a careful juggling act so as not to short-change one benefactor for another. Any gift was often seen as better than none at all, and the relationship was symbiotic, so long as educators were left alone and business generated goodwill.

More systemic involvement—at the policy or district level—required much more effort from both educators and businesses, with few companies able to meet the challenge. In the aftermath of *A Nation at Risk*, for instance, business involvement tended toward project-based efforts, rather than long-term relationships that focused on improved student achievement. Dale Mann's (1987) study of school-business partnerships in 23 cities found that, while superintendents were making new efforts to bring in partners, much of the chosen involvement was "peripheral," "special purpose" and "episodic" (Mann, 1987). At this point, most partnerships tended toward basic gifts and financial donations to adopt-a-school programs.

Fortunately, a lot has changed in 25 years. Mostly gone are the days when business talk equated students with "products," when vouchers and charters were synonymous with private takeover of public schooling, and when business was automatically "better." Today, venture capital has spurred new technologies and innovations to the education sector, and the field of social entrepreneurship has blossomed. Scores of businesses have moved beyond what Kolderie (1987) called "tinkering at the margins" of reform and what Mann (1987) characterized as low-cost, low-conflict support of education.

In recent years, the Eli and Edythe Broad Foundation and the Bill and Melinda Gates Foundation, philanthropic endeavors formed by notable titans of industry, have invested hundreds of millions of dollars in urban education reform and high school redesign. Private equity dollars and venture capital now flow to social entrepreneurship endeavors like charter schools, tutoring programs, and teacher and principal training programs. An urban superintendents program, a residency program for recent MBA graduates, and the Broad Prize in Urban Education bearing a $1 million prize are a few of the ways the Broad Foundation pursues urban education reform.

These foundations have engaged management consulting giants like McKinsey & Co. and the Boston Consulting Group in providing consulting support to resource-constrained districts. These firms leverage their private sector tools in the public sector context, often providing a portion of their assistance *pro bono*. They have invested in and developed expertise in the K-12 sector, lending strategic insights and frameworks to help to solve what, in an era of "dropout factories," may seem like intractable problems. Business schools in universities include social entrepreneurship courses and some even have partnerships with their schools of education to support cross-sector research in K-12 reforms.

Yet, behind these efforts lurks some tension in the movement to improve schools. "Strong-mayors" and superintendent "CEOs" are striving to overhaul bureaucratic systems, build portfolios of schools with greater accountability, and negotiate union contracts to facilitate these changes. Charter schools of promise are showing that autonomous leaders can build cultures of accountability to drive growth among underserved students. Longer days, frequent testing, and a passionate commitment to the underserved often accompany these beacons of achievement.

Results-oriented laws and state accountability systems that monitor achievement have led to more testing to measure progress. Money that once may have flowed directly to the classroom may now fund strategic plans, accountability measures, charter schools, choice, and voucher plans that to some tend toward more of a market-based rather than a student-oriented approach.

This major shift in business and philanthropic, not to mention federal, support for public education comes at a time when the field of education reflects more research-grounded practice with a laser-like focus on instruction and student achievement. Educators at all levels have stepped up their game, examining teaching, content knowledge, accountability, and curriculum (to name a few) while embracing management techniques as well. They carry a heavy load, trying to balance many actors and efforts and leveraging the most they can for their students.

The stakes are high for educators and business people. Educators are entrusted with building this country's greatest asset—its people. Businesses cannot survive without human capital. Yet, even with such import, the two sectors struggle with how to deliver a quality education to all children. Tensions between education and business reach back a century, to a time when the rise of industry drove the need for factory workers rather than farmers. Ongoing economic issues and threats to our nation's competitiveness have driven waves of business involvement for over a century. New cycles of partnering will continue to follow major events, conflicts and breakthroughs, presidencies, and nationally commissioned reports.

The work may never be finished, but with an improved understanding of shared history and a dependent future, education and industry can better leverage their respective strengths and priorities. As industry drives toward excellence and improved efficiencies, educators lead with a commitment and responsibility to equity and quality. Rather than operate in contradiction, these differing values may spur more fruitful cross-sector dialogue toward solutions.

Turnaround as strategy, still relatively new in educational parlance, is showing results in struggling schools. Longitudinal data may not yet be available, but more and more cases showing dramatic improvement, like those in the coming chapters, offer hope. As Karin Chenoweth noted in a commentary about her 2007 book *It's Being Done*, which catalogues high achievement in high poverty schools, principals leading these schools have overcome the theoretical arguments mounted against them. They are showing through instruction, expectations, and results that their schools defy stereotypes about circumstance and who can and cannot achieve; they make a difference for students.[2]

Cross-sector research also can lend insight as educators adapt turnaround to schools. To be sure, the private sector follows different rules and operates in a vastly different context where analysis of accounting rules, bankruptcy codes, and contract language might lead to bankruptcy, divestiture, revised financial modeling, or legal action. While corporate managers may employ different instruments and tactics on the path to renewal, there are some useful insights to distill from the business literature. The remainder of this chapter offers a targeted review of the cross-sector scholarship dealing with turnarounds and the demographic nuances in many of these schools. For additional resources about turnarounds see Appendix B.

INSIGHTS FROM THE LITERATURE

Across the spectrum of current research and programs, one common theme emerges, that is, the need to draw from different sectors when seeking solutions to complex issues (Viadero, 2007). The following literature review offers a brief examination of highlights from existing research on turnarounds in both the private and public sectors, as well as demographic considerations that are particularly relevant to school turnarounds.

The Turnaround Leader

It is now more commonly recognized that, in addition to teaching, leadership plays an important role in driving student achievement. In the case of turnaround, the leader's decisions often will distinguish success from failure. At the core, turnaround leaders are change leaders, and as such, John Kotter's definition of leadership versus management is useful.

> Management is a set of processes that can keep a complicated system of people and technology running smoothly. The most important aspects of management include planning, budgeting, organizing, staffing, controlling and problem solving. Leadership is a set of processes that creates organizations in the first place or adapts them to significantly changing circumstances. Leadership defines what the future should look like, aligns people with that vision and inspires them to make it happen despite the obstacles. (Kotter, 1996, p. 25)

While most agree that the leader of an organization does not act as a "gunslinger," providing the "silver bullet" that will save the day, the importance of a strong leader with specific skills is undisputed. What the education sector is still trying to understand is what competencies best define a school turnaround leader.

In the business sector, turnaround competence is so essential that the Turnaround Management Association (TMA) and its Certified Turnaround Professionals (CTP) designation is devoted to training and certifying talent that corporations can purpose to distressed organizations. Like certified public accountants or certified financial planners, the TMA develops turnaround professionals using a concrete set of principles and skills from a research-based "Body of Knowledge" that includes crisis management, and restructuring and renewal of troubled organizations, in addition to finance, accounting, and the law. TMA also teaches a process and a set of characteristics common to effective turnaround managers.[3]

Whether driving corporate renewal or student achievement, in addition to training leaders for turnarounds, scholars and practitioners agree that there exists a set of characteristics best suited for the challenge of leading an organization out of distress. While Kowel and her colleagues (2007) found no rigorous research on the characteristics distinguishing successful turnaround leaders from their ineffective peers, there is anecdotal evidence from both the private and public sectors of the qualities that prove most helpful in these situations, including a toolkit developed in 2008 by Public Impact for the Chicago Public Education Fund.[4]

Table 3.1 highlights characteristics presented from select corporate and education sector sources, including Hargreaves and Fink's (2006) work focusing on sustainable leadership, a critical yet under-discussed aspect of turnarounds. This is by no means an exhaustive list but does include a range of research-based characteristics for comparison purposes.

In describing the "complete turnaround executive," Slatter and his colleagues (2006) emphasize that such a leader is one that is committed to the long-term process of addressing the underlying causes of the distress, not just the need to quickly stabilize the organization. They caution against following one single leadership style and thus offer a set of leadership characteristics most common among the turnaround executives they studied.

In addition to these efforts, other studies lend further insight into what is required to be a successful turnaround leader. Joyce (2004) posits that the leader's role in turnarounds is more complex than the literature on transformational leadership might suggest. The intensity and stresses of the job require an emotional resiliency and fortitude beyond the typical leadership "know-how." The critical situational difference in the turnaround is time; thus, turnaround leaders must be both strategic and able to thrive amidst the details of the management environment.

In the absence of a substantial research base on successful turnaround leaders' capabilities, one that considers failed leaders as well, the business literature offers some common leadership actions that might translate into these characteristics: bias for action, focus on implementation, strategic orientation, the ability to handle organizational politics, coalition building, use of symbolic actions, shared ideas and values, and "will," which includes exercising powers skillfully and effectively (Paton & Mordaunt, 2004; Pettigrew & MacNulty, as cited in Paton & Mordaunt, 2004).

While it may be tempting for any turnaround leader to start with a clean slate of staff and initiatives, Paton and Mordaunt (2004) advocate for a "twin-track" approach allowing for the incorporation of the "old" with the "new." Such a practice leverages the introduction of new ideas and people with the networks and relationships and essential institutional expertise of existing staff and programs. Most essential here is the leader's ability to quickly diagnose strengths and weaknesses of the organization to focus people and actions on significant and immediate results.

In the private sector, turnaround operators come into distressed companies to bring a fresh perspective and a particular set of skills to ameliorate the situation. Change in leadership—or at least what Burbank (2005) termed "management augmentation"—is a given. They come in knowing they are short-term or interim managers and the expectation that they will achieve results is the reason they were tapped for the job.

Most important is that a different set of skills are needed to effect change when an organization is in distress than when it is prospering, a point that Joyce (2004) echoed in the public sector literature. Depending on the situation, this may require the replacement of existing leadership and some or all of the management team, which Walshe and colleagues (2004) cite as the first step in the public sector turnarounds.

The ranks of turnaround practitioners in business may include turnaround executives, financial stakeholders, and advisers, as well as the newer positions of chief restructuring officer and interim manager. Vital to turnaround leadership is the ability of a leader to recognize the range of expertise that may be needed and, where he or she is not confident, to address those limitations with other leaders on the team (Slatter, Lovett & Barlow, 2006).

This advice is echoed in Jim Collins' research. In his bestseller *Good to Great* (2001), Collins lays out the characteristics of a "level five" leader, someone who can take a company from "good to great." His notion of not just viewing people as general assets, but making the placement of the right people in the right positions a top priority, is essential in the work of turnarounds. Moreover, in a companion piece written for the social sector, Collins added the art of influence as central to a public or nonprofit leader's ability to achieve success, given the constraints often faced by managers in the public domain (Collins, 2005).

Collins' books have relevant lessons for any leader, but to the turnaround specialist his research can provide both comfort and motivation. Concepts like the "BHAGs—big hairy audacious goals" (Collins & Porras, 1994) and "the Stockdale principle" (Collins, 2001) of confronting the brutal facts while never losing faith can take on special meaning for an inspirational leader facing dire

Table 3.1. Turnaround Leaders—Characteristics and Competencies for Renewal

Slatter et al. (2006) p.10 *The Complete Turnaround Executive*	Public Impact (2008) p. 9 *Competencies for Turnaround Success*[1]	Hargreaves & Fink (2006) pp. 18–20 *Seven Principles of Sustainable Leadership*
Develop clear, short-term priorities and goals.	*Driving for Results Cluster*: These enable a relentless focus on learning results.	Sustainable Leadership . . .
Exhibit visible authority.	*Achievement*: The drive and actions to set challenging goals and reach a high standard of performance despite barriers.	*Matters*. It preserves, protects, and promotes deep and broad learning for all in relationships of care for others.
Set expectations and enforce standards.	*Initiative and Persistence*: The drive and actions to do more than is expected or required in order to accomplish a challenging task.	*Lasts*. It preserves and advances the most valuable aspects of learning and life over time, year upon year, from one leader to the next.
Decide and implement decisions quickly.	*Monitoring and Directiveness*: The ability to set clear expectations and to hold others accountable for performance.	
Communicate continuously with all stakeholders.	*Planning Ahead*: A bias towards planning in order to derive future benefits or to avoid problems.	*Spreads*. It sustains as well as depends on the leadership of others.
Build confidence and trust by being transparent and honest.	*Influencing for Results Cluster*: These enable working through and with others.	*Does no harm* to and actively improves the surrounding environment by finding ways to share knowledge and resources with neighboring schools and the local community.
Adopt an autocratic leadership style during crisis stabilization.	*Impact and Influence*: Acting with the purpose of affecting the perceptions, thinking, and actions of others.	
	Team Leadership: Assuming authoritative leadership of a group for the benefit of the organization.	

Table 3.1. Turnaround Leaders—Characteristics and Competencies for Renewal (cont.)

Slatter et al. (2006) p.10 The Complete Turnaround Executive	Public Impact (2008) p. 9 Competencies for Turnaround Success[1]	Hargreaves & Fink (2006) pp. 18–20 Seven Principles of Sustainable Leadership
	Developing Others: Influence with the specific intent to increase the short- and long-term effectiveness of another person. *Problem Solving Cluster*: These enable solving and simplifying complex problems. *Analytical Thinking*: The ability to break things down in a logical way and to recognize cause and effect. *Conceptual Thinking*: The ability to see patterns and links among seemingly unrelated things. *Showing Confidence to Lead*: This competency is concerned with staying focused, committed, and self-assured. *Self-Confidence*: A personal belief in one's ability to accomplish tasks, and the actions that reflect that belief.	*Promotes cohesive diversity*. It fosters and learns from diversity and creates cohesion and networking among its richly varying components. *Develops material and human resources*. It renews people's energy. *Respects and builds on the past* in its quest to create a better future.

[1]*School Turnaround Leaders: Competencies for Success*. Public Impact for the Chicago Public Education Fund, June 2008. The authors note that they "mapped" cross-sector research on leadership action with leadership competencies of successful entrepreneurs and other leaders to arrive at these leadership competencies. They expect to be able to validate and refine them with more research on successful and unsuccessful turnaround leaders (p. 9). Steiner, L.M., Hassel, E.A., & Hassel, B. (2008).

circumstances. In a time-bound turnaround situation where resources may be especially constrained, Collins' insight that leaders of great organizations not only decide what to focus on but what *not* to do, can be empowering to the turnaround principal inheriting an assortment of disconnected programs.

Cross-sector research notes additional characteristics such as the ability to handle organizational politics and the use of entrepreneurial and proven techniques (Paton & Mordaunt, 2004) as well as culture management, listening, and rewarding and recognizing achievement (Joyce, 2004).

It is undisputed that the turnaround leader must make decisions in a compressed time frame if he or she is to achieve success. Such time stress underscores the importance of being innovative and strategic while also managing details, of being a clear and confident negotiator who can communicate with internal and external stakeholders, and of being able to set clear objectives that delineate a forward path which employees can follow (Burbank, 2005).

Strong skills in both management and leadership are necessary, so that the pressure for stabilization does not outweigh the importance of establishing a future strategy, including processes and organizational frameworks that prevent slips backward into failure. This focus on strategy and process also guards against the tendency to define a turnaround in terms of its leader, rather than on the long-term results achieved.

Beyond the turnaround executive him- or herself are the key stakeholders supporting the work of turnaround. Mordaunt and Cornforth (2004) examined the role of boards in public sector turnarounds. They, too, emphasize the critical nature of a turnaround leader's skill set. They also acknowledge the emotional resiliency required to sustain a turnaround effort, especially in cases when a board must intervene. As the cases presented in this book will demonstrate, the work of turnaround is exhausting and even painful; it requires leaders who can fight through challenges with steadfast determination and an unfailing perseverance toward the mission at hand.

The Turnaround Process

Turnaround

> *A substantial and rapid performance improvement sufficient to reestablish business viability in the face of actual or impending failure. (Paton and Mordaunt, 2004, p. 209)*

School Turnaround

> *A dramatic and comprehensive intervention in a low-performing school that produces significant gains in student achievement within two academic years. (Mass Insight Education & Research Institute, 2007)*

Turnarounds in any context are about contending with and removing failure. Few would argue that the work of turnarounds is complex and multidimensional. But first, failure must be seen and acknowledged. With an unrelenting focus on profitability, business turnarounds seek "business viability." In the public sector, however, Paton and Mordaunt (2004) point out that stakeholders may show more tolerance for failure than private sector peers, since definitions of failure are less clear. They point out that chronic, not just impending, failure may need to be considered when defining turnarounds. State and national accountability systems like No Child Left Behind (NCLB) have gone a long way to improve on this, but cultures of failure can be pervasive and what is expected and tolerated for certain people and certain conditions may confound the urgency of turnarounds.

In certain respects, private sector failure is more noticeable, more easily detected. As Pearce and Robbins (1993) note, turnaround situations follow periods of prosperity and are marked by multiple years of financial declines. In the public sector, however, Walshe and colleagues (2004) note that the costs of failure currently acceptable to some stakeholders may be too low given the social necessity of public organizations such as schools and hospitals.

To be sure, the crosswalk between private and public sector turnarounds is complex, and comparative analysis is limited by the shortage of research in the public sector. Given different missions, cultures, and metrics, drawing lessons between turnarounds in these sectors is not necessarily clear-cut. Despite the challenges, however, scholars continue to draw from the more extensive literature of the management field as a means of providing frameworks and strategies for better understanding the public sector turnaround.

Diagnosis, Then Strategy

The context surrounding a turnaround often determines the strategy for the reversal of decline. To use a medical analogy, the triage that arrests life-threatening conditions must come first, with a more in-depth battery of tests, a full workup, and treatment to follow for a complete recovery. The diagnostic, or strategic, review must include an analysis of the current situation, including its root causes. Slatter and his colleagues (2006) present six objectives used in the private sector that may offer educators some insights. These include:

- assessing whether the entity can survive in the short run
- determining whether the organization can be viable in the medium and long term
- assessing the options available and identifying those that offer the best value to the various stakeholders

- diagnosing at a high level the key problems; evaluating whether they are strategic, operational, or both; and identifying the mix of strategies necessary for short-term survival
- assessing the positions of key stakeholders and their willingness to support the turnaround
- assessing the management in a preliminary fashion (who is part of the problem, etc.) (pp. 55–56)

Such diagnosis in the private sector may be more straightforward. For instance, Pearce and Robbins (1992) discuss causality for private sector failure as binary—external versus internal factors. In contrast, Paton and Mordaunt (2004) note that complex stakeholder interactions may be at work in the public sector, leading to a more politically charged environment for accomplishing turnaround.

Such complexity in the context of education might encompass the school's physical and human capital, social involvement, demographic conditions, district environment and supports, state policies, federal laws, other stakeholder pressures, and apathy. Yet, analysis of these initial conditions is paramount and might lead first to a district- or state-level decision about school closure, reconstitution, "charterization," or turnaround. In the latter case, a turnaround professional would come in to address the school-level operational and instructional challenges.

The assessment of conditions leading to failure, in terms of both causality and severity, is essential to designing an effective turnaround strategy. Understanding causality can help determine whether turnaround strategies need greater focus on operations, human resources, or external constituencies. This type of analysis can also uncover strengths among management and staff teams that will help them carry out the difficult work ahead.

The completion of a thoughtful and thorough diagnosis, by either an internal team or a third party, may allow specific intervention strategies to be matched to each of the various circumstances that produced the failure. Walshe and colleagues (2004) note that while the process might be different in the public sector due to the practical challenges presented by the political environment, governance, and accountability frameworks, the success of turnaround in any sector may rely most heavily on the alignment of strategies and actions with the contextual issues causing the decline.

Translating this to the education arena, states, districts, unions, and other entities increasingly are finding the need to change policies that hamper turnaround. While Race to the Top funds have spurred recent efforts, turnaround leaders often go above and beyond to ensure policy meets what works for students. Mel Riddile, winner of the 2006 National Association of Secondary

School Principals' "Principal of the Year" award for his turnaround of J.E.B. Stuart High School in Fairfax County, for instance, led his staff and community to adopt a year-round calendar that better served the needs of his student body. Such an effort required approval by the Virginia State Board of Education, which he sought and received.[5]

One important caution here, however, is that while the literature is clear that the turnaround leader needs the freedom to act amid the dire conditions he or she is presented, especially in the public sector, a single-school solution will not have lasting impact over the long run. District or system change, as the next chapter will address, is an essential element of sustaining turnaround success. Furthermore, a "turnaround zone" as Mass Insight (2007) suggests or a department dedicated to turnaround may offer the ability to examine similar conditions across schools within a district, region, or state and then identify the types of policy changes needed for sustainable improvement and prevention of future decline.

Stakeholder Engagement

Champions within the turnaround environment are essential to reversing the circumstances of decline. Stakeholder engagement, which also will be addressed in the next chapter, must be present to protect the turnaround from potential failures caused by the political machinery or any single stakeholder group's inability to reach agreement. Analysis of stakeholder interests and positions is critical to a turnaround leader's understanding how to align efforts toward desired and necessary changes.

States and districts embracing turnaround strategies must assess how to engage and consistently communicate with specialists and their constituencies, especially in the event of politically unpopular strategies. Understanding and thoughtfully addressing the conditions which have led to the school's distress—which may be even more complex in schools with chronic underperformance—are essential to providing the necessary support for long-term achievement.

Change Management Processes

Since dramatic change is the heart of any turnaround, the change management literature offers a number of useful frameworks that help organizations to focus on the strategies and actions that will facilitate the reversal of decline and stagnation. John Kotter's (1996) eight-step change process,[6] developed from research on both successful and failed transformations, offers one recognizable set of conditions necessary for change to take hold in the short term and to have lasting impact over time.

Kotter admonishes that all steps are important, and that skipping steps only creates the illusion of speed. Kotter's (1995) seminal article in the *Harvard Business Review*, "Why Transformation Efforts Fail," showed how each of these conditions, when not fulfilled, can contribute to further decline or transformation failure. Kotter is one of many researchers (e.g., Michael Fullan, Andy Hargreaves, Rosabeth Moss Kanter, Nitin Nohria) making sense of the messy work of change.

While the change management literature is relevant to turnarounds, a turnaround by definition includes urgency with regard to time and a focus on dramatic improvement that sets it apart. Among those considering questions of urgency and timing within the turnaround process, Bibeault (1982) was the first to discuss the multi-stage turnaround model. His process included situation analysis, management change, and the creation of an "emergency plan," followed by the more time-consuming "recovery" process.

Table 3.2 summarizes a few research highlights relevant to the stages of the turnaround process in the private sector and the actions found necessary for renewal to take hold in one education sector study.

Situation analysis, a more detached and objective process, leads to an understanding and acknowledgement of the severity of the problem, which is arguably more emotional, as it requires those involved in the turnaround to recognize and overcome denial (Boyne, 2004; Mordaunt & Cornforth, 2004). Collins (2001) calls this "confronting the brutal facts." Whatever the term used, the planning phase of turnarounds must include clear examination and acceptance of the current facts as well as the causes of the distress.

In the planning phase especially, honesty regarding the situation is paramount. Communication is also critical. If the severity of conditions is not well understood, then the interventions required likely may not be fully realized and thus not well implemented or, even worse, not implemented at all. Therefore "chartering" (Roberto, 2005), or setting a course for change that includes boundary setting and team design, is an essential part of the planning process.

Although planning is critical, implementation is the keystone of a successful turnaround, as Gibson and Billings (2003) found in their analysis of the corporate turnaround of electronics giant Best Buy. It was the engagement of a Change Implementation Team (CIT) made up of front-line store managers that helped create the processes necessary for the eventual turn. Employing a Change Implementation Scorecard to constantly monitor the pulse of the effort engages a set of tools that not only help diagnose problems but also assist in the processes of coaching and organizational learning, through which solutions to a multitude of implementation challenges are sought. In school turnarounds, the parallel might be the use of a leadership team and employing a balanced scorecard.

Table 3.2. The Turnaround Process

Turnaround Management Association (Body of Knowledge) Stages of the Turnaround Process	Pearce & Robbins (1993)	Ansell (2004) Review of School Turnarounds—Success Factors

• Management Change
• Situation Analysis
• Design & Selection of a Turnaround Strategy
• Emergency Action
• Business Restructuring
• Return to Normal
	• Retrenchment
	  • setting targets
	  • cutting costs
	• Recovery
	  • employing change management strategies to improve performance
		• involving of people with past expertise and experience in turnaround situations;
		• appointing of a new head teacher (principal), or more specifically, one with an experienced track record of success in improving schools of this nature;
		• planning thoroughly, identifying and addressing weaknesses and involving key stakeholders;
		• developing strategies and use of target setting and benchmarking for improvement;
		• monitoring the implementation plan carefully and regularly;
		• communicating and clarifying the individual roles of everyone involved on the leadership team; and
		• outsourcing specific tasks and functions that don't fit within the competencies of the school leadership, such as accounting and human resource management.

Efforts to mobilize financial and human resources for the short-term survival plan (e.g., a 90-day plan) and bring on key influencers, though not necessarily all stakeholders, are essential (Mordaunt & Cornforth, 2004; Paton & Mordaunt, 2004). Beer and Nohria (2001) posit that a combination of a "theory E," or use of external consultants, and a "theory O," a commitment to building organizational capacity, is needed to achieve transformation.

In the education sector, changes made in the implementation stage might include reorganizations, changes in program focus, negotiations of policy changes, alignment of curriculum, implementation of benchmark testing, targeted assessment and professional development, and close and regular observation of classroom instruction. Cosmetic changes to a school's exterior can provide a face-lift while longer-term maintenance issues are negotiated. Some schools in distress, however, must put immediate attention to more significant physical plant challenges such as rodent, water, mold, or sewage problems.

Paton and Mordaunt (2004) find that in public turnarounds stronger politics tend to exist, and so the need to provide additional freedom to take culturally sensitive or symbolic actions to restore basic institutional confidence is more pronounced than in the private sector research. If a principal needs to eliminate a popular volunteer program, change schedules and routines that involve parents and teachers in order to protect instructional time, or opt out of district or state policies that are impeding student success, then freedoms that facilitate such change while protecting the principal from repercussions from community leaders, school board members, or parents are essential.

If the planning phase can be described as charting the path forward, then the implementation phase consists of translating the map into actions that lead to the desired goals. Yet, as Gibson and Billings (2003) point out, "the map is definitely not the territory (p. 10)"; the map can offer a planned course of action directed toward the desired change, but as turnaround leaders know, they must also possess a level of flexibility to respond to emergent issues, making course corrections as necessary in order to maintain forward momentum.

Whatever the implementation strategy, the turnaround leader must move forward on a number of fronts simultaneously and decisively. Quick and symbolic wins can lay the groundwork for gaining momentum among internal and external stakeholders. Dual or "twin-track" strategies, such as those that combine innovations and efficiencies, will have stronger results than those adhering to a single-track approach.

Finally, leaders should focus on those changes that address underlying causes, engaging stakeholders in a way that defines change and success in terms of a team goal, such as student achievement, rather in terms of a single leader's efforts. As the cases presented will show, addressing inconsistent lesson planning and instituting and carefully reviewing interim assessments are just a few of the ways that turnaround leaders imbed strategies in the school that shore up a laser-like focus on student achievement. Such strategies also offer a last set of culture changes that can continue once the turnaround leader moves on.

Sustaining Improvements

Turnarounds should only be needed once in any organization. Unfortunately, that is not always the case. If a turnaround is accomplished successfully, the potential for sliding back into distress should be minimal. Yet, given the primary focus on arresting the decline, school, district, and even state leaders may not be putting enough emphasis on what Fullan (2006) called "the beyond turnaround solution."[7] Succession planning to ensure hard-fought change is sustained is paramount as turnarounds are scaled. Otherwise, "slide back" is inevitable and the hard-fought changes and resource investments are wasted.

Planning for sustainability cannot wait until the turnaround is complete. The timeframe to complete turnarounds varies though most agree that lasting change takes three to five years. While private providers suggest this is at most a two-year process, Paton & Mordaunt (2004) find that the timeline required to achieve sustainable change in the public sector may be incompatible with such estimates, given the public pressures and complex political structures involved. As the cases presented in this book will show, skilled turnaround professionals need at least three years—and more likely five or six—to address the complexity that drove a school's chronic underperformance and to ensure changes are imbedded into the culture and will not dissipate when the leader departs.

Thus, it is hardly surprising that programs and interventions designed to achieve immediate results might not provide the range of assistance individuals need when establishing the long-term changes that will prevent decline in the future. While scant research exists in this area, some have argued that lack of improvement or further decline results from either a focus on the leader as change guru or a lack of major policy changes that address the root causes of the initial distress (Fullan 2006; Harvgreaves & Fink, 2006; MERI, 2007).

In the business sector, approaches to succession planning and human resource management contrast sharply with such practices in education. Hargreaves and Fink (2006, p. 61) compare public sector approaches to succession with those in the private sector, and identify major differences in how leaders are developed. These differences include the notion of "growing your own" versus recruiting, strategic planning based on short-term views versus a long-term vision, and perspectives on succession as a cost versus those that consider it an asset.

Renewal involves longer-term actions that will reestablish strategic direction, vision, and the overall purpose of the organization, placing it not on the fast track to survival but on the longer-term pathway to performance (Walshe et al., 2004). The public sector literature offers few specific directions for achieving such renewal, perhaps due to the fact that turnarounds in education are a newer concept.

As Hargreaves and Fink (2006) note, sustainable leadership fulfills three key responsibilities: leading learning, distributing leadership, and attending to leadership succession, so that improvements outlive the leaders that put them in place. Embedding change into a new culture takes time; without plans to build on success over time lasting improvement may never be attained. Thus, turnaround leadership requires a careful examination of leadership transitions, on both the front end and the back end of the turnaround period.

In most cases, the leader that completes the turnaround will not be the leader that continues to sustain its growth. Given the distinct characteristics and skills needed to accomplish turnarounds, such leaders might be restless or otherwise underutilized if they remained in their turnaround school. These leaders may themselves have the need to move on to take on a new challenge, as the chapter 9 case study featuring turnaround specialist J. Harrison Coleman's fifth turnaround school will illustrate.

Consider the private sector parallel. A turnaround operator comes into a distressed company to employ a set of strategies and processes that lead to corporate renewal, after which another manager generally takes over. Turnaround operators in business are trained for interim assignments.

While education schools still train leaders as generalists to be employed in multiple school settings, this approach does not clearly develop a strong bench of leaders who will take over once the turnaround is complete. Nor does a generalist approach develop a talent team of leaders that can specifically address the needs of struggling schools. What the current approach fails to consider is that leaders skilled at long-term sustainable growth might be better able to take the school to a new level once renewal is achieved than the specially trained turnaround leaders that breathed new life into the school.

As this brief literature review demonstrates, turnarounds in education will be most effective if they incorporate knowledge from the management and leadership literature of all three sectors: business, public, and nonprofit. In addition, there are a few critical yet oft under-discussed factors at work in educational turnarounds that bear special attention—the socioeconomic and demographic challenges imbedded in the complex profiles of chronically under-performing schools.

THE ROLE OF POVERTY

In examining the national and state landscapes surrounding schools in distress, the intricate challenges of socioeconomics become readily apparent. Nearly 20 million of the nation's 73 million school-age children, or about 27 percent, come from low-income families; that ratio rises to 42 percent in the South (Douglass-Hall & Chau, 2007).

As such, careful considerations of the legacy of poverty are essential to understanding the environmental and systemic factors affecting student performance. While research has found poverty and other sociocultural factors such as ethnicity or low levels of parent education to be reliable predictors of low achievement among students (D'Amico, 2001), clear indicators of high achievement are emerging as well.

Karin Chenoweth's (2007) case studies of high-performing, high-poverty (HPHP) schools demonstrate that a strong focus on teaching, with emphasis on the outcomes of learning, is essential to achievement in the profiled schools. Individualized instruction with frequent opportunities for measured feedback allows teachers to continually adapt instruction toward ensuring that students indeed learn what is taught.

Similarly, Blankstein (2004) considers six principles for high performance. Second among them is "ensuring achievement for all students." He encourages educators to examine the school community's belief system regarding low-performing students; identify the overarching philosophy that unifies staff behavior; and build in "comprehensive systems" to facilitate student success.

Taking proactive steps to address the variables that have often become barriers to learning, such as low socioeconomic status, differences in learning styles, other languages spoken at home, and stressful family situations, offers the support that students need most to overcome those barriers.

The work of changing belief systems is complex and difficult. So too are the challenges involved in removing the myriad obstacles facing students. This work requires schools to move from a culture of compliance to one of complete commitment to students and their success.

Blankstein's model concludes with the principle of "building sustainable leadership capacity," a notion of particular import to the turnaround field given the accelerated cycle time of the change process. Borrowing from Goleman and colleagues' (2002) research into leadership styles and Collins' (2001) concept of the "level five" leader, among others, Blankstein posits that the most effective school leaders are those able to collaboratively build a culture in which "failure is not an option."

Clearly, there is growing evidence of what creates high performance in high-poverty schools. Understanding the complexity of conditions in these schools is paramount. After that, the task is to transform what has been learned into strategies that will create a culture in which success is the expectation, not the exception, in the most chronically under-performing schools and in schools with pockets of under-performing students. In states like Louisiana, where the size of the economically disadvantaged population is nearly twice the national average, at 61.4 percent,[8] or other states like Connecticut, where poverty is largely concentrated in urban centers, the factors relating to poverty that affect student achievement must be carefully examined.[9]

THE ROLE OF RACE

In the debate on underserved, underperforming schools, the role of race and ethnicity in student success is one of the most complex and difficult issues to discuss. Yet, given both the majority-minority makeup of the public school population in some states and districts, the pronounced black-white and Hispanic-white achievement gaps, and the racial legacies and ethnic tensions that stem from our nation's history, the role of race in underperforming schools cannot be overlooked for its own distinct effect beyond socioeconomic status.

Unfortunately, the topic of race—including racism, racial legacies, and racial stereotypes—usually falls at the end of the list of important topics when it comes to discussions about improving teaching and learning. This may be the case especially in a turnaround situation where there is a long list of other elements of the crisis boiling over at the surface. When discussions do happen, gender performance gaps and the role of poverty may seem easier to talk about than how skin color influences actions, especially in what some call a "post-racial" society.

Despite the seeming lack of conversation, there is generally agreement that a significant black-white achievement gap prevails at the national level. Thernstrom and Thernstrom (2003) write, "The average black and Hispanic student at the end of high school has academic skills that are at about the eighth-grade level" (p. 22). Since racial categories are social constructions and not indicators of innate genetic differences, it is important to understand the data and to talk openly about what may be impeding the achievement of students of color in their early years up through college.

The U.S. Census Bureau (2003) data on education attainment of the population 25 years and older by race, ethnic origin, and age underscore how those gaps translate into higher education attainment. While a third of the white population 25 to 29 years old and 60 percent of the Asian population held at least a bachelor's degree, only 17 percent of blacks and one in 10 Hispanics held such degrees. Also striking is the educational attainment of the populations 25 and over; for whites and Asians the percentages in the 25–29 group are clearly greater whereas in the black and Hispanic populations, the percentages of degree holders or even those having "some college" remain largely unchanged from the 25–29 to the 25-and-over age groups.[10]

State and federal accountability systems allow achievement gaps to be viewed in both socioeconomic and racial terms, so the data are there. Yet, many see race and poverty gaps as one and the same. However, take the case of Louisiana, for example. While the gap between economically disadvantaged and non-disadvantaged students in Louisiana remains significant, at a 24 percent statewide average, the black-white achievement gap is even more expansive, at a statewide average of 30.3 percent.[11]

Given this reality, the emerging field of turnaround leadership should support meaningful conversations about the distinct effects of race-based beliefs and attitudes on student success. Consider a study some years back of the Department of Defense (DoD) schools. DoD schools are an interesting example in part because racial diversity crosses all ranks in the military, more so than in most communities. Researchers from Vanderbilt University found that eight interconnecting factors contribute to student success in highly diverse schools. These included:

- centralized direction setting and localized decision making;
- policy coherence and regular data flow;
- financial resources linked to instructionally relevant goals;
- job-embedded staff development linked to student performance;
- small school size, conducive to trust and community building;
- academic focus and high expectations;
- continuity of care for students in high quality preschools and after-school programs; and
- a "corporate commitment" to public education and responsiveness to parents.

One additional interesting finding about race was that this study showed that in a 1998 NAEP reading test climate survey, 85 percent of African American students reported being "very positive" about teacher expectations, versus 52 percent nationally (Smrekar, Guthrie, Owens & Sims, 2001). What was it about that environment that changed student perceptions of teacher expectations?

Other researchers, like Beverly Daniel Tatum,[12] offer rich material by which to explore the role of race in students' experiences of school as well as how teachers and leaders can best address the complex historical legacy that accompanies these issues. Thomas Shapiro's (2004) research on wealth and asset creation, which reveals the hidden disadvantages experienced by minorities, particularly African Americans, in class mobility, provides another promising avenue toward understanding the intersection of socioeconomics and race.

Steele and Aronson (1995) present one more dimension in the complex list of factors surrounding the experience of students of color and their achievements. Their notion of "stereotype vulnerability" describes situations where students so fear confirming stereotypes related to achievement that they in fact "choke" in performance environments. Building on similar analyses of gender differences in math performance, Steele and Aronson add to an understanding of how a student experiences the schooling environment and expectations for achievement. Through this scholarship, turnaround leaders can enhance their knowledge and further develop their abilities to facilitate the dialogue so needed to create meaningful and sustainable change in schools.

The culture of underperformance may have both class and race dimensions that few understand well, and tendencies toward political correctness hamper needed dialogues about biases, however unintentional. Nosek and his colleagues' work on implicit associations[13] offers new opportunities to identify teacher and administrator blind spots in the ways they teach and manage students. Implicit assumptions at work in the classroom, for instance, may surreptitiously influence which students get called on and which get reprimanded. Without understanding or acknowledging such biases, however unintentional, school leaders and staff may be spending time focusing on interventions that have more to do with behaviors than content.

Despite major strides of the Civil Rights Movement, the War on Poverty, and more recent elections and policy changes, racism (systemic or otherwise) clouds progress on many fronts. Communities are still experiencing racism, even if for some it is more covert in nature. Perhaps dealing with overt racism was easier, and now the subtle biases, lasting tensions, and painful legacies are trickier to handle. Whatever the case, turnaround leaders cannot avoid these troubling histories and difficult conversations and thus must equip themselves with the self-awareness, knowledge, and skills to address, rather than avoid, issues that keep the achievement gap from closing.

Consider the turnaround specialist who started his principalship in a district that was the hub of the Massive Resistance Movement in Virginia. In 1958, public schools closed to avoid integration, a practice endorsed by the Governor that affected a number of communities across the Commonwealth.[14] Recognizing the importance and stubbornness of this legacy, this turnaround leader began by having his staff read a book about the history of their community. Confronting the racial legacies upfront allowed him to release an unspoken tension that had plagued his school for decades. Rather than let the issues fester, this leader acknowledged their importance to the communities' healing process, nearly 50 years later.

The work of school turnarounds requires leaders that can be passionate and compassionate, those who can look hard at the data and stand back and examine the bigger picture. It is work that needs leaders who can draw from educational research and management insights, from race and social justice research, and from economics, psychology, and sociology. Leaders equipped with a broad set of insights and grounded in the work of turnarounds across fields may be best able to accelerate results and find strategies and solutions to meet the needs of their schools and communities.

NOTES

1. See U.S. Department of Education. (2010). Voices from turnaround schools. http://www.ed.gov/blog/2010/05/voices-of-reform/. Accessed 9-30-10.
2. Chenoweth, K. (2007). "It's being done." *Education Week.* April 11, 2007.
3. Turnaround Management Association. (n.d.). "Overview of Body of Knowledge Course Content." http://www.turnaround.org/TMAccess/Materials.aspx. Accessed 11-4-10.
4. Public Impact. *School turnaround leaders: Selection toolkit.* Chapel Hill, NC: Steiner, L.M., Hassel, E.A., and Hassel, B, Valsing, E and Crittenden, S. http://www.publicimpact.com/publications/Turnaround_Leader_Selection_Toolkit.pdf. Accessed 10-15-10.
5. Liedtke, J., Fairchild, T., and Kelly, D. (2005). *J.E.B. Stuart high school.* Darden Case Collection. Charlottesville, VA: Darden Business Publishing. UVA- OB-0853.
6. Kotter, J.P. (1996). *Leading change.* Cambridge, MA: Harvard Business School Press. Kotter's eight-stage process (p. 21) includes: establishing a sense of urgency; building a powerful guiding coalition; developing a vision—a "picture of the future"; communicating the change decision; empowering others to act on the vision; planning for and creating short-term wins; consolidating improvements and sustaining the momentum for change; and institutionalizing new approaches.
7. See also MERI (2007) and Hargreaves and Fink (2006).
8. Standard & Poor's. www.SchoolMatters.com. "Louisiana Statewide Education Highlights" 2004 data. Accessed 9-10-07.
9. See Education Trust. (2010, January 6). *Gauging the gaps: A deeper look at student achievement.* Washington, DC: Rowan, A.H., Hall, D., and Haycock, K. http://www.edtrust.org/sites/edtrust.org/files/publications/files/NAEP%20Gap_0.pdf. Accessed 6-26-10.
10. http://www.census.gov/mso/www/pres_lib/2003Education/textmostly/slide15.html. Accessed 11-4-10.
11. School Matters.com. "Narrowing the achievement gap." Accessed 9-10-07.
12. See Tatum, B.D. (2003). *Why are all the black kids sitting together in the cafeteria? A psychologist explains the development of racial identity.* New York: Basic

Books; and Tatum, B.D. (2007). *Can we talk about race? And other conversations in an era of school resegregation.* Boston: Beacon Press.

13. Nosek, B.A., and Hansen, J.J. (2008). "Personalizing the Implicit Association Test increases explicit evaluation of the target concepts." *European Journal of Psychological Assessment, 25,* 226–236. For additional citations for papers on Implicit Associations see: http://projectimplicit.net/nosek/.

14. Sluss, M. (2009, July 19). "Black students recount early days of integration." *The Roanoke Times.* http://www.roanoke.com/news/roanoke/wb/212343. Accessed 6-26-10.

Section II

A Critical Path to School Turnarounds

Chapter 4

Approaching Turnarounds with a 2-S Model

Systems and Stakeholders

Give talented teachers a classroom and the instructional resources to engage students. Then leave them alone. Some would argue that more of this is needed in all schools and especially underperforming ones. Talented teachers. Instructional resources. Quietude away from the many distractions that interrupt the day—the loudspeaker, pullouts, paperwork, meetings.

In a tech-savvy, interconnected world, it is important for teachers to be quick, flexible learners that keep up with the latest content and pedagogical techniques with a laser-like focus on improving student learning. Yet, teachers may regularly be expected to implement new report cards, high-stakes assessments, and a variety of textbooks as well as keep up with technology and a myriad of different programs. It is no wonder they have difficulty finding time to strengthen lesson plans, analyze data, differentiate instruction, and collaborate effectively.

Enter the principal. This leader is expected to protect that precious classroom time, limiting interruptions that can mean the difference between students understanding the daily concepts and missing them. Hopefully, he/she is focused on strengthening the core program to ensure all students succeed, creating a schedule that allows for "double dipping" on targeted content or providing interventions that break down what otherwise may be especially difficult concepts for some learners.

The principal develops a schedule that maximizes instructional time and considers transitions and the need for recess, appropriate groupings, positive behavior, and other supports to help students and teachers thrive in the classroom—all the while managing buses, nutrition, and community involvement and integrating volunteers and after-school programs in a meaningful way to take learning to the next level. The work is exhilarating and at the same time exhausting as principals lead, motivate, and manage toward the many goals they must accomplish each day.

All too often, however, teachers don't have the opportunity to shut out the rest of the world, and principals cannot keep teachers from the many issues, offerings, and concerns that accompany any regulated environment. Federal laws, state regulations, and district policy changes focused on student achievement trickle down to the school and, ultimately, the classroom and students. Union contract requirements, and local bond issues, and desegregation orders are among the many other critical considerations that impact the classroom.

Sometimes these "gifts from above" enhance the teacher's portfolio of tools, and other times they are yet one more distraction or misaligned addition to a set of one-size-fits-all interventions. For the principal, they can be a welcome set of resources, especially if they help drive innovation and promote the school's vision. Yet, too often, they cloud the objectives, confusing the professionals, parents, and students on the receiving end. A well-intentioned grant, volunteer program, or district intervention can be onerous, requiring more rather than less work to ensure it enhances rather than detracts from the school's strategy and core program.

While it might be appealing for teachers to be able to shut out the rest of the world as they engage our students, it is not realistic. The resources a teacher may need are likely tied to content requirements and state standards and assessments. Each piece of knowledge builds on another, connecting classrooms to grades and grades to schools. Isolation, however tempting, discounts the important benefits of connecting learning across teams, subjects, and grades and into enrichment and intervention strategies and even to after-school programming. Transitions within and across grades and schools can mean the difference between a struggling student attaining a diploma or becoming a dropout.

Principals may want to close their doors and focus on accomplishing "to do" lists as well. Such uninterrupted think time may be similarly appealing for administrators managing the many details of school life. Yet, a visible principal engaged in the school's core business—teaching and learning—would be more likely to emanate a school's vision, build community, and mentor staff and students. Isolation is tempting for administrators too, especially when their plate is overflowing, but in the long run making connections among and across stakeholders and systems can accelerate improvements.

It may seem straightforward to focus on the principal as leader of the turnaround, to develop his or her capacity to effect swift change, and to reward his or her performance based on the achievement of targets. However, this approach overlooks both the system and the stakeholders working within it. Equally wrong-headed is a singular focus on teacher performance, with ties to assessment and even compensation. Ultimately, such a singular focus on the school or classroom leader will not produce or sustain the results needed to reverse the stagnation or decline in underperforming schools.

A WEB OF RELATIONSHIPS

Essential to any turnaround is acknowledgement of the interconnectedness of the teachers, schools, district, and larger community. Some might remember the experience of the New American Schools Development Corporation (NASDC). Business leaders created this private, nonprofit corporation in 1991 to identify and fund effective school-wide restructuring designs.[1] The corporation ultimately identified 11 school-wide models from hundreds of proposals. From 1992 to 1995, models were implemented in over 150 schools in 19 states.[2]

While the idea of model schools sounded promising to many, NASDC's approach initially focused on the school as the hub of change. Model schools can indeed spur innovation, but political changes and systemic influences can be difficult to overcome even for the most well-funded entities. A Thomas B. Fordham Foundation report entitled *The Evolution of New American Schools: From Revolution to Mainstream* offered this critique.

> Implementation was anything but smooth, however. Design teams varied in the progress they made in participating schools, in part because some designs focused on narrow changes in instruction and curriculum while others sought to introduce broader reforms in school governance, reforms that typically proved very difficult to implement. People in communities targeted by NASDC were often deeply divided. Principals worried that there was a mismatch between the design teams' student-centered approaches and the more traditional standards and tests being used by states and districts. NASDC reformers gradually discovered how arduous it is to change existing schools. (Mirel, 2001, p. v)

While NASDC (later NAS) leaders realized the importance of system change to the development and sustainability of good schools, the report noted that their efforts to scale up these models hit numerous political roadblocks and implementation challenges. Design teams may not have fully considered their largely disadvantaged urban student populations in order to realize dramatic gains. Despite a number of evaluations, the overall impact of NAS schools became difficult to assess.

Some may view the NAS experience as a cautionary tale for the charter school movement. Public charters, often with loose ties to a school district, can operate with relative autonomy from district bureaucracy and policies, hopefully spurring the innovation to spark new and unique products, processes, methods, or applications. Organizations that succeed in creating inclusive cultures where diverse thoughts, perspectives, and experiences are valued are also creating fertile ground for innovation.

Charter schools are able to do business differently because, by definition, they aren't bound by all the same rules. Billed by some the "research and development" arm of school districts, charters offer opportunities to redefine the student's experience, upending how teachers teach, what they teach, for how long, and with what rewards and accountability. While such practices may have been tried in more traditional schools, the unique ways charter schools can put them together often results in a school culture and operational structure much different than those in neighboring schools.

Yet, as with any research and development effort, the translation of an isolated success in the lab to a mass-marketed product can be tricky. Replicating specifications to the highest standards of quality is not easy in any environment and is proving even more complex in the public education system. Pockets of success are evident but scalable models are in short supply. A few charter management organizations, such as those discussed in Chapter 2 (KIPP, Achievement First, and Green Dot Schools), have been able to replicate programs (and, most important, results) and port strategies to different locations. The task now is to scale models like these to levels where they impact millions rather than thousands of students.

The question of whether charter schools can scale to a level of serving the many students in need remains unanswered. For instance, in New York City, a recent study (Hoxby, Murarka & Kang, 2009) provided a strong endorsement for the attention charter schools place on underserved students and for the environment and policies these schools offer (e.g., longer school year, more instructional time, focus on academic achievement). Evaluation results show that students attending New York City charters have made progress in closing the "Scarsdale-Harlem" achievement gap. Yet even with the positive trends, New York City Independent Budget Office reports that only 2 percent of all students attend charters, many of these concentrated in Harlem and the Bronx.[3]

Another recent study (CREDO, 2009) indicates that charter school results are more mixed across the nation. Much of this has been blamed on poor decision making around which groups get and renew charters. The National Alliance of Public Charter Schools has acknowledged that comparative data are still limited and continues to look for ways to better understand the impact and quality of charter schools across the nation.[4]

The need for turnaround continues to outstrip the capacity to offer a variety of solutions, including charter school success, on a large scale. Currently,

40 states have charter school legislation, and all states that have won Race to the Top monies have charter schools. Successful charters are an important part of the portfolio of solutions, especially as they test innovations while operating largely outside the system. Solutions that also fix the system itself—state and federal entities included—might have more promise for long-term, scalable success.

Facilitating turnarounds within districts can help to untangle the messy systemic influences at play. Removing obstacles and spurring improvement at a turnaround school can lead to the replication of good ideas and policies across a set of schools. In this way, turnaround schools within public school districts, more so than their charter counterparts, may be able to act as catalysts for needed change in the larger system. Jefferson Parish School System and Kate Middleton Elementary School, for instance, highlighted in Chapter 7, illustrate how one turnaround specialist and her district advocate, an accountability director, are developing and implementing novel assessment tools to inform instruction. These tools, developed initially for the turnaround school, are now being replicated in other schools throughout the district.

Finding and replicating a formula for turnaround school success, however, is not the point. Every turnaround operates within a unique context. Frameworks and tools can be utilized, ideas can be shared, research-based interventions can be implemented, data tools and instructional strategies can be employed, but the system and its stakeholders will always be different. In short, context matters.

The remainder of this chapter outlines the essential role that systems and stakeholders can play in the turnaround process. By taking a 2-S approach to turnaround, attending to the larger system in which the school operates, and engaging the stakeholders within that system effectively, turnaround leaders and their teams can stay focused on the "big picture" while solving the many problems afflicting their schools.

ATTENDING TO THE SYSTEM

System Influences

Understanding the larger organization in which the school operates is essential for any turnaround leader. Like a Russian nested doll, a principal can start with his students and build the nesting system around the student from the classroom, school, district, community, state, federal government, and, in our global environment, to the international community. This outermost layer is the system in which the student may eventually compete for jobs and resources, invest, or otherwise support.

Decisions made at any one of those levels can affect that student's experience—a new reading program is adopted, a redistricting occurs, a community deals with its racial history, unemployment rises, a country goes to war, federal or state laws and funding mechanisms change. With an eye to the larger system and context in which the school is situated, a principal can attend to the many influences impacting the turnaround. He or she may not have direct control over many or even most of them; however, she or he will have knowledge of how the system influences the teacher. Strategies then can be chosen with the system in mind.

Political will, an essential component in turnarounds, must be managed, and until a principal understands the web of connections—the ways to get things done, the issues to push first, the compromises that can be made while still accomplishing dramatic gain—they may find their ability to identify and address the root causes of decline limited, or the desired results not sustainable over time.

Imagine for a minute that the roof of the turnaround school is removed and its inner workings exposed. A turnaround leader would be able to see well beyond the surface issues of neglect and low expectations. The inner problems that elude parents or community members might be easily visible to the trained leader: a teacher engaging only half of her class; a classroom without age- and level-appropriate books; a pile of test data sitting on a desk, unused; a lecture-based science class with no hands-on materials; students roaming hallways; a playground without equipment; a library with a paucity of books; a school with no marquee; discipline run amuck.

With surety, the turnaround leader envisions a building freshly painted and equipped, enthusiastic teachers and engaged students, interested parents, and involved community members pursuing high expectations with an aligned curriculum, purposeful testing, analysis and dialogue, shored up after-school programs, books and support services—all clearing a path toward accelerating student achievement. The vision is broad and yet specific, and it draws on a system of interconnected elements, organizations, policies, and processes.

The set of strategies for addressing the decline are sensitive to these interconnections, and must be carefully monitored so that unintended consequences are minimized and systemic effects—the connections externally—can be managed appropriately. Change takes time, and a turnaround leader knows that time is not on one's side. Seeing and understanding the larger system, the interconnections of classrooms, grades, and resources takes time upfront, but is an investment that ultimately saves time when the turnaround plan can be executed and system influences and stakeholders can be leveraged to accelerate the process.

Lessons from Systems Theory

This systems approach has its roots in systems theory. It was biologist Ludwig von Bertanlanffy who first challenged the scientific method's assumption that systems could be broken down and analyzed as discrete parts and assembled in a linear fashion. Instead, von Bertanlanffy (1968) proposed that systems were made up of components that interacted in a non-linear fashion. General systems theory emerged from there and began decades of influence on scholars, scientists, and practitioners.

A systems mindset can ensure that turnaround leaders plan changes in ways that consider and anticipate how the changes they pursue impact their schools, their school communities, and their districts. These leaders implicitly embrace systems theory, which recognizes the interrelationships between and among groups, organizations, or actors that work together to produce results.[5] Turnaround leaders understand, for instance, that changes made in one classroom impact others; how grade level changes affect the rest of the school; how requesting exceptions to district policy may be viewed; how state and district policies may further, or disrupt, their turnaround plan.

A turnaround leader who views herself within the broader system that includes the district, state, and federal governments seizes the opportunity to consider environmental conditions that contributed to failure in the first place, along with conditions and resources necessary to support the turnaround plan. Such a focus also allows for the integration of other relevant programs, initiatives, and resources to augment the turnaround, and, as important but less often carried out, a careful examination of policies and programs and the elimination of ineffective or duplicative initiatives.

Likewise, turnaround leadership at the district level focuses on how the entire enterprise supports student learning. District administrators work within the larger system and often enable or impede turnaround efforts by attention (or inattention) to the interconnected drivers of change at the school level. Broward County Public School district, two-time finalist for the coveted Broad Prize in Urban Education, has spent more than five years developing a culture of what it calls enterprise accountability. Broward's Enterprise Accountability System for Education (EASE) takes a system level view to align all organizational elements toward accelerating student achievement.

Through an initial focus on executive development that fostered cross-functional discussions, senior leadership identified organizational "silos" that effectively separated the direct service side of the enterprise (i.e., instruction) from the support side (i.e., operations). Superintendent James Notter and his team targeted efforts toward streamlining instruction and enhancing service operations to best meet student needs. All members of the enterprise—from purchasing to transportation to nutrition and social services—share in the urgency to accelerate student achievement.

The Broward EASE system combines process management and a balanced scorecard with project management and a knowledge environment to build organizational capacity toward accelerating student achievement.[6] It is this kind of system-level attention that encourages transparency, cross-functional collaboration, and innovative solutions that build and sustain turnaround success.

Systems-Oriented Leadership

Margaret Wheatley's powerful discussion of interconnectedness in her management research brings a systems approach to leadership and "the new science." Decades before global warming came into common parlance, Wheatley (1992) talked about the ways in which the sciences have embraced quantum physics and chaos theory. She discussed the "butterfly effect," which describes how a butterfly flapping its wings in Tokyo could influence a tornado in Texas. Her leadership lessons included how minor disturbances in one place could create major changes elsewhere, and how chaos rules but order can prevail.

Wheatley's notion of leadership may strike an important chord for those working in turbulent environments. She argues that incorporating chaos theory allows a leader to "stop describing tasks and instead to facilitate process" (p. 38). Processes can provide order in a system while also creating nimbleness, allowing room for organizational learning and the adaptation to new and changing sets of conditions.

The system is ever important, and strong leaders analyze and leverage the interactions and relationships embedded within the system to create more opportunity for dramatic improvements. These leaders attend to systems and processes that eliminate slack and leverage connections between discrete elements. For example, they might focus on how on-time and well-managed buses deliver students "ready to learn"; how after-school programs offer more time for reading or other interventions; or how meeting protocols create more meaningful professional development experiences. They still must analyze and address the discrete elements within the system, like math achievement, Title I funds, or IDEA requirements, but those that focus on how these are connected to the core business of the school can move achievement appreciably.

Turnaround leaders can operationalize a systems approach by putting programs and processes in place to bring consistency and structure to what may be an ever changing set of conditions, students, and circumstances. This

Approaching Turnarounds with a 2-S Model 73

will be evident in the case studies presented in later chapters. For instance, as Aretha Eldridge-Williams' case study illustrates, a belief system, including performance expectations, can offer a backbone of support to students during crisis. J. Harrison Coleman's case brings a relentless focus on consistent lesson planning, and the cases from New York City employ various district-supported structures and protocols to shore up student achievement.

While a turnaround leader may not immediately see how to engage this larger system most effectively, these leaders view the district central office as an integral part of the system. They recognize the influential role of district policies, procedures and supports (not to mention political cover) on the principal's ability to affect and accelerate improvements. Likewise, savvy districts and states recognize the role they can play in furthering (or impeding) turnaround and make it their business to clear a path for school renewal.

Perhaps most important, while keeping the larger system in mind, the turnaround leader attends to the schoolhouse and its community of teachers, staff, and administrators to create a supportive learning environment, the relationships that lay at the heart of the system. Also touching the system are the foundations, associations, support organizations, community advocates, and parents whose important influence on the turnaround should not be minimized. These actors within the system influence the change with their action (and inaction). They are the stakeholders that both define and work within the system in which the turnaround specialist must operate.

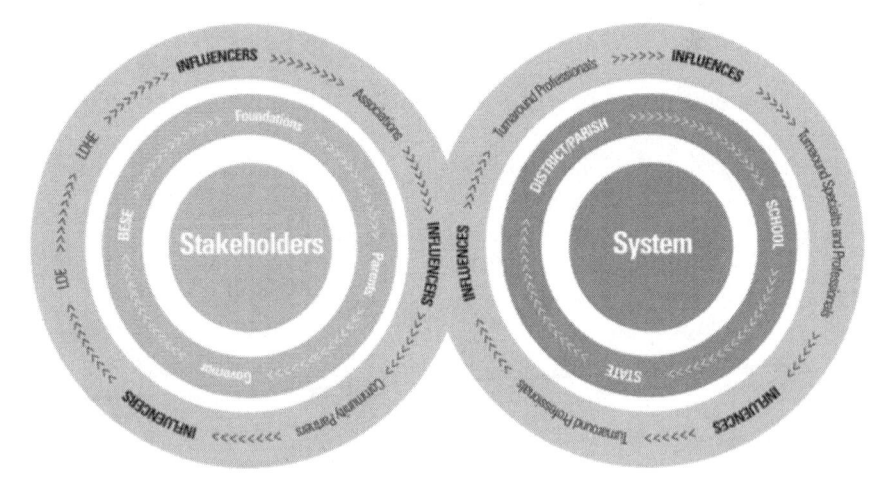

Figure 4.1. Systems and Stakeholders (2-S) Approach.
Source: Tierney Temple Fairchild, PhD, for EduLead and Louisiana Department of Education, April 2008.

ENGAGING STAKEHOLDERS

> "Leadership is always dependent on the context, but the context is established by the relationships that we value. We cannot hope to influence any situation without respect for the complex network of people who contribute to our organization."
>
> —*Leadership and the New Sciences* (1992, p. 144)

The second element of the 2-S approach is stakeholder engagement. Stakeholder engagement is a defining element of turnaround. Who is engaged and how they are involved in turnaround says something about a leader's values. Stakeholder communication must be carefully planned to build a supportive environment in which the principal and his or her team of turnaround professionals can transform the school.

Leaders might begin by recognizing that the word "turnaround" may have negative connotations for some stakeholders. To others it may create expectations for overnight improvements. Understanding how stakeholders view the school and its turnaround is an important aspect of how the turnaround leader approaches the challenges in the school and community.

Addressing each stakeholder's needs with due diligence and individual care can be time consuming. It requires both fact finding and analysis. Leaders need to probe beneath the surface to uncover hidden bias and assumptions that may be contributing to the decline. They need to look at the facts of how the stakeholder groups engage with the school and, as important, they must account for, and manage, perceptions.

Perceptions cannot be ignored or underestimated for the ways in which they drive what others see as the truth. A savvy turnaround leader can build his/her credibility by taking the necessary time to analyze stakeholder interests and potential opportunities. This fact-finding mission can bring crucial information to complete the web of relationships and influences that envelop the school.

Ascertaining the "story" or "stories" of the school is an essential building block for establishing a communal understanding of the history of decline and the challenges of transformation. Listening without judgment can be a powerful mechanism for establishing credibility as a leader. For some parents, teachers, and students, a turnaround leader comes with heightened expectations of the change they have longed for; for others, a new leader may be one of many and expectations for real change are low.

Collecting the "stories" of the school's stakeholders can help the leader build a complete picture of what has occurred and what needs to change. These individual stories, weaved into a collective story, can have the powerful effect of involving stakeholders that otherwise would have been on the sidelines.

Take the example of a turnaround school in East Baton Rouge, Louisiana. Two common and colorfully dressed figures waiting outside this elementary school are the mother and grandmother of two students. Clad in matching hot pink suits, they refer to themselves as the "Bubblicious" women. They are quick and comfortable in sharing with visitors what they like about the changes that have been instituted since the arrival of their turnaround specialist. They speak knowledgeably about the addition of student clubs, business partnerships, content workshops for parents as well as night hours for the computer lab.

These women are influential stakeholders in their community. They echo their leader's messages of hope and can articulate the strategies at work. This parent and grandparent talk with other parents. Through their engagement in the school and presence in their neighborhood, they spread these messages throughout the community, which then increases stakeholder buy-in.

Talking with stakeholders openly and honestly can also engender tremendous goodwill and accrue public relations benefits that help restore a school's reputation. Turnaround leaders don't shy away from the brutal facts or difficult conversations. Instead, they use them as an opportunity to acknowledge past mistakes and make a fresh start. They offer stakeholders a new story that includes messages of hope and expectation along with strategies for accelerating achievement that align and engage stakeholders in support of turnaround. The complete school story can be one that recognizes the history, the failure, the frustration and then turns toward the future, creating a vision that stakeholders see as attainable.

Stakeholder engagement is a manager's responsibility that links the values of the school with the interests of its constituents in ways that positively impact teaching and learning. Understanding and valuing stakeholder interests and experiences requires intense listening and dialogue. Stakeholder interests are not likely to be aligned, and thus turnaround leaders must strive to appreciate these complex stories and perspectives and to work toward building common ground based on the moral imperative of providing all students a high-quality educational environment.

The stakeholders engaged in and influencing a school turnaround are likely quite varied. Within the obvious groups of teachers, parents, and students, a turnaround leader may find it helpful to break these groups into supporters, skeptics, detractors; seasoned or unseasoned; influential or without voice. Stakeholders within the school like support staff, bus drivers, cafeteria workers, or maintenance and security officers, when considered and aligned to the vision, can be critical supporting actors in the turnaround. Community members and organizations might include religious organizations, volunteers, after-school programs, and business or other leaders. They too can be analyzed and mapped for connections, influences, and support.

The superintendent, other district administrators, and the school board, as well as principal colleagues will have a vested interest in the turnaround's success; some may have designs on its failure. The director of accountability, technology, or human resources, for instance, can help a turnaround leader clear the path for needed changes or create obstacles or fan resistance, even surreptitiously. Associations, unions, nonprofit organizations, philanthropic partners as well as state leaders are important stakeholders as well. They may control funds or messages and hold sway with other influential district, state, and national leaders that also have a stake in a turnaround's success. Community leaders, those representing the interests of racial or ethnic groups, or state and local agencies may help make connections essential to restoring order, leveraging resources, and furthering achievement.

These stakeholder groups and their respective influences may change with each turnaround. Contexts vary, histories vary, laws and policies vary. What is most important is that the turnaround leaders define, analyze, communicate with, and ultimately engage school stakeholders so that interests are aligned toward a vision that accelerates student achievement.

Lessons from Stakeholder Theory

Stakeholder theory has most notably been applied in the private sector. In his seminal work, Freeman (1984) built on the notions of stakeholders seen in systems theory, strategic planning, organizational theory, and corporate social responsibility and linked stakeholder theory to the strategic management of the firm.

Offered as a competing theory to maximizing stockholder returns, stakeholder theory is premised on two important questions: What is the purpose of the firm? And what is management's responsibility to its stakeholders (Freeman, 1984)? At its core, stakeholder theory challenged the notion that a firm's purpose is to maximize stockholder returns and that management's primary focus should be on short-term financial returns as evidenced by stock price.

Freeman offered a strategic framework for attending to those constituencies that had a "stake" in the firm. Mapping the range of stakeholders, understanding their various interests, and communicating with and negotiating the necessary trade-off between them would bring greater value to the firm. Implicit in the theory is that all stakeholder interests cannot be maximized at the same time, yet, over time, greater value can be driven from considering and balancing the interests of various groups, rather than attending to the interests of one (i.e., stockholders).

Stakeholder engagement in a turnaround situation can have a multitude of positive effects on a school. The very process of communicating with various groups, no matter how disengaged or contentious, creates dialogue that can lay the foundation for building trust. Communicating openly can build a more complete history—a catalog of perspectives that allow leaders to not only better understanding the nature of the decline but to more effectively address conditions that may have caused (or will in the future again cause) decline in student achievement.

Finally, stakeholder communication can pull leaders back from the tendency to firefight. Communicating with stakeholders can lead to better problem solving, assistance with addressing particular problems, or leveraging resources and influence to affect needed policy changes. Stakeholder communications build out the system to create a web of interconnections that allows for more strategic decision making and, hopefully, more sustainable results.

One recent extension of stakeholder theory to the strategic management and ethics field is the notion of Company Stakeholder Responsibility (Freeman, Velamuri & Moriarty, 2006). While educators may not learn about corporate social responsibility in their master's programs, most educators know the powerful benefits that schools accrue from corporate social responsibility programs.

The notion of Company Stakeholder Responsibility can apply to any organization, not just large corporations. Considering the complexity and urgency of turnarounds, Freeman, Velamuri and Moriarty's 10 Principles of Company Stakeholder Responsibility (p. 11) offer some important insights:

1. Bring stakeholder interests together over time.
2. Recognize that stakeholders are real and complex people with names, faces, and values.
3. Seek solutions to issues that satisfy multiple stakeholders simultaneously.
4. Engage in intensive communication and dialogue with stakeholders, not just those who are "friendly."
5. Commit to a philosophy of voluntarism—commit to managing stakeholder relationships yourself, rather than leaving it to government.
6. Generalize the marketing approach.
7. Never trade off the interests of one stakeholder versus another continuously over time.
8. Negotiate with primary and secondary stakeholders.
9. Consistently monitor and redesign processes to better serve stakeholders.
10. Act with purpose that fills your commitments to stakeholders. Act with aspiration toward your dreams and theirs.

Considering the many stakeholders operating within a school turnaround environment, it may be useful to view them as primary and secondary stakeholders Teachers, parents, students, and staff are primary groups of interest and each of these can be further divided into subgroups if views and or values diverge significantly within these constituencies. Secondary stakeholders, such as unions, administration, the school board, other district schools (especially feeder schools), and community groups, extend beyond the school. State officials, grantmakers, federal officials, and universities may also have a stake in the school's success. Each of these groups has perspectives, histories, insights, and opinions to share, and each has an interest in seeing the school dramatically improve.

Yet, each stakeholder group may have different views as well as a different level of readiness for the type of change a turnaround leader must bring. Some teachers may not be ready for the type of schedule changes, instructional oversight, curriculum changes, or accountability measures that will better serve students. Some parents may be so disengaged that they are skeptical of the turnaround strategy and a new leader's commitment to their community and the well-being of their children in particular.

Likewise, school boards may not be ready to empower leaders to utilize resources, hire (and remove) staff, and implement a turnaround strategy that addresses chronic failures that may have been perpetuated at the district, board, and state levels. Unions and state leaders may not be prepared to negotiate the necessary trade-offs that may require concessions that affect "the way things have always been done." A turnaround leader's challenge is first to define and map the interests of primary and secondary stakeholders and then to engage and coalesce stakeholders toward a vision that considers, leverages, and serves what is in the best interest of students and the well-being of the school.

The Systems-Stakeholder approach presented in this chapter can support the strategic management of any school situation, but it has particular relevance for turnarounds, given the sense of urgency and the levels of complexity involved. By understanding the history and importance of systems and stakeholders, a turnaround leader can create order out of the chaos that he or she discovers. He/she can focus on processes that facilitate excellence while allowing for the necessary flexibility in a dynamic school environment. Furthermore, he/she can leverage the skills and interests of stakeholders to maximize the value students receive in the classroom, both in the near term and consistently over time.

The 2-S approach undergirds a turnaround design, with the goal of ensuring that the turnaround principal effectively considers both the influences (the system) and the influencers (stakeholders) during the development and implementation of the turnaround plan. With a dual focus on both the system and the stakeholders operating within that environment, turnaround leaders and their constituents can understand the larger organizations in which they operate and the stakeholders they must engage to create dramatic change.

Turnaround specialists can be successful at the principal level by engaging a community of professionals at the state, district, and school levels. These relationships then become the professional learning community that offers a support network to facilitate real transformation and sustainable achievements in a turnaround situation.

NOTES

1. http://www.ncrel.org/sdrs/areas/issues/students/atrisk/at61k50a.htm. Accessed 6-24-10.

2. Mirel, J. (2001). "The evolution of new American schools: From revolution to mainstream." Thomas B. Fordham Foundation. http://www.edexcellence.net/doc/evolution.pdf. Accessed 6-27-10.

3. New York City Independent Budget Office. (2010, February). *Fiscal Brief,* p. 2.

4. National Alliance for Public Charter Schools (2009). Public charter school dashboard. http://www.publiccharters.org/files/publications/DataDashboard.pdf. Accessed 6-28-10.

5. See von Bertalanffy, L. (1968). *General system theory: Foundations, developments, applications.* New York: Braziller; Kuhn, A. (1974). *The logic of social systems.* San Francisco: Jossey-Bass; and Kuhn, T. (1970). *The structure of scientific revolutions.* Chicago: University of Chicago Press.

6. http://www.broward.k12.fl.us/ease/. Accessed 11-15-10.

Chapter 5

The 3Es of School Turnarounds
Environment, Executive, and Execution

Leading turnarounds requires a careful detangling of the causes of decline and the conditions stifling student success. Frameworks, processes, and tools that drive a critical path to stabilization and growth are strategic necessities for the turnaround principal and relevant stakeholders. Organizing for action is essential.

First, educators need to consider a myriad of conditions surrounding the turnaround to "prepare the environment" for the change that is coming. These conditions exacerbate the dysfunction and, if they are not considered and addressed, could present barriers during implementation.

Second, educators engaging in turnaround must tap into the latest research-based interventions, curricula, and technology applications to strengthen their plans to bring dramatic change. Fortifying what happens inside the classroom during instructional time, is the core of turnaround. It is interaction of the "who" (the teachers) and the "what" (the curriculum) that leads to engaged students.

Principals and teachers need to access instructional supports and engage in quality professional development that strengthens and builds capacity for the turnaround. "Developing the executive"—including the turnaround principal, district administrators, and a school leadership team—will attend to the essential human capital component of the turnaround, which is not only critical for turnaround to occur but also for the change to be sustained over time.

The first phase of "developing the executive" is ensuring that the turnaround principal, district administrators and school leadership team are well selected and developed to carry out the difficult work of leading school renewal. The next phase includes a focus on developing the entire school staff in ways that support turnaround. Finally, the development of a suitable successor is essential. This individual will learn about the turnaround but also will understand how to strengthen and increase performance so that the school never experiences decline again.

Once the environment is prepared and executives primed for the challenge, turnaround leaders at all levels must "focus on execution" and achieve results. Implementing plans, adjusting for unforeseen conditions, and further strengthening a team of professionals to have the knowledge, expectations, and fortitude to overcome the conditions of decline is the hard work of turnarounds.

It is here where tools like the 90-day plan and the balanced scorecard, both of which will be discussed in chapter 6, offer principals the means to plan, monitor, and communicate the nuts and bolts of the turnaround strategy. Inside these plans, a myriad of strategies must be carefully chosen and implemented to collectively target instructional challenges, engage stakeholders, and build a safe, secure, and orderly environment that affirms student success.

The 3Es framework presented in this chapter offers turnaround leaders and supportive players a set of discrete yet interrelated components—Preparing the Environment, Developing the Executive, and Focusing on Execution—around which the turnaround strategy can be planned, implemented, and updated. As new elements and conditions arise, training and development shifts commensurately, and newly considered implementation actions follow.

The 3Es framework is intended to provide a structure for considering and organizing essential elements in any turnaround. In its consideration of context and conditions (environment), human capital requirements (executive), and strategic goals and actions (execution), the 3Es do not prescribe a turnaround plan; rather, they offer a set of interconnected supports around which a turnaround specialist can reflect, analyze, and organize what is essential for achieving the dramatic results that will reshape the possibilities for a school community.

PREPARING THE ENVIRONMENT

Educators may find it more workable to view the turnaround school as a discrete entity, isolating its malaise from other, higher-performing schools as if to quarantine the contagion. Those that embrace the 2-S approach know how important it is for stakeholders to address the conditions of underperformance within the system affecting the school. Some of these conditions connect to the larger system of district, state, and federal policies, procedures, and regulations. Others are based in the school and its surrounding community. Many offer "quick wins" or symbolic victories that shore up the credibility and commitment necessary to tackle more complex instructional issues.

In order to ensure that the road on which the turnaround leader travels is well paved, turnaround stakeholders can prepare for the turnaround by attending to the following key elements, organized into state and district conditions and school and community circumstances.

State and District Conditions

Selection of Schools

While it may seem obvious, state and local officials must first be able to distinguish a school in need of turnaround from other schools in the district. State accountability systems vary, but there are overarching performance indicators common to all—student achievement, attendance, and graduation rates chief among them.

A student performance–based criteria that is easily communicated to the public can clearly delineate high-performing from low-performing schools. Some states, like Florida, assign a letter grade to each school based on student performance; others, like Virginia, have detailed school and district report cards. Districts can create even more transparency by posting similar trend data on each school's website. States that openly report which students are performing at or above basic levels may reveal a wider pool of schools in need of turnaround, especially in schools that in aggregate look healthy but in reality carry significant achievement gaps.

The choice of turnaround as a strategy for school renewal may be a complicated one. Which schools should be closed versus converted to charters versus given a turnaround principal are difficult questions for district and state leaders to answer. The availability of strong charter organizations, the condition of the physical plant, the size and trend of the school population, the availability of skilled leaders, and the community and political landscape are just a few considerations that may affect this decision. Whatever the determination, student welfare should be paramount and, thus, a commitment to address the impediments to achievement is essential.

Selection of schools can be further complicated by a resource-constrained environment and a district with multiple schools in need of turnaround. If resources are not available for all schools, officials must determine how to apportion resources to ameliorate declines in achievement. With many underperforming schools to fix, there is all the more reason for the district to have completed a thorough analysis and to have a system-wide plan for accomplishing turnaround in multiple schools.

Selecting Turnaround Leaders

Once eligible schools for turnaround are identified, state and district officials must determine whether they have the pipeline, or supply, of turnaround specialists needed over a course of years to support these distressed schools. As the turnaround field evolves, state and district leaders will become savvy on how to select and train leaders specialized in turning around low-performing schools.

A careful analysis of student achievement data at the school level, for instance, could surface numerous existing turnaround leaders who have done the work of turnaround without the title. This was the case with J. Harrison Coleman, a turnaround specialist who completed two turnarounds before being selected for the Virginia School Turnaround Specialist Program. One of Principal Coleman's turnaround schools is featured in chapter 9.

As noted in chapter 2, states like Louisiana are tackling the supply and demand question by developing the capacity of universities to deliver a state-supported turnaround specialist program. Districts like Chicago are creating a portfolio of approaches to school renewal and considering how best to select this new cadre of leaders. Other important development programs like New Leaders for New Schools and the NYC Leadership Academy rigorously select and develop leaders capable of transforming struggling schools.

One key challenge for states and districts as they address the supply side of turnaround leadership is geography. The development of these leaders is especially critical in hard-to-staff areas where the local community may be resistant to outsiders and where the supply of talent may be thin.

To meet the demand for these leaders, eventually search firms will choose to specialize in finding and placing turnaround leaders; universities will develop specializations in the principalship to develop turnaround leaders; and district officials will know what turnaround talent looks like in their local community. Until then, however, states and districts must continue to refine the competencies of these leaders so that principals are able to self-select into or be tapped for this work.

All school leaders are not, cannot, and will not be successful turnaround leaders. Anyone that has interviewed candidates for this type of work knows that turnaround leaders stand apart from their peers. Their skill set is grounded by an unwavering belief that all children deserve the opportunity to be taught in a rich educational environment, no matter their circumstances. They bring confidence to the school, knowing that students can achieve at high levels despite sometimes desperate conditions.

They know that such leaders take action and make tough calls without regret because they know they are working to meet student needs, no excuses.

They know that a thriving school community with the highest of expectations can overcome the worst of circumstances.

As the field of school turnaround leadership develops, districts and states will hone and validate the competencies that strong turnaround leaders must possess. Meantime, some districts, like Chicago, have developed resources to fill this void. Public Impact's *Turnaround Leaders: Competencies for Success* (2008a, June), funded by the Chicago Public Education Fund, offers a set of competencies for turnaround leaders. Public Impact also offers selection toolkits for turnaround leaders and turnaround teachers.[1] Given the urgency of turnaround, these tools offer a starting point that can be refined and validated over time.

State/District/Specialist Memoranda of Understanding (MOU)

Once eligible schools are targeted for turnaround and leaders are selected, expectations must be discussed and set. Expectation setting is important for any new leader, but in turnarounds written agreements are especially helpful. Because the work is urgent and the circumstances complex, and political and other forces working against a school's success can fuel major tensions, leaders can benefit from creating mutual understanding of the parameters around which to accomplish the job.

A Memorandum of Understanding (MOU) outlines the expectations of each major entity/team involved in the turnaround (i.e., state, district, school). It serves as an agreement between the district superintendent, board, and the turnaround leader, and in some cases, state officials. It can go a long way toward preparing the environment for the dramatic change inherent in a turnaround strategy. While it will not supplant a contract between the district and principal, it can supplement the contract, offering a set of responsibilities for each party.

Any principal entering a turnaround environment should have some type of MOU, to be signed by a state official (if appropriate), the local superintendent, and the turnaround leader. Ideally, the state or district would have a standard MOU template that offers a menu of options from which each district superintendent, and turnaround specialist candidate could jointly select based on their individual circumstances.

The menu offers a set of assurances to each of the major parties involved (state, district, principal) so that once the turnaround is underway, there is clarity when inevitable conflicts or disagreements arise. Such assurances may include the following:

- expectations for participation in executive development programs,
- coaching assistance,

- timing and latitude around a plan or scorecard deliverables,
- degrees of freedom or autonomy granted to principals,
- performance goals and incentives, and
- expected length of the turnaround engagement.

In order to give the turnaround leader's role transparency and teeth, MOUs should be negotiated and signed by personnel during the hiring process. (See Appendix C for a sample Memorandum of Understanding.)

Not every state will be involved in this process, but for those engaged in the work of turnarounds, states can lend significant weight to the mandate for change. States willing to examine policies and procedures can greatly facilitate the turnaround process. For instance, they might offer flexibility or special assistance around the development and submission of School Improvement Plans, use of Title I or Title II funds, use of audits, and other state resources like targeted intervention programs.

Offering performance-based incentives or an endorsement in turnaround leadership can attract and motivate those leaders doing this difficult work. It can also send important signals to reluctant stakeholders. Such messages may provide important political cover for the turnaround principal to do the essential work of leading a school out of distress.

Degrees of Freedom

Perhaps the most important district consideration in preparing the turnaround environment is what level of autonomy the turnaround leader will have in executing a strategy to reverse the decline or stagnation. In the private sector, it is not uncommon for turnaround operators to be given a set of parameters around which to complete the work. Within those boundaries, operators can then act with relative discretion to alleviate the conditions causing the decline. Constant back-and-forth with management "higher-ups" only serves to delay action that trained turnaround operators know they must take.

For some reason in schools, as in the political realm, stakeholders can find numerous reasons to delay turnaround. The potential harm to a child's education seems to fade when difficult conversations and negotiations are required. Unions, school boards, and district and state leaders must provide the turnaround leader the necessary decision-making authority to act swiftly and carefully in the interest of students. The cost of inaction is damaging.

The urgency of turnaround may be a hard case to make when schools have been underperforming for years, when low expectations pervade, or when student body after student body have missed the opportunity for a high-quality learning environment. Some blame the community, or the parents of "those kids." Finding that urgency, what Kotter (1996) called "the burning platform," can serve as a call to action for policy makers and other district administrators to give turnaround leaders the necessary resources to accomplish dramatic change in three years.

Degrees of freedom may include discretion over a budget and the authority to hire and remove staff in order to meet the school's needs. Without compromising *due process* and offering the opportunity for staff to lead and grow with the turnaround, districts and states can support principals by working with union leaders on revising evaluations and dismissal procedures. Recent examples in New Haven, Connecticut, Newark, New Jersey, and Washington, D.C. offer encouragement that the environment is being prepared by both labor and management so that all principals can be successful.

District superintendents and turnaround principals should have conversations upfront so that the "degrees of freedom" (e.g., staff hiring, removal) are outlined in the MOU in advance of finalizing this agreement. With a clear sense of what to expect, district superintendents and boards will spend less time fielding questions and managing frustrations from turnaround principals in a pressurized situation.

All too often, a turnaround leader's efforts can become stymied by politics within the organization. Middle managers may pick at one decision here, another there, with or without realizing the cost to the turnaround process. Whether the source is cronyism, jealousy, or ignorance, these distractions cause undo stress and fan resentments. Degrees of freedom and MOUs clear the way for a turnaround leader to do what he or she has been trained to do. These freedoms may not seem as crucial as they actually become once the leader is engrossed in the complex problems that led to the distress.

If the district has more than one school in distress, then carving out a "turnaround zone" or separate unit may be beneficial. This is especially helpful if the district can articulate how these schools—and their leaders—will operate differently. Similar to a set of charter schools, these schools would be granted degrees of freedom to meet student needs and to address the complex issues causing the underperformance.

Turnaround Leadership Endorsement

Once turnaround specialist candidates complete the turnaround (including meeting or exceeding established performance goals and MOU requirements), the State Department of Education and its administrative credentialing arm can offer an add-on endorsement that provides a credential for turnaround accomplishment. This is important to address in preparing the environment for the expectations it sets and because of its potential use as a recruiting tool.

Louisiana offers such a credential, the Turnaround Specialist Endorsement,[2] which is linked to success in the state-run Louisiana School Turnaround Specialist Program. The endorsement is valid for five years once candidates complete the program, verify continuing learning units, achieve performance targets, and are recommended by the Louisiana employing authority. In the race to find talent, Louisiana can capitalize on the attractiveness of such a credential as it recruits principals to lead turnarounds in the state. (See Appendix D for more information on Louisiana's Turnaround Specialist Endorsement).

Louisiana's endorsement is based on the Virginia School Turnaround Specialist program's performance-based credential. Under Governor Mark Warner, Virginia awarded the credential after principals successfully accomplished three measures: program completion, goal attainment (including AYP and/or growth targets), and superintendent recommendation or committee review. Whatever the relevant measures, credibility of turnaround leaders can also be established if and when they dramatically improve student achievement and stabilize the school environment (including discipline, attendance, and/or staff turnover).

Incentives offer another important means to prepare for the turnaround. While they will be awarded based on performance, like the endorsement, they can offer important motivation for turnaround leaders. Such incentives may be reserved for turnaround principals but can also be designed to include awards for staff and/or school-based awards (per student) that continue to facilitate improvement. Whatever package of incentives is offered, it is important that these rewards reflect equitably across leaders and schools.

Programs like the federal Teacher Incentive Fund or the Teacher Advancement Program (TAP) as well as district-based programs like the Executive Principal in New York City, while not directly related to turnaround, can both enhance and further motivate principals and teachers eager to take on the challenge.

The state can also build a set of incentives for the principal, school, and even staff that offer motivation and resources not otherwise provided. These might include recognizing pay scales across districts or offering bonuses for meeting certain milestones. Governor Warner's Virginia program included both principal incentives and school-based awards. While incentives may be awarded at the same time as the endorsement, they should not be part of the endorsement program. The ultimate end-goal of any incentive is to further student achievement.

Other Enabling Conditions

The state and district can further stakeholder buy-in to the turnaround by thoughtfully addressing key policy and procedural conditions under which schools operate. Wherever possible, these should be outlined in the MOU. First, chronically underperforming schools are often overburdened with too many interventions, requiring too much paperwork. The state can ease paperwork requirements by streamlining plans like the School Improvement Plan, the 90-day plan, and balanced scorecard.

Second, the state can provide information in the MOU about which programs might offer supplemental support to the school (e.g., Title II, Reading First, and Algebra Readiness) and whether the principal has discretion to eliminate or opt out of such interventions or programs. Third, advanced consideration should be given to alignment opportunities that might offer turnaround leaders needed assistance with challenging issues like staffing shortages. In these cases, creative solutions might be fashioned by leveraging other district, state, and federal programs to support turnaround schools.

Finally, the district and state can offer personnel to support the turnaround process. These supportive players may be separate entities, like the "lead partners" that Mass Insight (MERI, 2007) recommends. Such partners may be a nonprofit organization contracted to recruit, develop, and manage the turnaround leaders in a district, much like a charter management organization. They also may be central office administrators, "shepherds" at the district level and even the state level, assigned to guide and advocate for the turnaround leader; or they may be external consultants, trained mentors, or coaches skilled at supporting turnaround leaders.

In Louisiana's program, superintendents assign a "district advocate" to offer guidance and support where needed. This person must be carefully chosen and is likely not the direct supervisor or assigned mentor. Rather, it is someone who has a direct relationship to the superintendent and can clear the path, removing procedural and other obstacles that inhibit momentum.

Ideally, these enabling conditions are agreed to and outlined upfront. In reality, however, changes for many districts and states come more slowly, and so having savvy professionals at the state and district levels is a crucial asset. Chapter 7 offers insight into this concept, as Aretha Eldridge-Williams' district advocate in Jefferson Parish is a critical partner in supporting her turnaround.

Selection of these supporting role players cannot be taken lightly, for their appointment can be a critical signal to stakeholders about the change that is coming. Whether current personnel or contracted turnaround partners, these individuals and entities can be essential advocates for and guides in solving an array of problems that impede turnaround. For even with the best of intentions, bureaucratic inertia can be a powerful force that requires real political savvy to navigate.

School and Community Circumstances

Prior to launching a turnaround strategy, the principal can gather information and begin to address the circumstances surrounding the state of affairs of the school and community. While a number of conditions can and will be part of the execution stage of the turnaround, assessing the environment is an essential precondition to preparing an effective strategy.

School Setting

Many turnaround leaders find their buildings in disrepair. From broken toilets to mold and spores growing in the classrooms, various unseemly conditions affect turnaround schools. These buildings may be health hazards or at the very least nameless structures that do little to emanate a culture of learning.

As Camille Wallin demonstrated in P.S. 42–Claremont Community School in the Bronx, New York, whose story is told in Chapter 8, careful and swift action to clean up the messes of previous administrations can literally and symbolically provide a facelift that speaks to the care, quality, and seriousness of the principal in improving student success. The state of the physical plant and school environment sends important messages to students, parents, and staff about the value of the students and the teachers.

When J. Harrison Coleman, another principal featured in this book, joined Stephen H. Clarke Elementary School in Portsmouth, Virginia and the Virginia School Turnaround Specialist Program, she brought photographs of her school's condition with her to the executive program at the University of Virginia. Coleman seized this opportunity to share the Polaroid photographs with a high-level state official in attendance, who was aghast that such conditions could be tolerated in any school. It was a risky political move for Coleman, one that likely embarrassed her district, but the urgency of her mission was foremost on her mind. She would not rest until her building was repaired and presentable for her students. Moreover, state officials played a role in hastening improvements when they scheduled a press conference for the Governor at her school just weeks into the school year.

Physical plant improvements can be "quick wins" that build credibility. They are an essential element of turnaround, but only the beginning. A facelift is insignificant if not coupled with an equally if not more aggressive instructional remake. Wallin's story illustrates how turnaround leaders utilize every opportunity—starting with the cosmetic and leading to the more complex instructional and capacity building challenges—to drive home a vision that includes the highest expectations for improving student achievement.

Staff Morale

Chronically underperforming schools inevitably suffer from low morale. In some cases, the learning environment has been so neglected—physically and emotionally—that faculty members are demoralized, effectively paralyzed by the circumstances around them. This is not to say that the faculty and staff—a small or even large portion—are not part of the problem. Nor is it to say that there aren't teachers and others working to the best of their abilities, waiting to be freed from the grip of low expectations and excuse making.

Continuous messages of underperformance can have a deleterious effect on the school's ethos. Teachers and students come to embody the labels they have been given, and parents, even if they know better, may learn to expect less from their children and the schools. Comparisons to other schools, other neighborhoods, the other side of town, cannot be helped. Turnaround leaders, however, know how to instill pride in the students, the school, and the community. Each of the principals featured in this book takes issue with such low expectations, offering insights into how best to challenge assumptions in the school and community about what is possible.

In some districts, entire faculties may have to be replaced immediately. In others, all faculty may need to reapply for their positions. Still others, especially those in hard-to-staff areas, must make do with current resources. Thus, the turnaround leader, as she/he prepares the environment, must identify the leaders and detractors to turnaround quickly and make some swift and noticeable changes that will improve faculty and student morale. In essence, the turnaround leader must ensure that the faculty and students believe they can and will achieve significantly.

Community Milieu

Wrapped up in the school culture of underperformance may be a community in distress. Turnaround leaders often find that their school is located in a community experiencing underemployment, poverty, crime, or other conditions that add to the school's achievement challenges. The surrounding community itself may have become so accustomed to the school's circumstances that little hope remains.

It may be a community on the other side of town, segregated from its more affluent and high-performing peers. It may be a community in which parents, perhaps teens themselves, experienced limited success in school and now see their children in similar situations. It may be a community with a challenging history—a turbulent racial past whose scars are still fresh, or an isolated rural community or Native American reservation grappling with poverty and its effects.

Other communities may not be in obvious disrepair, but what is going on inside the school is blighted or unequal. In these communities, where underperforming schools may look presentable from the outside, there may be a lack of knowledge that some schools (or students) aren't performing even close to their potential. Or worse, these schools (or students) are viewed not to be as worthy of equitable resources as their peers. These schools may be located in communities that may not see the underlying gaps in achievement or whose members' voices are not heard.

The school's racial and/or economic history is likely an under-discussed yet critical component of the environment facing the turnaround leader. Acknowledging and, where possible, addressing the conditions of the community strikes at the heart of turnaround. Conversations in the barber shop, visits to churches, meetings with community leaders, and walks in the neighborhood can offer a turnaround leader insights—and relationships—book knowledge cannot replicate.

Getting the community involved may surface some circumstances or questions a principal cannot answer, though mostly the community's involvement, however sparse, can unseat strong forces at work in the school. As Aretha Eldridge-Williams' case will describe in chapter 7, a community's support can be a positive force toward ameliorating challenging circumstances. Tanya John, the turnaround principal featured in chapter 10, also demonstrates the power of home visits, reaching into the community to connect with parents, and sharing a culture of high expectations.

Analyzing the Data

Preparation of the environment for turnaround cannot be complete without significant attention to the school data. Trend data will help reveal when the school experienced its decline, which can lead to questions and answers about what may have caused the decline.

Classroom and student data over a few years will help the principal identify which faculty are meeting and exceeding the challenges as opposed to those that may be paralyzed or contributing to the underperformance. Examinations of data across subpopulations—and in particular, students with special needs—will help identify those incidents where students may have been assigned in disproportionate numbers to a particular school or schools.

In preparing the environment, faculty absenteeism may indicate morale challenges. Low student attendance may signal ineffectual teaching, lack of consequences, disruptions at home, or simply a lack of understanding how attendance and homework relate to learning and achievement. Discipline referrals and data give a sense of classroom management, student engagement, potential gang activity, or other community challenges. Promotion and graduation rates provide information about the history and current state of achievement and may indicate a lack of basic reading or numeracy skills.

A full scan of the school data—including how accessible and disaggregated the data are—will provide the turnaround leader a roadmap to the most troubling issues and a set of baseline indicators that comprise the school's culture of performance.

Many turnaround leaders do their best analytical work observing in the classrooms. They often couple regular classroom observations with interim assessments and review of lesson plans to build a complete picture of what student learning looks like. These instructional snapshots reflect years of master teaching and seasoned feedback and pave the way for a level of consistency that elevates instruction.

As each case in this book demonstrates, data-informed decision making is an essential tool for turnaround. These early assessments and observations may vary based on school environment, district practices, and state accountability, but they are singularly focused on preparing for an instructional overhaul that unleashes teachers and benefits students.

DEVELOPING THE EXECUTIVE

This book starts with the premise that turnaround leadership needs to become a subspecialty of the principalship. As such, those leaders taking on the challenge of leading the renewal of schools in distress must develop and hone a unique set of skills that are different from the skills of leaders of flourishing schools. Turnarounds require a set of leadership competencies that allow principals to accomplish the hard work of reversing the decline and stagnation of student achievement in a time-compressed manner. As Bryk and his colleagues (2009) found in studying urban schools in Chicago, strong leadership—strategic, instructionally focused, and collaborative—is one of the five major ingredients to urban school success.[3]

To develop the necessary leadership capacity to effect school turnarounds, school districts and states can draw on the field of executive development in business for guidance, focusing on the turnaround specialist as executive. Executive development in the private sector involves selecting and developing leaders based on a set of leadership and functional competencies. In its most successful application, executive development is linked to succession planning, where senior management regularly review leadership success and plan for the growth and movement of talent to optimize performance.

Human resource development organizations utilize talent development data to build upon or locate a host of options that meet specific executive development needs. From leading business school executive education shops to the Center for Creative Leadership to business strategy gurus like Ram Charan or Jim Collins, corporations invest significant resources into building and sustaining a pipeline of talent to enhance company performance.

In the education sector, executive development programs of the caliber provided to major corporations have only recently become available. University partnerships drawing on the executive education houses at major business schools such as those at Harvard and the University of Virginia offer to school executives the types of programs previously reserved for business executives. The Wallace Foundation, for example, has long had a leadership development focus, and in 2006 awarded grants to these universities to extend executive development to district and state leaders as well.

In order to build district capacity at the school level, attention to recruiting and training turnaround leaders and then identifying and building successors to retain and extend turnaround results is paramount. With strong leadership at the school, principals can then build a cadre of teachers capable of doing the hard work of turnaround. Thus, the second "E" of turnaround is all about developing and employing talent effectively.

Turnaround Specialist Selection

The selection of leaders is among the most critical elements of the turnaround. Effectively selecting candidates with the leadership characteristics necessary to be successful in a turnaround environment is paramount. Effective recruitment and selection will allow for a focus on honing and strengthening existing skills rather than building new competencies. Any state, district, or third-party entity interested in building a candidate pool must clearly define eligibility using selection criteria and outline a process by which to attract and secure candidates.

Eligibility

Superintendents want to find the most experienced and capable turnaround specialist principals. Unfortunately, a local supply of such experienced talent may not be available. If regional or even national recruitment does not surface high-quality candidates, then it may be appropriate to extend the pool to include principal leaders who may not yet have effected a turnaround but exhibit the leadership characteristics most associated with successful turnaround managers.[4]

Given this potential lack of supply, district leaders may benefit from an initial focus on two types of turnaround specialist candidates, with subsequent efforts focused on successor candidates. The first type are the "experienced leaders" who have demonstrated success in turning around schools in distress, as measured by student performance and, where possible, other organizational indicators of renewal. These leaders may be found within public, charter, or independent schools, locally and nationally. This was the case for J. Harrison Coleman (featured in chapter 8), who went through the inaugural cohort of Governor Warner's Virginia School Turnaround Specialist Program.

The second type might be called "emerging leaders," credentialed principals who either show promise in an eligible school (with three years or less tenure) or show promise through other experiences that illustrate a strong match with the defined leadership characteristics. These leaders may be ones ripe for selection into programs like the NYC Leadership Academy or the Louisiana School Turnaround Specialist Program, as other case studies featured in chapters 7, 8, and 10 show.

First-year principals may not be the best candidates for schools in distress, especially if they have not been in a complex school environment previously. These principals already have to overcome the challenges of being new to the position, and thus adding the extra burden of turnaround may not be prudent. That said, leaders who have apprenticed within underperforming schools as assistant principals or administrative interns from organizations like New Leaders for New Schools or the New York City Leadership Academy should be ready to assume the challenge. In these cases especially, mentoring and coaching assistance can be a valuable support mechanism.

A high degree of caution should accompany principal candidates with administrative tenure longer than three years in a selected school. At some point a principal has had the opportunity to make change and may have become part of the problem. Following the widely held notion that change takes three to five years, principals who have not made dramatic improvement in that timeframe may not be the best fit for turnaround situations. Whatever the criteria chosen, leaders must have the necessary leadership qualifications and competencies to meet the challenge.[5]

Attention to Successors

One area that has received almost no attention in the emerging field of school turnarounds is the selection and preparation of successors that follow the turnaround specialists' tenure. These are the individuals that have the all-too-important job of sustaining turnaround results. If turnaround leaders are the principals who take the school from "abysmal to good," then the successors must be principals skilled at taking the school from "good to great."

Superintendents taking the long view will engage in succession planning to consider which educational leaders might best continue the growth once the turnaround specialist's work is done. Turnaround leaders and other district support players may also take the initiative to develop and mentor candidates as well. Successors may include assistant principals in the school, district administrators, or other principals who understand the fragility of turnaround and are prepared to shore up the transformation and take the school to the next level.

Identification of potential successors will allow superintendents to plan for and develop this additional cadre of leaders to meet the post-turnaround needs of their schools. Consideration of this important role should begin during the turnaround. Successor candidates ought to have separate selection criteria and leadership competencies, tailored to the contribution they will make in sustaining the gains made in student achievement and overall school improvement. Turnaround without succession planning risks long-term failure.

Executive Development Programs

While a leadership development program alone cannot drive and sustain transformational change, an executive development program specially designed to meet the needs of turnaround professionals can go a long way toward preparing principals and their teams for the tasks ahead. Given how much will be demanded of these leaders in terms of time, emotional resiliency, team building, and sheer multi-tasking, programs that offer these leaders high-quality, innovative, and engaging development experiences are small investments that can reap tremendous rewards.

Programs like those developed at University of Virginia and Harvard, and in states like Louisiana draw on cross-sector curricula with a set of analytical tools and strategies most likely to facilitate their leadership success. These programs offer a few examples of those that engage participants across districts and states for multiple sessions over years to ensure they have the necessary support from peers, faculty, and coaches to meet the turnaround challenge.

Developing and strengthening professional networks, these programs can bring together cohorts of participants that learn from the faculty, learn from fellow participants, and learn from case studies of relevant businesses and schools undergoing similar challenges. Programs like these are increasingly building collaborations between schools of business, education, and even public policy to draw on those with research knowledge and experiences in turnaround leadership across the public and private sectors. These programs are just a few that have specialized in executive development for educators.

As noted in chapter 2, they are not the only or necessarily the best models. Charter management organizations like KIPP and nonprofits like New Leadership for New Schools and the NYC Leadership Academy develop and manage similarly focused programs in partnership with universities or faculty or by using in-house talent. These principal development programs are among a distinct group of others that have specialized in preparing principals for leading schools out of distress. Each has its own theoretical underpinnings, methods, and pedagogy that build the necessary capacity to meet the leadership challenge.

Developing a Cadre of Turnaround Professionals

Involving more than just the principal in the executive development experience is an important element of most programs. Developing leadership capacity of a district "shepherd" and a core school leadership team extends the learning to a group of critical stakeholders that can affect and support dramatic change and plan for sustainability. A district administrator or other "turnaround partner" able to remove obstacles, advocate vigorously, and bring tools and assurances that hasten improvements is critical.

Likewise, a few lead teachers or staff members highly focused on student achievement and driven to support the principal's efforts can also accelerate the infusion of new practices. Sharing knowledge, discussing ideas, and reflecting on data are all critically important to the turnaround team. Networking with peers from other districts or schools and conducting benchmarking visits are also ways that the leadership team can drive instructional improvements.

This in-class and, perhaps more important, out-of-class networking can spur innovation and offer emotional and other support from like-minded peers facing similarly challenging circumstances. Extending the turnaround expertise beyond the specialist principal to those that can support achievement at all levels of the education system also builds capacity for sustaining the improvements.

Building a team of professionals at the district, school, and even state and community levels capable of supporting the turnaround underscores the importance of identifying the system and engaging relevant stakeholders in the transformation process. Including these stakeholders in the executive development experience both acknowledges their essential roles and offers them the opportunities to learn together and network with peers. Where resources and time don't allow for participation in a program, these stakeholders might benefit from joining in a retreat, site visit, or reading group that can build their understanding and capacity to support the turnaround vision and the difficult work of change.

Attending to Succession

As noted earlier, making the transition from turnaround school to growth school can cause a level of instability that results in "slide back" in student achievement, or worse, a return to a culture of decline. One additional team member most programs have not yet considered is the potential successor. This person may be one of the current school team members, or could be someone external to the school. Identifying and preparing these leaders to sustain the turnaround likely will require an entirely different executive program. This program might expose these sustainers to the work of turnaround but also might develop them for the challenges of ensuring stability and driving new growth.

Ideally, states, districts, and nonprofits engaged in turnaround efforts will design or participate in two interconnected programs, one focused on preparing the leader and his/her team and another preparing the successor for the hand-off that sustains improvements. Such a "dual-track" endeavor would acknowledge the primary role of the turnaround specialist in putting in place the conditions necessary to facilitate dramatic improvements, while at the same time recognizing that successors need to build their leadership capacity in understanding the turnaround process and how best to support continued growth.[6]

Accessing Case-Driven, Cross-Sector Coursework

Schools of education and traditional providers of professional development are not well known for their use of case method pedagogy or cross-sector literature. Yet, adult learning scholars have long espoused the benefits of engaging adults in interactive dialogue and experiential learning. Using case studies from the private and public sectors allows participants to engage in examinations of situations relevant to them.[7]

Visiting schools and even businesses that have been turned around can offer opportunities for examining best practices and discovering techniques or ideas that are portable to another school context. This type of experiential learning excursion might facilitate the observation and discussion of the school's leadership, culture, and environment that reinforce classroom content. As Principal John's case illustrates in Chapter 10, these visits can help bring new ideas and cohesion to a leadership team implementing turnaround strategies.

Program content can address a variety of leadership topics. It may draw on fields and specialized skills including organizational change, turnaround leadership, guiding instruction, teamwork and communications, data analysis and decision making, stakeholder engagement, ethics and inclusiveness, conflict resolution, or building and sustaining high performance. As the turnaround field develops, executive training and other professional development programs will be able to draw on research to best prepare these leaders to lead and sustain dramatic school improvement.

Performance Requirements

Most executive programs, even in the private sector, do not tie development opportunities to expected results. However, in the ever-urgent landscape of school turnaround, states, districts, and executive program providers engaged in this work cannot effectively develop turnaround specialists without defining what constitutes a turnaround. These stakeholders—and especially the turnaround specialist principal—must understand the competencies around which curriculum has been developed and the results expected in order to best determine how the specialist's success will be evaluated.

A set of performance targets, some required plan (e.g., 90-day plan), and a means to monitor progress (e.g., the balanced scorecard) are three essential elements that undergird an executive development program for turnaround leaders. A robust turnaround plan will allow for attention to both short-term and long-term indicators of progress. Meeting or exceeding performance metrics should be required for candidates to receive a Turnaround Leadership Endorsement (as discussed in the previous section).

Developing executives capable of succeeding in the turnaround environment is an ever-apparent necessity as the demand for turnaround specialists across the nation increases. The supply of successful turnaround leaders is insufficient, and so more providers—universities, nonprofit turnaround partners, state education agencies—need to engage in this work and refine the leadership competencies and essential metrics of success. Moreover, as the field develops, program content will benefit so that leaders learn to execute those core essentials that facilitate turnarounds.

FOCUSING ON EXECUTION

Turnaround leadership requires a relentless focus on execution. Analyzing, reflecting, and planning all lead toward executing a clearly articulated vision and plan for action. Yet, turnarounds are about unearthing problems and delving deeper and deeper until each is solved. Plans need to be fluid and turnaround leaders must be able to make continual adjustments to meet changing conditions. That said, a well-researched and thought-out plan for the first 90 days can be a critical map to gain the type of "quick wins" that signal positive change is underway.

Core Essentials

Without a rigorous research base of successful and failed turnarounds in the K-12 education arena, a clear path to turnaround cannot be articulated. However, there are both anecdotal and research findings that can guide turnaround leaders to the core essentials they need to execute their turnarounds. Specific actions will vary depending on context. Conditions differ in urban, rural, and suburban locations, for example; content and student development change from elementary to middle and high school environments; and some schools have significant community challenges while others are in physical disrepair.

Few turnaround leaders would argue that a set of core essentials undergirds the work of turnarounds in various contexts. In the private sector, the Turnaround Management Association certifies managers against such essentials. Such strategic drivers for school turnarounds might include: principal leadership; quality teachers and instruction; rigorous core content; a culture of high expectations and performance; interim assessments that lead to data-driven and differentiated instruction; targeted and effective professional development; high expectations for all students; programs and interventions aligned toward student achievement; and school and community support.

Some turnaround leaders may find that their situations resemble urban school or high-poverty environments, and thus, execution strategies can be informed by research on high-performing high-poverty schools or Bryk and his colleagues' (2009) analysis of urban school success in the Chicago public schools. One well-publicized finding of Bryk's study, for instance, is the interaction of five core elements—strong leadership, welcoming attitude and community connections, developing of professional capacity, a nurturing and safe learning environment, and strong instruction and materials.[8] Some leaders and policy advocates focus energies on one or more of these essential elements; yet, the strongest improvements were found in schools embracing all of these.

Plans and Tools

Organizing and communicating plans can make a significant difference for turnaround leaders. Some business tools, which will be discussed in the next chapter, can provide organizing frameworks around which turnaround professionals can develop and execute strategies. In a turnaround environment, for instance, early wins can give a school the jumpstart it needs to accelerate improvements. Thus, the first 90 days can set a course for dramatic change.

Turnaround plans centering on the first 90 days, and subsequently updated every 90 days, can outline targeted areas, goals and objectives, tasks, and responsible parties as well as success indicators. As Michael Watkins' (2003) book *The First 90 Days* demonstrates, the effective development and implementation of a 90-day plan, especially during that initial transition, can build critical momentum for the journey ahead and achieve those essential "quick wins" that lead to longer-term successes.

The balanced scorecard (BSC) is another tool that educators from schools to state departments of education are finding useful. Kaplan and Norton (1996) designed it to monitor financial performance, customer relationships, internal business processes, and organizational learning. Initially developed to counter a singular focus on stock returns, the balanced scorecard is adaptable to any organization seeking a multi-dimensional approach to strategic action and measurement.

Educators have adapted scorecards to address and monitor four similar strategic areas as well. Charlotte-Mecklenburg schools in North Carolina showed notable gains as an urban district employing the balanced scorecard and a project management focus as its improvement plans.[9] A balanced scorecard may be used for an entire school district or for an individual school. East Mecklenburg High School (Charlotte, NC) included the following four key strategic areas in their 2004–2005 school improvement plan: (1) attaining high academic achievement for all students, (2) creating a safe and orderly environment, (3) ensuring community collaboration, and (4) ensuring equity in all schools.[10]

Many states and districts are utilizing balanced scorecards to support performance monitoring. The BSC offers turnaround professionals a tool that not only outlines goals and measurable objectives but also provides an effective means to communicate the core essentials—including ambitious performance targets—to a variety of stakeholders.

Finding that critical path to turnaround in any school environment can mean the difference between success and stagnation. For a turnaround leader, knowing what works in the classroom is essential and understanding how to develop and motivate teams—be they leadership, staff, or community—can turn stress into positive change for students. The next chapter will offer some business tools that leaders can adapt, including one new tool that will be introduced to help turnaround leaders ensure they are working toward that critical path.

Communicating plans and actions is an oft-overlooked area of turnarounds. Plans and data are important, but open lines of communication can make the difference between stakeholders' understanding and embracing change versus opposing or sitting on the sidelines of change. Communications planning is another tool that will be discussed in chapter 6. Focusing on execution requires a leader's careful observation and near constant communication so that all stakeholders—especially staff and students—have clear expectations for performance, as well as the tools to achieve it effectively.

Flawless execution may not be realistic in the school setting, given the many changing variables and circumstances; however, executing flawlessly does not necessarily mean adhering to set plans. Adaptability is critical to effective implementation. Executing and monitoring plans with fidelity, meeting commitments, making necessary adjustments, and communicating progress will help the turnaround specialist gain credibility and accelerate results.

Ongoing Support

While plans and tools play an important role in the project management aspects of turnaround, professionals benefit greatly from ongoing support of peers, district leaders, key stakeholders, and even skilled coaches. This is helpful throughout the turnaround, but can be especially critical during the implementation phase. The principalship can be an isolating experience and when tough leadership decisions must be made, sometimes there are few people who can offer guidance or understand the potential consequences, much less help a turnaround leader manage the politics of change.

One benefit of developing more programs that nurture leaders for these types of situations is the potential for ongoing support. Most leadership programs, especially those preparing new leaders, stop short of offering support beyond the initial coursework. Even with the best preparation and mentoring, turnaround principals can benefit from implementation support (e.g., coaching) that helps them accelerate the change necessary to effect the turnaround and to create a path toward sustainability.

Given the complexity that these principals face in their school environments and the time pressures inherent in a turnaround initiative, it can be especially helpful to offer a set of supports that build internal capacity in the turnaround arena. This assistance can offer much-needed day-to-day support for the specialists and their professional colleagues. Such a network might include three major components.

Turnaround Specialist Network

Experienced turnaround operators know how to renew chronically underperforming schools. They understand how to prepare the environment for change, how to develop a set of capable leaders in and outside the school, and they know how to remain steadfast and true to their vision and resilient under implementation challenges. They also know that their peers can offer insights and innovations that can help them solve problems. They know how to learn and adapt ideas quickly to their own situations.

During the first cohort of the Virginia School Turnaround Specialist Program, a brash and confident African American female principal from an urban elementary school near Virginia Beach sat next to a quiet, white male middle school principal from a coal-mining county in southwest Virginia; they exchanged ideas, began to troubleshoot their respective political challenges, and discussed interventions for failing students in their equally struggling, yet vastly different, communities. Despite the little they had in common, they offered each other all they had of themselves, revealing doubts and anxieties that few others might understand.

Were it not for the program, these principals would not have met and been able to confer and shore up hope for their own capabilities and the futures of their schools. Networks of turnaround principals can span districts or state "turnaround zones," or be nurtured by existing charter management organizations, nonprofits, or alternative preparation programs. They may even form as interest groups in national organizations. Such networks provide powerful opportunities for principals and even other turnaround professionals to network, share best practices, and build a professional learning community.

Leveraging technology applications such as online learning communities or Blackboard can help turnaround leaders gain ideas and support in their time-compressed and geographically dispersed situations. Such networks can also benefit districts and states in identifying and developing a ready supply of professionals, especially as specialists and support players inevitably move to new roles.

Strategic Support

District or central offices provide a critical lifeline for turnaround specialists and their teams. Superintendent and board support not only clears the path for the turnaround to begin, but can remove barriers during implementation as well. Allocating scarce resources, displaying confidence in the leader, and expediting purchase orders or maintenance requests are just a few vital ways district leaders can shepherd the turnaround. Such leaders may also provide important political cover or a sounding board for turnaround leaders as they work through resistance from various stakeholders.

It is important to note that while the necessity for district support is clear, the number and types of leaders engaged with the turnaround specialist may vary greatly depending on the context. Small rural schools, for instance, may have or need only one district shepherd, and in some cases it is the superintendent. In medium to large school districts support and involvement by the superintendent is equally as important, though one or more trusted others may oversee turnaround success.

Sometimes outside strategic support in the form of consultants, turnaround management partners, or executive coaches can provide a level of expertise beyond what district administrators or a network of turnaround professionals within the organization is able to offer. These external resources may bring scalable tools and insights that address implementation challenges. Outside experts can also be valuable confidantes for turnaround professionals facing highly politicized situations, and they can be contracted to bring knowledge, insights, and a level of confidentiality that may otherwise be difficult to obtain.

Community Support

Community stakeholders at the local and state levels can be critical advocates for the turnaround as it is being executed. They can also lend support for sustaining its achievements once the turnaround is completed. Thus, in keeping with the notion of creating a cadre of turnaround professionals, communities may benefit from considering ways in which such critical stakeholders can gain expertise in and ultimately strengthen the turnaround.

A turnaround leadership team might ask themselves a variety of questions to leverage the system and maximize stakeholder resources and support. Are there business partners that might be engaged in targeted interventions or fundraising projects? Can religious leaders be sought out to counsel or mentor youngsters having discipline challenges? Can business professionals or scientists come to talk about careers or to judge a competition? Can these leaders give voice to needed policy changes?

Principals may choose to set up a school council that is involved in monitoring the school turnaround plan and can assist in eliminating barriers while advocating and supporting change. Select parents and community members known for getting the word out could be especially helpful to communicate positive change and brainstorm solutions to stubborn problems.

Parents themselves are often a difficult group to involve in any school, and may be more noticeably absent or disgruntled in one that is chronically underperforming. Often, these schools are located in distressed areas where parents are challenged to keep their own lives from unraveling, much less get involved in a school's problems. These parents may not have been successful in school themselves, and so they may not readily see the value for their own children. Community walks, home visits (with appropriate others), ongoing school performances, and tangible "rewards" for participation are just a few ways some principals engage parents that sit on the sidelines of their child's school experience.

Whatever the avenue taken to secure parent and community support, schools—and children—benefit from all stakeholders being engaged in their success. A confident leader knows he or she does not have all the answers; building and expanding a team of active supporters makes culture change more viable. Involving others in solving problems not only helps produce stronger results but also builds trust that can live beyond the turnaround.

Performance Metrics

As stated earlier, the turnaround environment demands highly transparent accountability for success. This is based on the urgency for students and allows educators to document the history of failed interventions. In addition to meeting and sustaining national and state achievement measures, interim measures like discipline referrals, curriculum alignment, and use of instructional time to gauge turnaround progress can help provide a more complete sense of the health and well-being of the school. Both the balanced scorecard and the Turnaround Value Chain (detailed in the next chapter) are tools that can support this monitoring process.

Any turnaround plan must include a thoughtful set of performance metrics by which turnaround specialists can enhance leadership competence and demonstrate success. Principals, district leaders, and relevant others must identify what specific performance targets and improvement indicators are important for each individual school. "Value-added" performance measures are an attractive and innovative means to evaluate turnaround success for their focus on individual student growth rather than grade performance. Such growth testing models also offer principals and teachers real-time results for individualizing and improving instruction.

A set of accountability metrics may include: performance metrics (a set of annual student achievement measures that define the turnaround); interim measures (a set of indicators that may go beyond student performance to climate, discipline, attendance, parent engagement that can be defined and monitored throughout the turnaround); and turnaround indicators (a combination of student performance metrics and two- or three-year indicators of renewal). Linking the short-term turnaround to long-term success is also vital to sustaining improvements; thus, turnaround indicators might also include whether a succession plan has been developed for the post-turnaround environment.

Executing the turnaround successfully requires a dual focus on the immediate issues that drive low morale and performance and the extenuating circumstances that stand in the way of sustained student achievement. Research-based interventions and a set of "core essentials," organized and communicated through effective tools and plans, bolstered by support networks and monitored with transparency through a set of appropriate metrics are all elements that must be embraced. These are the mechanisms that highly capable and courageous leaders stand ready to employ so that they can confront conditions at the root of underperformance and activate the "flywheel" that accelerates success.

NOTES

1. Public Impact. (2008, June). *Turnaround Leaders: Competencies for Success. Part of the Turnaround Collection from Public Impact.* Funded by the Chicago Public Education Fund. See also *Leaders for School Turnarounds: Selection Toolkit; Teachers for School Turnaround: Competencies for Success;* and *Teachers for School Turnarounds: Selection Toolkit.*

2. Louisiana Department of Education. Bulletin 746. Item 710. HISTORICAL NOTE: Promulgated by the Board of Elementary and Secondary Education, LR 35:645 (April 2009), p. 64.

3. Bryk and his colleagues (2009) offer four lessons, as cited in Debra Viadero, D. (2010, January 27). Scholars identify five keys to urban success in *Education Week*, including a welcoming attitude toward parents, and formation of connections with the community; the development of professional capacity, which refers to the quality of the teaching staff, teachers' belief that schools can change, and participation in good professional development and collaborative work; a learning climate that is safe, welcoming, stimulating, and nurturing to all students; and strong instructional guidance and materials.

4. See Public Impact's work on turnaround leadership competencies (2008), as well as states like Louisiana, South Dakota, and New Mexico and districts such as Philadelphia and Chicago that have developed or participated in leadership development programs and can offer insights into this process.

5. EduLead. (2008). *Louisiana school turnaround specialist program: White paper,* prepared for the Louisiana Department of Education. See pp. 12–13, 19–20 for a preliminary list of leadership characteristics as well as Public Impact's (2009) *Leaders for school turnarounds: Selection toolkit.*

6. EduLead. (2008). *Louisiana school turnaround specialist program: LSTS blueprint. Version 2.* Prepared for the Louisiana Department of Education. EduLead recommended a dual-track program that included a track for turnaround specialists and another track to prepare successors to sustain the turnaround (p. 15).

7. Case collections at the Harvard Business School and the Darden School of Business, for instance, offer a variety of examples in disciplines like organizational behavior, strategy, decision analysis, and communications, especially relevant for the turnaround context.

8. Viadero, D. (2010, January 27). "Scholars identify five keys to urban school success." *Education Week.* http://www.edweek.org/ew/articles/2010/01/27/19cesr.h29.html. Accessed 1-27-10.

9. http://pages.cms.k12.nc.us/gems/eastmeck/SIPAll.pdf. Accessed 6-27-10.

10. Ibid.

Chapter 6

Leveraging Management Tools

Applying business concepts to the public sector is not new. Site-based management, for example, followed a trend toward decentralization in industry. The total quality management movement in industry found its way into schools eager to identify and apply best practices to improve performance. The Baldrige Performance Excellence Program and Baldrige Quality Award, well known in industry circles, added education and health care to its service categories in 1999. Run out of the National Institute of Standards and Technology (NIST), an agency of the U.S. Department of Commerce, this systems approach to performance management now offers frameworks, programs, and networking opportunities focused on how quality management systems can improve performance.[1]

Outsourcing is a more recent adaptation, which helps ensure that an organization focuses on its core business, leaving other necessary functions to a strong set of suppliers.[2] These suppliers become partners in the delivery of a quality education for all students. Transportation, food services, and information technology are just a few departments that districts might have outsourced.

Management tools offer districts valuable strategic frameworks. For instance, many schools, districts, and even states are now turning to project management techniques and balanced scorecards to chart a course for change and to monitor and measure progress. To business professionals, project management is an essential managerial skill and now school systems like Charlotte-Mecklenburg, North Carolina, and Broward County, Florida, two Broad Prize[3] nominees, are incorporating it into their business practices and competencies.

In managing turnarounds, leaders need the kind of efficient, root-cause problem-solving tools and processes that will help them plan, monitor, and communicate their strategies broadly. This chapter will first discuss two widely used private sector tools that have gained traction in turnaround schools and districts; the latter part of the chapter will propose additional business tools that, if well adapted, offer turnaround leaders additional applications and communication strategies to accelerate improvements.

THE 90-DAY PLAN

Leadership transition is a costly business. Ineffectual leadership can bring multi-million-dollar payouts for football coaches and business executives, but for most leaders the only payout is at best a recommendation that helps secure a new job. Replacing a leader involves recruiting, securing, and training a new leader for the job, paying for someone to "act" in the position during the search process, and managing the organizational fallout left by the failed attempt.

Leaders coming in from the outside have it harder; failure rates can top 50 percent and costs have been shown to be more than twenty times base compensation.[4] In 2009, *The New York Times* estimated that fixing failing schools could cost $3–6 million per school.[5]

Often, leadership transition can be underestimated—and underappreciated—for its ability, when successful, to set a positive course for change and the acceleration of results. Harvard Business School professor Michael Watkins' (2003) book *The First 90 Days* zeros in on this leadership transition challenge. Watkins argues that carefully planning for and managing through leadership transitions can turn an organization's haphazard "sink or swim" process into one that accelerates the organization's ability to reach the "break even" point where a leader moves from consuming to creating value.

In most environments, the first 90 days are as much about learning as they are about acting. Strong leaders can quickly assess the situation and the employees, and execute strategies that create early wins that propel change into lasting improvement. Each situation and leader is different, and thus, Watkins focuses on frameworks such as the "breakeven point" and the "diagnostic framework for managing change." He employs analytic tools like STARS, that focus on organization and action planning that helps match strategies and organizational strengths to situations, while identifying obstacles and opponents.

In a turnaround situation, those first 90 days are especially critical. Franklin Delano Roosevelt's first 100 days redefined the post-WWI and Depression era. Faced with a paucity of hope in a nation paralyzed with high unemployment, failed banks, and other dire conditions, FDR pushed through a historic 15 major pieces of legislation to turn America toward a new, positive era of growth. Those 100 days have become a bellwether for all presidents. They give the populace a means to get an early sense of what the new administration can and will do over the next four years.[6]

For turnaround schools, the first 90 days maps the first half of the school year. This valued tool can help a turnaround leader set a course for change and outline a limited number of pursuits that will stave off further decline. It can help a leader and his/her team to distinguish between the things that must get done and what could be done. From items in the early period of transition, when the focus is on preparing the environment, to those that develop the staff, to instructional strategies necessary to execute dramatic change in student performance, the 90-day plan can provide an essential roadmap for leaders, teachers, and other key stakeholders.

The 90-day plan is more than a strategic roadmap; it is a communications tool. This is critical for a number of reasons. First, creating a plan that involves key staff and other stakeholders can involve others in the ownership of and accountability for results. A 90-day plan not only articulates the goal and strategy, but also the expected result and "owner" of the initiative. This simple planning tool can facilitate communication between a new leader and staff and relevant stakeholders.

Second, once fully developed, the 90-day plan can be used for discussions with internal and external stakeholders. It not only communicates the vision and expected early wins, but it also offers an opportunity to easily discuss the most critical issues affecting the school. In this regard, the plan can aid a leader in gaining important feedback from key stakeholders.

For those wanting to assist the school, the 90-day plan can illuminate what is most critical so that external stakeholder efforts support, rather than detract from, those priorities. As will be described in the next chapter, Principal Aretha Eldridge-Williams used the 90-day plan faithfully with her staff to guide her turnaround of Kate Middleton Elementary School. (See Appendix E for a sample 90-day plan from Kate Middleton Elementary School.)

Beyond its important role in publicly articulating the strategies and actions needed for turnaround, it can provide a template for a turnaround leader's confidential plans. For instance, some turnaround leaders keep a separate 90-day plan for the more sensitive issues like staff development and evaluation strategies. The time-bound nature of the plan can be an important mechanism for monitoring performance issues. Most "corrective action" plans allow three months to achieve agreed-upon improvements to performance, and thus, the tool can help principals create and monitor human capital action plans.

While assisting the turnaround leader in easing the transition the organization inevitably undergoes as a result of his or her arrival at the school, the 90-day plan also offers important benefits for strategically outlining initiatives, monitoring their progress, engaging key staff, and communicating priorities to relevant stakeholders.

There is nothing to keep turnaround leaders from revising the plans each 90 days in order to re-engage the leadership team, assess performance, celebrate victories, brainstorm solutions to obstacles, and outline new priorities and expected results. Conducting what the military terms "after-action reviews" also can be a means to discuss how the targeted goals were (or were not) met. These facilitated conversations are used as both a learning and project management tool. As structured debriefs, they encourage immediate feedback and learning around intended versus actual results.[7]

The use of protocols,[8] as two of the cases in the upcoming chapters will illustrate, offers turnaround leaders additional means to bring structure and consistency to their efforts. Protocols can serve as codes of conduct for many aspects of instructional practice. In professional development sessions, for instance, use of protocols can provide teams a set of conversational guidelines that spur listening and create the space necessary to challenge thought and build more productive collaborations. Turnaround leaders and their teams may find after-action reviews and/or protocols helpful complements to the 90-day plan.

Whether the 90-day plan is used only in the beginning of the turnaround or continuously revised, it is not just the tool itself but the process that leaders and their stakeholders engage in that is critical to its usefulness. In education especially, it is easy to spend many hours fighting "fires." Having a tool that facilitates strategic conversations and commits staff to a plan of action can mean the difference between modest and dramatic gains in a school. At the very least, it can chart a course for how best to arrest the spiral of decline.

Educators are not lacking in plans—strategic, school improvement, emergency-based, instructional, to name just a few. The 90-day plan offers turnaround leaders a tool and process for building effective short-term, transparent, and accountable plans that communicate a vision not only in what they contain but also by the fact that they are completed and revisited often. Many leaders find these plans so successful that they update the plans each 90 days throughout the school year. They commit the leader and staff to actions, timelines, responsible parties, and expected results so progress can be met and monitored.

THE BALANCED SCORECARD

Another strategic management tool gaining traction in the education sector is the balanced scorecard. Developed in the private sector as a means of extending firm performance and accountability beyond financial metrics, the balanced scorecard addresses the often difficult to quantify areas of intangible assets. Like stakeholder theory with its emphasis on broadening those with a "stake" in the firm beyond stockholders, the balanced scorecard is a strategic management tool that tracks business performance in four inter-related domains—financial, customer, internal business processes, learning and growth—in effect, creating a more balanced accountability system (Kaplan & Norton, 1996).

Recognizing that sole reliance on financial metrics for measuring performance had become ineffective in managing and monitoring complex firms, a number of executives began to work with Kaplan and Norton in a study group to understand and create a system that better served the needs of the firms. They questioned how to measure and reward not only short-term but also long-term performance, how to motivate and account for internal as well as external drivers of success.[9]

The balanced scorecard that emerged from this effort was conceived as an enhanced performance *measurement* system but evolved into a performance *management* system. The balanced scorecard offers firms a means to translate mission and strategy into a comprehensive set of measurable priorities that include not only financial performance metrics but also the essential drivers of financial performance across the four perspectives.

The balanced scorecard gained a foothold in the education sector in 2001 in the Fulton County school district outside of Atlanta, Georgia.[10] Charlotte-Mecklenburg school district in North Carolina implemented the balanced scorecard as well. Dr. Beverly Hall, the American Association of School Administrators (AASA) 2009 National Superintendent of the Year and superintendent of the Atlanta public school system, with her cabinet and school board, employed the balanced scorecard as an executive leadership tool in her pursuit of a strategic turnaround of the Atlanta school district.[11]

In the education sector, the balanced scorecard offers a level of transparency across many critical priorities for districts and schools not typically available through standard strategic plans and reporting. Such transparency drives greater accountability and the alignment of priorities across domains. This can be especially fruitful for state agencies and districts driving multiple initiatives toward improved student achievement.

The "perspectives" relevant to the private sector have been adapted to the K-12 arena. Perspectives at the school level may include student performance, school/community relations, learning and growth, and school process. Through initiatives like those at the Wallace Foundation or the Council of Chief State School Officers, state agencies, school districts, and even individual schools are employing the balanced scorecard to align and enhance performance management.

For turnaround schools, the balanced scorecard can be helpful both as a strategic management process and as a communications vehicle. The Virginia School Turnaround Specialist Program, for instance, developed a previously used online balanced scorecard tool for turnaround principals to upload and update measurable priorities. A companion to the 90-day plan, the scorecard set forth annual targets for student achievement, instruction, professional development, community engagement, and building processes. The 90-day plan becomes the short-term action plan that supports the balanced scorecard's aggressive and targeted improvement initiatives. (See Appendix F for a sample balanced scorecard.)

Together, these tools offer clear roadmaps by which to communicate with stakeholders. Some districts[12] post their scorecards on their websites, which enhances transparency and may also serve to build greater trust among constituencies. For both internal and external stakeholders, the balanced scorecard offers a comprehensive view of the school and, hopefully, a cogent set of initiatives that will bring about the necessary and dramatic change.

The scorecard is often monitored with a stoplight system. Red, yellow, and green arrows mark progress from baseline indicators toward agreed-upon targets. This allows stakeholders to easily distinguish victories from obstacles and monitor whether initiatives are on track. With a designated "owner" for each project, there is little room for obfuscating responsibility.

Like the 90-day plan, the balanced scorecard is more than just a collection of desired goals, targets, or planned actions. The 90-day plan requires strategic conversation focused on accelerating leadership transition and securing initial wins that will generate further positive change. A project management system undergirds the balanced scorecard, driving new processes for leading and managing change.

In the private sector, project management is a required competency for many executives, managers, and professionals. Corporate training departments offer courses to teach managers how to plan, execute, monitor, and adjust an initiative to attain desired results. From "chartering" a project to outlining goals and objectives, customer requirements, and metrics, project management processes can bring to the balanced scorecard the kind of prioritization and organization necessary to manage the complexity of turnaround.[13]

Employing a "project management oversight committee" (PMOC) to lead and monitor implementation helps leaders to maintain the scorecard as a "living document." The PMOC, whether at a turnaround school, a district central office, or a state agency, must be committed in its pursuit of excellence and consistent in its approach. This means meeting regularly and communicating often and being as objective as possible in its decision-making practices. Project leaders report in to the PMOC about how initiatives are progressing toward set targets. The PMOC can mitigate issues, clearing a path forward when obstacles arise that leaders cannot easily remove.

Skeptics might wonder what the balanced scorecard and PMOC process do that a cabinet meeting or department retreat cannot. Advocates could point to the rigor and structure of the process, for one. When consistently applied, it can align initiatives, help avoid derailments, make measurable goals and results transparent, and keep politics at bay, while maintaining a laser-like focus on student achievement.

The balanced scorecard as a process is a rigorous endeavor; however, it is not without its limitations, especially in the pursuit of turnaround. First, training is essential to ensure the scorecard is enacted as a process instead of a piece of paper. Learning how to organize and manage complex projects and competing priorities and objectives, within a highly politicized environment or with a staff experiencing low morale, can seem overwhelming. Those that use the scorecard know that there is an important investment of time upfront needed to build capacity to use the tool successfully and then ongoing efforts to use the tool consistently.

A second limitation lies in the time and technology it takes to manage the balanced scorecard. A turnaround leader is operating with a heightened sense of urgency and in an environment that requires fast-paced decision making. Many may not see they have the ability to spend significant time managing the scorecard. Technological challenges can slow the process, especially when a school's or district's technical capacity and support are limited. Such challenges should not prevent a scorecard process from being used if leaders see its value, but planning for the time necessary to implement it properly—including contingencies for technical difficulties—can save a tremendous amount of time and frustration for teams using the tool.

A third limitation is how the balanced scorecard interacts with other tools. The balanced scorecard does not replace the district's strategic plan, but at the school level, it may be able to replace a school improvement plan. Most important is that states and districts streamline these management tools so that turnaround leaders in particular can realize their added value. Otherwise, the balanced scorecard adds one more potentially onerous and cumbersome responsibility on an already taxed set of committed leaders.

Finally, the balanced scorecard, like any tool, must facilitate success. A balanced scorecard process that drives people to spend more time managing it than leading the strategic initiatives in it can take away from the accountability and communications benefits of employing such a tool. The tool is not the answer; the people leading the turnaround are, and thus, the tool cannot manage the people.

People must manage the tool, using it as a lever for accelerating change at whatever level of the education system it is employed. They cannot rely on the tool but rather must use it to have often difficult conversations about aligning initiatives and priorities, to commit to aggressive plans for action that benefit students, and to monitor progress and communicate the vision for turnaround.

When implemented well, the balanced scorecard tool and process offer the opportunity to shift a culture toward leading through complexity in an organized, integrated, highly accountable, and transparent fashion. It can be "cascaded" throughout an organization, from state department of education to school district to turnaround school, mapping and aligning strategies for improvement and transparency at all levels of the system.

As a performance management system, the balanced scorecard requires training and support—and thus the precious commodity of time—in order to realize its potential. Should it be employed in year 2 or 3, once the initial action plans are underway? Or should it be at the core of the turnaround and culture change? It is this tension that makes it a promising opportunity—and a potential drain—in achieving turnaround.

THE COMMUNICATIONS PLAN

It may be too dramatic to suggest that turnarounds hinge on effective communications; however, successful turnaround leaders know how integral clear and strategic messaging can be to facilitating turnarounds. Communications, in fact, is an essential component of good leadership. Communicating early and often has almost become cliché in leadership. Leaders often drive change by putting forth persuasive arguments targeted at particular audiences receptive to the messages. Small wins build momentum that drive the cycle of success.

Yet, many times, leaders become distracted, fighting fires as they flare up, living in the moment of the crisis and hoping their messages are consistent. In chronically underperforming schools, as leaders face numerous discipline, operations, and academic challenges, the latter method can often rule the day. In this way, ineffective communications can be the undoing of a turnaround in progress.

For the turnaround leader, a communications plan can be a critical tool to reflectively plan messages and manage the flow of information in a turbulent environment. (See Appendix G for a communications plan template.) In a school demoralized by underperformance or paralyzed by violence or economic hardship, communications planning can go a long way toward shoring up the necessary support to move a culture of failure toward becoming a culture of excellence.

Most schools have strong orientations when it comes to crisis or emergency planning. Providing a safe and secure environment is paramount in a school setting. But few school leaders take the time to thoughtfully plan, document, distribute, and manage the messages that must accompany turnaround strategies.

Turnaround communications starts with the vision for the school. What will the school look like when the turnaround is accomplished? This is the forward-looking, optimistic yet realistic view of the school environment, the staff and students working within it, and the community's support of it.

Communicated with passion and conviction, this vision can become a powerful mantra for change. It is a "pitch" that any turnaround leader needs for that two-minute elevator ride with a critical stakeholder—whether dignitary or parent—to garner their support and motivate them toward action. It is this message that gets repeated so often that the forward direction is clear.

A communications plan helps leaders articulate specific goals that facilitate scorecard or 90-day plan objectives. It can provide a critical path to reaching key stakeholders and delivering a set of critical messages that will allow for optimal communications and transparency during the turnaround. With a goal articulated, the plan also sets forth specific communications objectives, along with the strategic actions targeted to relevant stakeholders and the medium by which that message may be delivered (e.g., website, letter, board presentation, PTO/PTA meeting, grant application).

Communications professionals understand how to target messages to reach intended internal and external customers. They know the impact they are seeking and employ written and verbal materials to achieve desired results. Turnaround principals don't have the time or resources to hire professionals to assist them. Like many other aspects of their job, they must learn and do for themselves in order to drive the needed change. Tools like these can go a long way toward organizing ideas, mapping issues, and carefully considering how to support turnaround effectively.

A communications plan may be a critically important tool, not only for the turnaround principal but also for the superintendent, turnaround partner, or state officials supporting the turnaround effort. Schools experiencing chronic underachievement and pursuing a turnaround strategy (as opposed to closing altogether) may be mired in politics, flailing in mixed messages, bogged down by a myriad of unaligned programs, or stagnating in a set of low expectations or self-fulfilling prophesies. In these contexts, communications planning can be especially helpful for setting a new tone.

The communications plan ensures that a turnaround principal considers thoughtfully the perspectives of each major stakeholder, honing in on the best ways to deliver messages, build trust, and promote fruitful relationships. While no set of communications can guarantee a successful turnaround, developing a communications plan offers the opportunity for the turnaround principal and leadership team to reflect on a number of issues.

Teams might consider how best to position the school, how to engage critical stakeholders (especially students, staff, and parents), and how best to manage the critical and often overlapping details of executing a turnaround strategy. Moreover, when the inevitable crises come, communications planning can help leaders anticipate opposition or garner support.

With a clear set of targeted messages that support the turnaround strategy, leaders can also help stakeholders stay focused through the turbulence of execution. Such messages should not be viewed as scripted but rather as essential talking points that reinforce rather than detract from strategy. The business of turnaround is multidimensional and time sensitive; taking the time to articulate a compelling vision, develop a set of initial messages that can be incorporated into various communications, and create communications goals and objectives with strategic actions and materials can give a turnaround leader an important edge when an unexpected crisis unfolds.

For many turnaround leaders such messages flow naturally, no script necessary. They speak passionately, preaching the gospel of high expectations and an unwavering commitment to teaching and learning. Surely, for these gifted leaders, a communications plan would just slow them down. Possibly.

Considering the importance of having these messages repeated, leaders may find that a communications plan allows them first to write down what they say so eloquently every day; second, to plan how best to share those messages—which mediums are best (e.g., newspaper, newsletter); and third, to target the optimal message carriers (i.e., stakeholders).

With planning comes reflection, and with reflection comes the chance to step away. With that step away, a new or different perspective can sharpen focus and lead to greater clarity and urgency, and ultimately hasten results. The communications plan complements the 90-day plan and the balanced scorecard so that the turnaround leaders and relevant stakeholders can consider more fully the scope of the turnaround and the strategic actions they (and others) will need to manage to best support the execution phase of the turnaround.

THE TURNAROUND VALUE CHAIN

Through researching and working directly with turnaround leaders in Virginia and Louisiana, it is clear that principals doing this difficult work need a set of tools that help them to quickly hone in on the variables they need to employ for their context. These principals need to zero in on a path that ensures all major stakeholder groups and elements impacting students are addressed. They need to know the territory of turnaround and the levers available that will add the most value for their students. One final management technique turnaround leaders can use to assess and pursue a critical path to change is a new tool developed by the authors specifically for these time-compressed and challenging situations: the Turnaround Value Chain.

The value chain (and "value chain analysis") has been widely used in the private sector as a means to identify the activities essential to creating value in a firm. Michael Porter's (1998) research into how firms create and sustain competitive advantage offers a relevant framework adaptable to the turnaround environment. Stephen Preece's (2005) value chain application to the arts sector presents one example of the value chain's organizational relevance to the nonprofit context.

The Turnaround Value Chain presented here is a K-12 adaptation that posits the activities (i.e., influences) and actors (i.e., influencers) likely to contribute and sustain turnaround success in schools. At its core, the Turnaround Value Chain is a graphical representation of the elements that ultimately create value for students in a chronically underperforming school, such that student achievement is dramatically improved. Specific applications and considerations for these major activities and actors may vary by context, but likely will need to be addressed in some way.

Based on a synthesis of research and experience, the Turnaround Value Chain attempts to frame the critical drivers of accelerated improvement in schools. It points to the set of core essentials any turnaround leader must consider. The "influences" are separated into primary and secondary activities, while the "influencers" include key stakeholders necessary to achieve and sustain success.

The primary *influences* and related activities in this model include:

- *Instructional Excellence*—high-quality teachers who are working effectively in teams and individually and collectively meeting the needs of their students;
- *Aligned Curriculum*—a standards-based curriculum which is aligned across grades and subjects with appropriate interventions and remediation;
- *Assessment for Continuous Improvement*—regular and interim assessments used to guide instruction, differentiate teaching, support struggling students, and help prepare for state and national assessments; and

- *Supportive Climate*—attention to basic and developmental needs that allow students to be engaged learners (e.g., safety, discipline, nutrition, essential services, equity, trust, high expectations for all students, particularly those who because of economic circumstances or racial background have been the subject of low expectations).

Influences playing a supportive or secondary role in this model include:

- *Governance*—strong and aligned governance to guide policy and be supportive of the turnaround;
- *Leadership/Management*—capable turnaround leadership that is empowering and decisive, as well as detail- and execution-oriented;
- *Outreach to Parents and Partners*—open communication to parents and partners in ways that engage and leverage community support;
- *Diagnostics*—data analysis of student achievement measures as well as indicators of the "health" of the organization (i.e., culture); and,
- *After-School/Enrichment*—opportunities that support and engage students that are also aligned with curriculum standards, and attendance and performance goals.

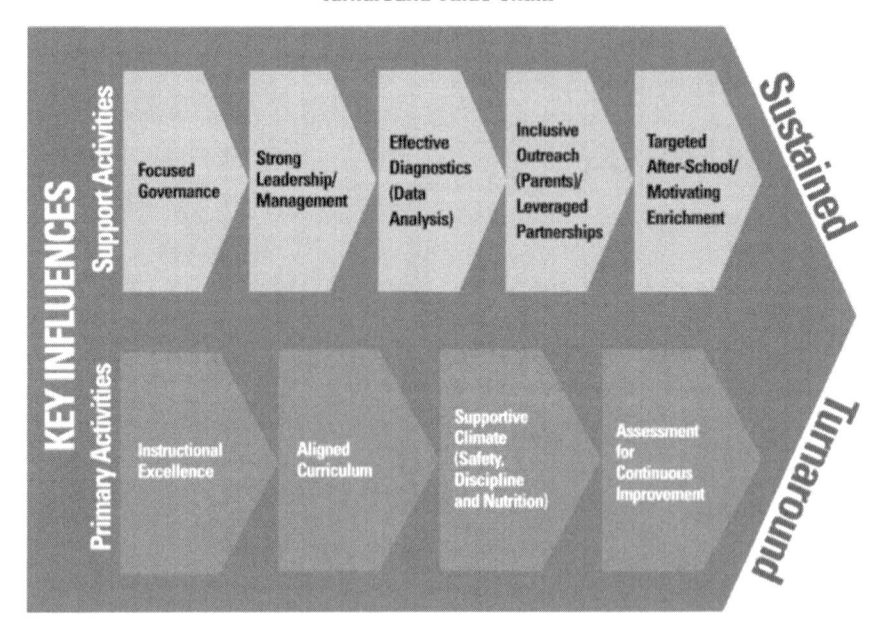

Figure 6.1. Turnaround Value Chain—Key Influences.
Source: Tierney Temple Fairchild, PhD, for EduLead and Louisiana Department of Education, April 2008.

Leveraging Management Tools 119

The principal influencers and their activities include:

- *Principal and Assistant Principal*—leading inclusively and decisively;
- *Teachers and Staff*—motivating students and modeling a professional learning community;
- *Students*—focusing on being successful and confident learners, engaged meaningfully in the school;
- *Central Office Administrators*—addressing turnaround specialist priorities, removing obstacles, and including advocacy where needed;
- *Parents and Community Members*—engaging with the school in support of the turnaround;
- *School Board*—building policy and governance supports for the turnaround;
- *State Department of Education Officials*—attending to the enabling conditions that drive transformation; and
- *Other Partners and Advocates*—consultants, philanthropic partners, nonprofit organizations, service agencies, places of worship, and others leveraging their work to further accelerate the turnaround.

Turnaround Value Chain

KEY INFLUENCERS

Supportive Partners: School Board → District Leadership → Central Office, State Support → Parents, Community and Other Partners → Supplemental Services Providers

Primary Drivers: Highly Qualified Teachers → Other Instructional Staff and Specialists → Cafeteria, Safety and Building Staff → Turnaround Specialist, Principal, AP

→ Sustained Turnaround

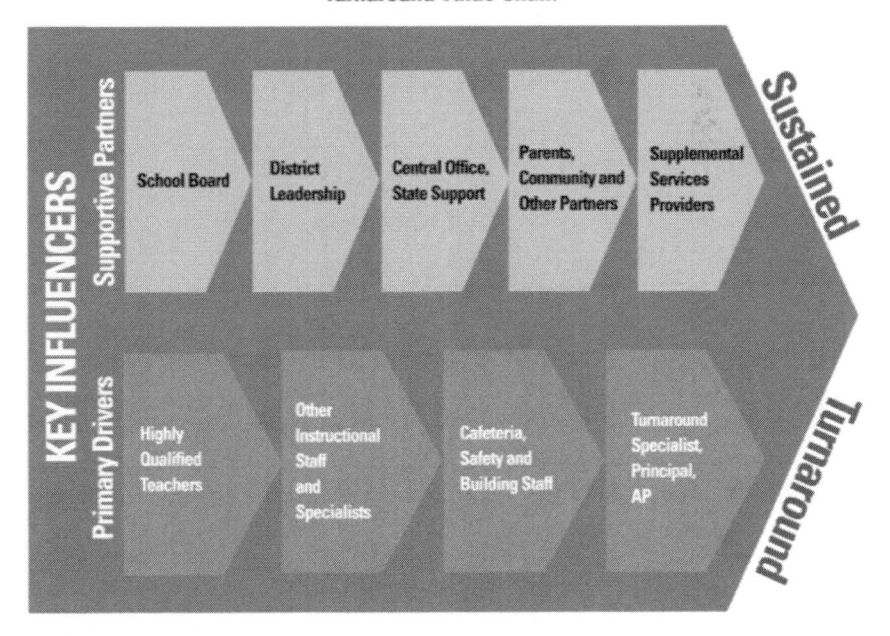

Figure 6.2. Turnaround Value Chain—Key Influencers.
Source: Tierney Temple Fairchild, PhD, for EduLead and Louisiana Department of Education, April 2008.

This model offers leaders a critical path to facilitating turnaround. With further research and validation, the Turnaround Value Chain (TVC) could offer a number of potential applications for facilitating school turnarounds. For example, a TVC could be used as an analytical tool for turnaround situations. In this application, turnaround leaders and relevant stakeholders might conduct an initial strategic assessment of their current situation relative to that which will be important for turnaround success. Here, the TVC would be used as a pre-assessment tool where the turnaround specialist and teams use the TVC to analyze these elements as they develop a turnaround plan, attending to how best to leverage stakeholders in its development and execution.

The Turnaround Value Chain might be further developed as a diagnostic instrument to assess whether a school is a good candidate for turnaround leadership. In this application, each of the elements in the value chain might be given a positive or negative assessment, and a score and scale could be developed to consider when the intervention is necessary and desirable. If a school has considerable negatives, it may be a better candidate for reconstitution, for example, while if it has numerous positives, another, less intensive intervention might be employed. Most important, since it is not yet a validated diagnostic tool, the Turnaround Value Chain should be used to offer insights into which schools might benefit most from turnaround.

Moreover, the Turnaround Value Chain has the potential to be used by the principal, district advocates, or turnaround partners during the turnaround process. For instance, the Turnaround Value Chain might offer a useful framework to provide feedback on turnaround progress. It encapsulates essential stakeholders and strategies known to accelerate school improvement. While it does not focus on performance targets or other metrics, the Turnaround Value Chain offers a critical path toward the influences and influencers that can facilitate turnaround success and may be adapted based on context to include the latest research-based strategies that accelerate student achievement.

The TVC focuses not only on the "what" but also on the "how" and offers a means to understanding that turning around a school requires much more than improving test scores. In depicting the primary and support activities as well as the partners necessary to achieve turnaround, the TVC lays the groundwork for turnaround specialist candidates and relevant stakeholders to have an essential dialogue about how to effect these drivers and how to stop those activities that are impeding success. It is a tool that can enhance the preparation of administrators being trained for the challenge of turnaround.

The Turnaround Value Chain zeroes in on the critical path to success and, as such, can help those influencers of turnaround—as well as those preparing to be teachers and administrators—create and deliver on an aligned, systemic, and transparent set of influences that impact student success.

Management tools and frameworks help professionals think strategically, organize for action, and articulate and monitor desired results. The 90-day plan, balanced scorecard, communications plan, and Turnaround Value Chain offer a set of tools with which turnaround specialists can develop and implement strategy. They draw on management practices that can facilitate the kind of alignment and transparency that brings coherence to a set of endeavors that drive toward results. They guide process but do not dictate actions, which may vary based on the environment.

While there are a number of other tools, processes, and frameworks to augment those highlighted in this text, what is most critical for the turnaround leader and his/her team is that they select and utilize tools with fidelity. Many tools exist; few are employed well enough to become institutional systems or processes woven into the fabric of the school, an essential issue in the post-turnaround environment. They take time upfront to understand and employ well, but such an investment is rewarded when results are realized and processes become imbedded in the school's culture. Careful selection and consistent implementation of tools like those described in this chapter will help turnaround leaders more effectively develop plans, communicate progress, and accelerate learning.

NOTES

1. http://asq.org/learn-about-quality/malcolm-baldrige-award/overview/overview.html. Accessed 10-15-10. The Baldrige Criteria for Performance Excellence include leadership; strategic planning; customer and market focus; measurement, analysis, and knowledge management; human resource focus; process management; and business/organizational performance results.

2. Moynihan, A. (2002, October 11). "Outsourcing enables owner to focus on core business." *The Business Review* (Albany). http://www.bizjournals.com/albany/stories/2002/10/14/focus10.html. Accessed 6-26-10.

3. The Broad Prize for Urban Education was established in 2002 and is awarded each year to honor urban school districts that demonstrate the greatest overall performance and improvement in student achievement while reducing achievement gaps among low-income and minority students. The $1 million prize is the largest education award in the country given to school districts. http://www.broadprize.org/about/overview.html. Accessed 3-30-11.

4. Watkins, M. (2003). *The first 90 days*. Boston: Harvard Business Press.

5. Dillon, S. (2009, June 1). "U.S. effort to reshape schools faces challenges." *The New York Times*. http://www.nytimes.com/2009/06/02/education/02educ.html?pagewanted=1. Accessed 6-25-10.

6. Chung, J. (2009, April 20). "History's verdict: What 100 days can reveal." *The Wall Street Journal*. http://online.wsj.com/article/SB124096652262466393.html. Accessed 6-25-10.

7. After Action Review process (AAR): "Learning from your actions sooner rather than later." http://www.mindtools.com/pages/article/newPPM_73.htm. Accessed 6-22-10.

8. National School Reform Faculty. (n.d.). "Why protocols?" http://www.plcwashington.org/study-groups/protocols/intoduction-to-protocols/why-protocols.pdf. Accessed 6-24-10.

9. Nolan, Norton, and Co. (1991). *Measuring performance in the organization of the future: A research study*. Lexington, MA. Executive Summary.

10. Kaplan, R.S., and Miyake, D.N. (2010, February). "The balanced scorecard." *The School Administrator*, *67*(2), 10–15.

11. Ibid. See also http://www.atlantapublicschools.us/18611010892250280/site/default.asp. Accessed 6-28-10.

12. Fort Wayne, Indiana school system's Balanced Scorecard is posted on its website, http://www.fwcs.k12.in.us/Home/BSC_DISTRICT_082508.pdf. Accessed 6-24-10.

13. http://www.pbs.org/makingschoolswork/dwr/nc/pughsley.html. Interview. Accessed 6-26-10.

Section III

Turnaround Leadership in Action

Chapter 7

Consistency and Compassion in the Face of Chaos

Kate Middleton Elementary School
Gretna, Louisiana
Aretha Eldridge-Williams, Principal

It was Aretha Eldridge-Williams' first week of school as the new principal of Kate Middleton Elementary School in Gretna, Louisiana. The school sat just over the bridge from New Orleans, across the Mississippi River on what locals refer to as the West Bank. Although bordering the Orleans school district, the school was part of Jefferson Parish, and Principal Eldridge-Williams knew her new school was the first thing that greeted visitors to her community. Yet, it had no marquee, no way of sharing its name or the pride she hoped to instill in its Jaguars learning inside.

Kate Middleton Elementary School had served many purposes since the main structure was built in 1951. It started as a neighborhood elementary school, and with the addition of buildings, it became a junior high school; later it served as a kindergarten center and at one point it also housed the parish's special education department. Now, it was a pre-K to fifth grade elementary school with its own separate library and gymnasium.

In 2000, census data showed the area around Kate Middleton to have twice the percentage of poor families as the national average. Forty-five percent of the population was of color, mostly black or African American (36 percent of total). While 70 percent were high school graduates, only 11 percent carried bachelor's degrees or higher.[1] And that was before Katrina.

PREPARING THE ENVIRONMENT

Principal Eldridge-Williams began her tenure in 2005 as the school's third principal in three years. Eldridge-Williams was taking over from a retiring principal that had been there just one year; her predecessor was principal of the elementary school for two years. During those three turbulent years, the school had been listed as "School Improvement" Level 1 and Level 2 under Louisiana's accountability standards; prior to that it was labeled as a "School in Decline."[2] As Eldridge-Williams took on the turnaround assignment, she observed the physical learning environment she inherited as a collection of worn buildings that had served many functions—not an ideal setting for delivering a high-quality elementary school experience.

Among her first decisions as a turnaround principal was to defer physical plant upgrades. "Knowing some of the history . . . I knew there might have been some changes that I wanted to make, but right then, I knew that changes to the physical plant weren't going to be a priority."

Based on an examination of a number of data sources, Ms. Eldridge-Williams found some disturbing trends that drove her immediate focus inside the classroom. Students had "basic minimum" scores and staff turnover was high. Louisiana's accountability data provided Eldridge-Williams with some confirmation of the long road ahead; all schools in the state were expected to reach a School Performance Score (SPS), a measure of test scores and attendance for elementary schools, of 120 by 2014.[3] Kate Middleton Elementary School's SPS in Spring 2005 was 53.8, which was only a slight improvement from the 45 and 48.4 scores received in 2003 and 2004, respectively.[4] She suspected much of the staff attrition had to do with the economic circumstances of the families the school served.

> Because of the population that came into the school, it was a difficult environment to work in. . . . I'm not certain if the teachers had the know-how, or the leadership had the know-how, I didn't know about that. I knew I was going in alone. . . . I began thinking about my trust situation and who I could trust.

Principal Eldridge-Williams found it challenging to identify the colleagues she could depend on to give her an objective sense of the "nuts and bolts" without editorializing or inserting their own "ill feelings" about the state of the school. She relied on a fellow principal confidante on the outside, but knew no one with experience at Kate Middleton, except one teacher on staff. She had worked with this teacher at a previous assignment in federal programs and was comfortable with her high standards and ethics.

"She really gave me a clear picture of what was going on in the school," Eldridge-Williams reflected, notions that she then validated herself through data and further observation.

As Kate Middleton's principal, Eldridge-Williams began her tenure walking around and listening a lot. When the school year started, she was anxious to begin the turnaround process. Her immediate plans involved arresting the turnover in staff and building up her instructional program to target literacy. But just a week into the school year Hurricane Katrina hit, and Eldridge-Williams' plans changed dramatically.

Trial by Fire

No one could imagine what the people of Louisiana, much less Principal Eldridge-Williams, would face in the aftermath of the hurricane. When the initial word came that the hurricane was coming ashore, she and her staff prepared the buildings as best they could, storing loose materials and moving external items indoors.

With news of the impending storm getting worse, and since the evacuation wasn't immediate, Principal Eldridge-Williams called in her custodial staff and had their assistance in making some final preparations to the building. Eldridge-Williams, however, didn't leave it to them to finish the job; she and her son came back in and tried to stave off potential damage by loading as much computer equipment into the gymnasium as they could.

Eldridge-Williams was extremely committed to the school but at some point in her preparations—and as news worsened—she realized that she also had to tend to her own elderly family members. "We fled in our RV, my husband [Malcolm], our senior parents and me," she said. Like many, they drove inland to escape the storm.

Once the storm had passed, Principal Eldridge-Williams was anxious to find out the status of her school. She had only a cell phone and laptop to communicate with her colleagues. Telephone connections were limited. When she finally got through to Gretna police, she learned that she could not return to that area immediately.

At first, officials said it would be a few days before they could return; a week, then two, then three went by before they were permitted to come back to the school. Meantime, available district administrators were called to a meeting in Baton Rouge, where Eldridge-Williams heard from her superintendent. It was there that they reviewed emergency protocols for their eventual return, such as checking the buildings for damage and reporting problems to maintenance. Superintendent Roussel told them to return as soon as possible and prepare for the re-opening of schools on October 3rd.

On September 19th Eldridge-Williams and her husband returned.

> We returned to the school by night. The police opened the school. . . . As we drove in, it was complete serenity . . . [the] only thing in view was a blinking red

light on the bridge. We started to walk around and could immediately see that the damage was severe. The primary building seemed to be the only building left intact. . . . So, we began mopping.

Little did Principal Eldridge-Williams know that the parking lot of Kate Middleton Elementary School would become her home for the next nine months. Their own home in New Orleans was uninhabitable, and so she received district permission to plug in her RV to the school's source of electricity.

Eldridge-Williams and her husband became the school's "plant people" and building maintenance was now her top priority. The National Guard was called in to take away fallen trees. The Board of Health came to condemn the mold-ridden library and cafeteria, and they discarded all the damaged books. Tables were moved inside the gym, and it became a place for work and eating.

Having multiple buildings was an asset now, and Eldridge-Williams used every available space to create a suitable environment for teaching and learning. Eldridge-Williams and her husband were managing the maintenance issues, but in order to open the school again, she needed teachers and students. Teachers started to come back; however, eight teachers and six paraprofessionals were forced to relocate because their own homes were destroyed. They never returned.

Before the storm, the school enrolled 349 students. Post-Katrina, the school lost nearly two-thirds of the students, and just 108 students, pre-K through fifth grade, returned to the school when it reopened on October 3rd.

Eldridge-Williams needed to get the word out that her school was open, yet she knew that part of her challenge was communicating with parents. She reached out to media contacts to create a few public service commercials inviting people into the school.

As families found places to live, more and more students enrolled in school. The devastation still crippled the New Orleans area. By October 28th, 289 children were enrolled at Kate Middleton. In November, that number swelled to over 400. One of the first schools to reopen, Kate Middleton was now operating at full capacity.[5]

Once again, teachers were in short supply. "Some came, and some couldn't handle it," she said. Eighty-eight percent of her students were on free or reduced-price lunch, one indication of the school's poverty. After the storm this number jumped to 94 percent, according to Eldridge-Williams, among the highest in the parish's 88 schools. Students were living in drug-infested neighborhoods where violence often prevailed. The community was on edge and her strongest teachers were often lured away by schools nearby that could offer more stability. Something had to be done to bring focus to the school.

"The Kate Middleton Way"

Before the storm, Principal Eldridge-Williams tried to set a welcoming tone with high expectations for students, parents, and staff. Her turnaround plan for the school included a vision that every child would succeed at high levels in an environment that emanated pride. During an ice cream social she held early on as a way for staff to get to know her, Eldridge-Williams was pleased to hear one teacher, one whom she knew, describe her to the others.

"I can tell you, [Principal Eldridge-Williams] will not ask you to do anything that she wouldn't do," Eldridge-Williams recalled the teacher saying. This comment exemplified the type of culture she wanted to create at Kate Middleton, one in which she and others would lead by example and dig in to do the hard work of change.

After Katrina, the physical repairs to her building as well as getting students back in school consumed Eldridge-Williams. Once she and the custodial staff had triaged the building maintenance issues, she had to re-engage with parents, teachers, and staff members. In effect, she was building a new team with largely new students. Teachers were hired by the central office, and so she had little control over who came to her building. This meant she had to spend more time emphasizing high expectations for all students, since her early observations led her to believe that not all teachers had shared her views about student achievement.

While teachers were critical to student success, Principal Eldridge-Williams believed that all staff and community members were vital to realizing Kate Middleton's potential. Eldridge-Williams and her new staff developed a vision by which they hoped to create a highly productive learning environment. They called it "The Kate Middleton Way." She explained.

> The Kate Middleton Way is: Everybody is polite, all the time. We greet each other with a hug and a handshake. They have a code of conduct—come to school on time, be prepared and ready to work, and are asked to give the teachers 100% of their attention. If they respect themselves they will be respected.
>
> Our vision is to build and sustain a learning community that embraces high expectations for all staff and students; to create an educational learning environment where teachers are encouraged and supported while implementing a challenging curriculum; and to create an educational community that teaches our students how to learn and how to apply knowledge learned to their own lives and experiences.
>
> Our mission is that the Kate Middleton community believes that all children will learn and reach their fullest academic potential through rigorous child-centered curriculum.

Principal Eldridge-Williams communicated this to everyone—staff, students, families, and community members. She invited the bus drivers to come introduce themselves, to see and learn about the school. She recalled one driver's comments: "No one has ever invited me in before. . . . I have learned more in these weeks than I have in a lifetime."

As the Kate Middleton Way became imbedded in the school's culture, it became more than a vision on paper or a code of student conduct. It was the way in which they worked together. It meant never giving up, always pursuing excellence, overcoming obstacles and even bending the rules, if necessary, to ensure students received all they needed.

DEVELOPING THE EXECUTIVE—"WALK WITH ME"

A self-described "hard-working, hard-driving" leader, Principal Eldridge-Williams had her own physical challenges, and yet her team soon learned that she would go above and beyond to support them first. Her motto with her staff is "If you want to talk with me, you have to walk with me."

She saw her main responsibility as observing and improving instruction, so she would rarely be found in her office. She conducted regular walkthroughs of classrooms to see how well lesson plans were being implemented and to assess student engagement, and she took other teachers on "learning walks" during their planning time so they could observe teaching strategies in action. "I always [carried] a note pad in my pocket so that I could write them afterward," Eldridge-Williams said.

When the children in one classroom were disruptive, for instance, Eldridge-Williams stepped in to listen and observe. After assessing the situation, the principal determined that much of this was due to the children's distressing circumstances, not the teacher's instructional challenges.

For many of her students, the aftermath of the storm placed enormous stress on an already impoverished community, which affected behaviors and lowered academic performance. Children's emotions ranged from sad to scared, and some acted out in anger.

Knowing this, Eldridge-Williams was able to coach her teachers. Yet, as conditions in some classrooms worsened, she also knew she needed to seek outside assistance.

"The student population was rough, and the male population in particular was unsettled," said Eldridge-Williams. The teachers were challenged and discipline actions ruled the day in many classrooms.

So Principal Eldridge-Williams reached out to a minister and asked him for help. She explained the situation and he replied, "I understand. I'll be back tomorrow." The next day he came with a list of names of potential mentors for the boys. The minister had assembled over a dozen professionals—professors, businessmen, social workers—all willing to lend an afternoon a week to mentor the boys. They focused on academic areas that the teachers had requested and connected them to their job experiences, and they modeled through their professional manner and dress an alternate path to what these boys may have been exposed to in their neighborhoods.

Eldridge-Williams sought out as many opportunities as she could to bring the world to the school and her students. After the storm, Scholastic was in the area and, with a professor's recommendation, they did a story on Kate Middleton Elementary. "They walked with me and talked with me and created a beautiful story for kids," she recalled. They assembled a story called: "The Kate Middleton School: Portraits of Hope and Courage After Katrina."[6] Because of the story, various schools throughout the country collaborated with Kate Middleton students as pen pals. Technology brought the world to the students.

Eldridge-Williams had a sense that technology could be a bright light for her students. She established a technology lab and asked the mentors to help the teachers in the lab. The mentors began their work in October and clocked over 1,180 hours from then to the end of May. Eldridge-Williams nominated the mentors for a national award, which they received from the International Reading Association. When she gave the plaque to them at the church, she was met warmly with the pastor's own reflection. "'You see, everything doesn't come in dollar bills. We have a jewel here.'"

Developing a Learning Community

Principal Eldridge-Williams built a school environment that had "no doors." She wanted doors open so that she could readily and easily observe and learn from the teachers.

Eldridge-Williams regularly observed and worked with the teachers to identify not only their weaknesses, but also to focus on their strengths. She told them individually that she was considering making some moves the following year. She saw how the teachers interacted with students and found ways to further develop them. She used materials that inspired her from her participation in the University of Virginia School Turnaround Specialist Program, a program her state and district had selected her to attend.

She chose Jim Collins' *Good to Great*[7] so that they could learn about some of the strategies she was employing, like "getting on and off the bus" and into the "right seats." She always included a story along the way, such as "The Fourth Little Pig" or "The Nine Blind Mice." The stories always were linked to what the teachers were experiencing or what Eldridge-Williams needed to talk about.

> I brought new things to them. It was changing their mindset from having a meeting just for the sake of a meeting to a data-focused meeting. They came to understand that meetings were held for focused discussions about expectations and for content presentation about teaching and learning, classroom management, suggestions for improving, and candid discussions without placing blame. I still conducted face-to-face, individual meetings—because I needed to talk about what I observed. It would not be an evaluation but it was more to say, "I'm concerned about what I observed." I'd then give [the teacher] the opportunity to clarify the intent of the lesson.

Eldridge-Williams spent a large amount of time conferencing with her teachers—almost all individually—to help them succeed in the classroom. Her meetings were always focused and to the point, with clear performance expectations.

FOCUSING ON EXECUTION—LITERACY FIRST

Principal Eldridge-Williams told her staff that she viewed herself as a teacher first—a reading specialist, as opposed to their principal. She brought a focus on making sure everyone believed that every student would be able to read. Math was just as important, but literacy came first.

With that underlying philosophy, she set out to make everyone a teacher of reading. "All of you who consider yourselves a social studies teacher, you are now a social studies *and* a reading teacher. If you're a PE teacher, now you're a PE *and* a reading teacher. You're a math specialist *and* a reading teacher," she said. Since the storm had destroyed nearly all of her books, she established the goal of putting 1,000 new reading materials in each classroom.

With a strong literacy focus, all teachers and staff were to read to the children or have the children read to them every day. "We can't control what happens after hours but we can control what happens here."

Eldridge-Williams surveyed staff and students about what books they liked. She chose books that would help teachers "explain a lesson" when they couldn't get their hands on the real piece of material or equipment. She knew that children in poverty suffered instructionally because of lack of exposure and that they would need "replicas of the real deal"—like a cathedral they might never have seen.

In her second year, the school received a Reading First grant. Eldridge-Williams made certain that all her reading teachers received proper training, including PE teachers, and they built new teacher relationships during the process. She encouraged collaboration across peer groups and designed teams to maximize the strengths of her faculty. The teachers taped themselves so they could listen to their questioning during the lesson. Eldridge-Williams then held individual conferences to discuss the quality of their questions and how they could improve, and she encouraged them to reach out to peers as well.

Eldridge-Williams encouraged faculty to think creatively and modeled this with her staff. She instituted a number of awards, including the Goose Award (Get Out of School Early Award for teacher attendance) and the Golden Box (for out-of-the-box thinking) to further motivate her team and reinforce "the Kate Middleton Way."

In an effort to buy a marquee for the outside of the school, the teachers developed lessons around the bake sale that included measuring and money. After numerous bake sales, Kate Middleton raised four thousand dollars and purchased a marquee to publicize Kate Middleton's accomplishments. This allowed the parents and community members to become more informed about the activities of Kate Middleton, and community members began to build a partnership with the school.

The staff continued to link schoolwork to what was happening in the school. For instance, when students were not happy because the cafeteria kept running out of pepperoni pizza, Eldridge-Williams asked the teachers if they could help solve the problem. Classrooms made bar graphs showing "likes" and "dislikes" of different pizzas. The teachers seized the opportunity to have children solve the problem, and the data were shared with the cafeteria. The result: more pepperoni pizza at lunchtime. It was a "quick win" for kids. As important, it clearly demonstrated that examining data is a way to improve any situation.

Building Parent and Community Involvement

In 2006, Kate Middleton's tardy rate was 25 percent. Eldridge-Williams noted, "The population was not accustomed to having to come to school on time." She had to engage the parents to help them understand that she meant business about attendance. She started "Coffee Talks" and invited the parents. In the beginning just a few parents came, but that was okay with Eldridge-Williams. She knew they'd share the information and become voices for the school and community. The attendance grew steadily each month and tardiness declined. Now, two dozen parents regularly have coffee and talk with the principal.

Assembling a parent-teacher organization proved more difficult. Some parents worked more than one job, others felt uncomfortable leading the organization, and transportation was an issue. "They'll come to see their kids perform," said Eldridge-Williams, "and so we began to conduct parent meetings prior to performances."

To counter the lack of involvement, Eldridge-Williams would elicit support from parents and the community wherever and whenever possible. She made several public service announcements, highlighted students in the paper, and showcased many students through student performances. Over time, the school's motto became "High expectations in all areas. No excuses."

To address student attendance or performance deficits, Eldridge-Williams made home visits with a social worker and a police officer. She would explain to the parents that children couldn't pass and be successful if they weren't in school. She brought the student's test results and the class assignments they missed.

Eldridge-Williams also knew that the school environment was a reflection of the school community. Her school vicinity wasn't "bright and shiny" like higher-performing schools in other, more desirable neighborhoods. In fact, when she first arrived at the school, she called the mayor about the unsightly apartment complex across the street and the nefarious activities that went on there. As a result, the police stepped up their presence, the building changed hands, and the illegal activities abated. Still, the area around the school grounds was unkempt, and the apartment complex was often littered with beer bottles and trash.

One day, Principal Eldridge-Williams went to the complex and began knocking on doors. One door opened and she made her case.

> We are across the street and we are teaching our children to keep our environment clean. Could you help us by picking up your trash? Please pass this on to those in the complex to pick up their trash. We'd appreciate it. Some use words that we don't use. Could you do that behind your doors? And could you turn down your music? We're trying to teach kids there's another way, and we could really use your support.

After her visit, that tenant spoke to the owner. The owner then sent a flyer around with all the things they could do, such as where to park and where to put trash. "He hasn't backed down on his word," she noted with satisfaction. "The owner has beautified the complex with plants, grass, and trees. He supports our efforts to keep our environment clean."

Extending her appreciation and continuing to stress a commitment to the community, Principal Eldridge-Williams invited the owner over to the school's spaghetti dinner, and he brought people from the complex with him. The linkages Eldridge-Williams made with community members went both ways; it meant that her students would respect them and their property. Her students do not walk on their grass, and they help to keep the school environment clean.

One more way in which Eldridge-Williams embraced her surroundings was through what she called "Community Walks." On these walks, she brought staff into the neighborhoods just to say "hello" and talk with the community. They talked with parents or chatted with neighbors sitting outside. Either way, Eldridge-Williams used these opportunities to make connections, extend Kate Middleton's messages, and build a shared sense of responsibility for the school's success.

School Leadership and District Support

Principal Eldridge-Williams began the Louisiana School Turnaround Specialist Program (LSTS) with a cohort experience at the University of Virginia's (UVa) program in 2008.[8] The state required her to have a Memorandum of Understanding in place to outline the responsibilities she would undertake in the turnaround. Staffing support was the most critical issue and yet, the district had limited control because the courts were enforcing a desegregation order to racially balance the schools.

Still, Eldridge-Williams established a school leadership team committed to changing instructional practice. Commitment meant helping teachers understand the vision of the school. Teacher leaders showed their peers sample lessons, modeled best practices, and offered new interventions.

One of the most critical stakeholders at Kate Middleton was the "district shepherd," the central office staff person assigned to accompany and support the turnaround specialist candidate throughout the two-year program. Karen Herndon, Principal Eldridge-Williams' district shepherd, was also Jefferson Parish's Director of Accountability. Herndon attended monthly school improvement meetings and was the liaison to the state for the 88 principals in her district. She reported to the district about Eldridge-Williams' progress in weekly meetings and offered support and advocacy where needed.

As the district shepherd, Herndon was especially helpful in providing interval assessments and developing reports that met the school's needs, including a set of "data-driven support materials" to champion "the Kate Middleton Way" (TKM Way). These data included Louisiana iLEAP/LEAP results with three-year trend data by subject area, grade level, and subpopulation. This comprehensive data set also provided interval assessments by classroom with district, school, teacher, and class summaries, and had sample assessments attached for reference. The principal and shepherd met every Tuesday to examine data and to brainstorm solutions to problems.

Using Essential Strategies

In addition to interval assessments and Louisiana state data, Eldridge-Williams relied heavily on a few tools to create the transparency she saw as essential to leading turnaround. They used DIBELS[9] results to monitor reading progress with green, yellow and red charts. Student cards were displayed and tracked on a "data wall." Cards were placed on the chart according to their need for intervention. For example, a green card denoted students achieving the "benchmark" or meeting expectation; yellow meant they were approaching basic and in need of "strategic" support; and red flagged those students performing unsatisfactorily and needing "intensive" intervention. Test scores were kept on the back to ensure student privacy.

Even though Reading First targeted K-3, they implemented the program school-wide with two hours of uninterrupted reading. Reading blocks were staggered, allowing the reading coach to offer support. Using Title I funds, Middleton hired five highly qualified interventionists for groups struggling. Students in need of intensive support would get a total of three hours of reading per day.

With her leadership team, she developed a 90-day plan, which included major systemic issues (e.g., balanced scorecard implementation and monitoring, faculty engagement, master scheduling), data-informed decision making (e.g., data wall, interval assessments, data analysis and reflection, focused professional development, tutoring and intervention, laser focus on math), and improving the environment (e.g., safety, food preparation, campus appearance, faculty restrooms).

She regularly reviewed and updated the plan, noting whether they were on target to meet expectations. Eldridge-Williams highlighted deliverables in green, yellow, and red to easily convey their status with the plan.

"Turning Up the Heat"

A benefit of Principal Eldridge-Williams' time in the UVa program was the opportunity it afforded her to reflect and plan. She also learned how to take more risks. One conclusion she drew during the executive program was that she needed to consider students in the middle. "There's a lot going on for special education and even for gifted students but not for students in the middle." In addition to strengthening current programs, her focus turned to this.

She also began taking more risks, especially as the district lauded her success. For instance, she took over the school schedules. This gave her the chance to look at the schedules and to change them so that she could leverage every instructional minute and assign teachers to best meet the needs of the students.

With a few years under her belt, she and her teachers decided they needed to "turn up the heat." She requested one more degree of effort from her staff to make a difference in the students' lives. Staff members began to mentor the most challenged children, especially homeless and foster children. Some took on three or four children; they committed to nurturing them academically and emotionally, and sometimes offered clothes and food as well. With a high poverty population, Eldridge-Williams knew that plenty were in crisis but "some *really* needed them."

They started to turn up the heat on attendance, on academic performance, on parent involvement. She and her leadership team placed visual reminders everywhere, with a thermometer to show the progress and photos to generate interest and excitement.

> We changed the length of time for rewarding students. Waiting for nine weeks to reward students, especially in high poverty environments, is far too long. We began rewarding students every two weeks with easy things like a popcorn party, movie, freeze pops after lunch, or free time to play for a class reaching its goals. We posted the data outside the classroom.

Eldridge-Williams and her staff linked motivation and rewards to build confidence in their students. They also implemented a highly effective after-school enrichment program both to develop students in their talents and to encourage positive behaviors and attendance. Eldridge-Williams gathered some data about student interests and, with Title I and grant funds, added dance and music enrichment to Middleton's sports offerings. Participation was contingent on on-time attendance and adherence to the Positive Behavior Support[10] guidelines used throughout the school day.

At one point, however, Eldridge-Williams realized she was attending to the students but not the teachers. She started asking local businesses for donations, trinkets, cosmetics samples, breakfast cards from restaurants, books, and gardening supplies. She gave teachers small rewards as she observed what they did—and how they did it. Eldridge-Williams observed classrooms every day and looked at the data to better understand their progress. Because she was in the classroom all the time, she knew what the teachers were doing.

MEETING AND SUSTAINING TURNAROUND

Five years into her tenure, Eldridge-Williams knows she can't leave. She hasn't reached her thousand-book goal yet; she's only at 600. "Keep the students and teachers engaged and you'll get what you're looking for," she says. The multiple data sources show improvements but not enough to satisfy this principal. She knows they can do better, and hopes for more stability in her population over time.

Despite the many changes in staff and students at Kate Middleton, the data are encouraging. Since 2006, iLEAP reading scores (ELA) for the third grade went from only 18 percent of students meeting "Basic" or "Above Basic" levels to 53 percent reaching these levels in 2008.[11] The numbers of students tested in general assessments went down from 2006, largely a result of the population fluctuation post-Katrina.

Third-grade math achievement also saw notable improvements, with nearly 70 percent of students at "Basic" or "Above" in 2008 (up from 21 percent in 2006). Social studies and science scores improved as well.

In fourth grade, ELA achievement also rose, from 27 percent at basic or higher in 2006 to 56 percent in 2008. Similar gains were made in math during those two years; scores jumped 31 percentage points, from 23 percent at basic or higher to 54 percent.[12]

Eldridge-Williams saw even greater improvements in her fourth and fifth graders, since a number of them had been with her since the early grades. iLEAP results for 2009[13] indicated that over 60 percent of fifth graders were at or above basic in reading, including a few students that achieved mastery. Fourth-grade LEAP math and ELA scores similarly grew to over 60 percent of students reaching proficiency—this as the number of students tested increased by more than 50 percent.[14] This still wasn't good enough for Eldridge-Williams, though, even if student turnover masked some of the progress. She and her team relied on interventions and interval assessments to meet the needs of all students, no matter when they enrolled at the school.

For student attendance, Eldridge-Williams and her team set a goal of 98 percent for the 2009–2010 school year. After the second week, it reached 95 percent. In the 90-day plan, she set the goal with the students that helped "keep the momentum." If students reached the attendance goal, they would get a party. Flags hung outside each classroom that had perfect attendance that day, a visual reminder to create healthy competition and build school spirit.

Eldridge-Williams feels that she has grown tremendously during her turnaround. She learned from books like *Good to Great* (Collins, 2001), *The Five Dysfunctions of a Team* (Lencioni, 2002), and *The Knowing-Doing Gap* (Pfeffer & Sutton, 2000) and uses her 90-day plan religiously. She has even cascaded the plan to the teachers so that once they have developed the school plan, they are now having teachers focus on how that works in their own classrooms.

Eldridge-Williams continues to place a high value on developing her staff. Her 90-day plan includes "focused professional development" and a "book study" with the intended result of bringing "meaningful planned and executed engaging lessons for all students."[15] Her plan also illustrates her urgency to address ongoing challenges in math. Four of the 16 focus areas directly relate to math, with efforts ranging from providing appropriate "early bird and twilight tutoring for students based on achievement data" to offering "job-embedded professional development in math" with a consultant and "math strategist," to software training "to help teachers design appropriate test items," to creating weekly grade 4 GLE online assessments.

She worked closely with her district shepherd to design, deliver, and monitor meaningful data reports. Principal Eldridge-Williams views turnaround leadership as another way to look at what education has overlooked.

> We have to stop making excuses and saying that there is only one way to do something. Often we think we know what to do, but we don't always do it. It has taught me to take risks and do the things I know I'm in control of—and let someone know why I'm doing it, like my district shepherd. I look at the data and attendance and show them why I make the decisions I do. The shepherd is that important middle person to help central office know why I'm doing what I'm doing. I can make arguments to do what I need for my school.

Ongoing Challenges to Sustaining Turnaround

In 2008, due to a court order enforcing desegregation called the Dandridge Consent Decree,[16] boundaries changed and many students and parents who understood "The Kate Middleton Way" are no longer in the school. While some parents moved as their homes were repaired, others have moved in and out as a result of what the principal refers to as "Dandridge"—which, among other items, requires compliance with "student attendance zones" that balance the district's population and ensure students attend the schools in the communities where they reside.

To keep track of the new and returning students, she and her team devised a dot system on their DIBELS data cards to monitor who has moved in versus those that have been at the school. The population was already highly mobile, but in 2008 they saw 40 percent of the students change. Each school also had to have racially balanced staff ratios, and so Principal Eldridge-Williams lost seven teachers and received seven new people. Third-grade iLEAP scores for 2009, which declined from the previous year, seemed to reflect that upheaval. Despite these changes, they pressed on with their 90-day plan.

Eldridge-Williams continues to work closely with district shepherd Herndon. She invited central office administrators, board members, and district principals to show how their use of data and the 90-day plan might be utilized in other schools. With Herndon's support, many of Principal

Eldridge-Williams' practices are now being replicated district-wide. Her collaboration with Scholastic continues as well. Based on experiences in leading through the turbulence of Katrina, she is working with Scholastic on a national crisis management curriculum for schools.

Eldridge-Williams and her school community continue to see the fruits of their hard work and perseverance. With an SPS of 74.6 in 2008, Kate Middleton Elementary School received an Exemplary Growth distinction, becoming a one-star school and shedding the label of "Academically Unacceptable." Further, in 2010, the school was one of 24 finalists for the Panasonic National School Change Award, which recognizes schools for having "significantly changed."[17]

What Principal Eldridge-Williams most values is that the children can see what's changed at the school and have higher expectations for themselves. She reflects, "They want to know I'm expecting more of them."

The urgency of her turnaround mission for the school means that Principal Eldridge-Williams doesn't hold any ill will toward those who are working at cross-purposes. "I don't have that kind of time," she stated. "When you want something you have to do whatever it takes while being ethical and true to self. It's by no means the end but we have done our best and I've learned a lot."

NOTES

1. U.S. Census Bureau, Summary File 1 (SF 1) and Summary File 3 (SF 3). *American FactFinder Fact Sheet: Zip Code Tabulation Area 70053.* Accessed 6-10-10.

2. Louisiana Department of Education. *Bulletin 111: The Louisiana School, District and State Accountability System.* "School improvement" refers to federal NCLB law, a label reflecting a school's failure to meet subgroup performance; the "school in decline" designation was assigned to schools with negative School Performance Score growth (more than 2.5 points).

3. Louisiana Department of Education. *Bulletin 111: The Louisiana School, District and State Accountability System.* A School Performance Score (SPS) is calculated based on test scores as well as attendance, dropout rate, or graduation rate. Scores range from 0.0 to 120.0 and beyond; a score of 120.0 indicates a school has reached Louisiana's 2014 goal. (Louisiana Administrative Code, August 2010, p. 1.)

4. Jefferson Parish Public School System (JPPSS) Accountability Department. *JPPSS District Composite Report* (compiled July 2010). Note: In the Spring of 2006, the district and all JPPSS schools were given the label "Severe Impact" by the state due to Hurricane Katrina. Schools gaining or losing 25 percent or more of their student population received the label "Severe Impact." JPPSS rolled back into the accountability system in the spring of 2008 with the label "New District and New Schools." As a "New District" or "New School," School Performance Scores prior to Hurricane Katrina were no longer considered valid.

5. Taylor, D. (2005). *The Kate Middleton Elementary School: Portraits of hope and courage after Katrina*. Supplement to Scholastic, Inc. New York: Scholastic, Inc.

6. Ibid.

7. Collins, J. (2005). *Good to great and the social sector: A monograph to accompany good to great*. New York: HarperCollins.

8. Louisiana participated in UVa's Turnaround Specialist Program for two years before launching its in-state version in 2010. Principal Eldridge-Williams was part of the second cohort.

9. Kate Middleton Elementary School. (2010). *Dynamic indicators of basic early literacy skills (DIBELS) progress monitoring document.* Testing occurs three times a year, after which the student's card, based on student performance, may or may not be moved to indicate green-benchmark, yellow-strategic, or red-intensive.

10. Positive Behavior Support is a behavior management system used to manage challenging behaviors and decrease the need for punitive actions. http://www.pbis.org. Accessed 9-27-10.

11. JPPSS Accountability Department. (2009, February 10). *The Kate Middleton Way: Data driven support materials.* Grade 3 iLEAP data, p. 2.

12. JPPSS Accountability Department. (2010, July 10). *iLEAP/LEAP/GEE Combined Archive Multiyear Summary Report 2-5-2009.* Grade 4 iLEAP data.

13. Louisiana Department of Education. (2010). *2008–2009 Principal Report Card: Kate Middleton Elementary School.* Spring 2009 iLEAP Test, Performance by Achievement Level, p. 3.

14. JPPSS Accountability Department. (2010, July 10). *iLEAP/LEAP/GEE Combined Archive Multiyear Summary Report 2005–2009.* Grade 4 iLEAP data.

15. Kate Middleton Elementary School. (2009). *90-day strategic plan: The Kate Middleton Way.*

16. *Lena Vern Dandridge, et al., vs. Jefferson Parish School Board, et al.* U.S. District Court No. 14-801. http://www.jppss.k12.la.us/dandridge-information. Accessed 6-10-10.

17. Kate Middleton Elementary School. (2010). Schools are nominated and evaluated across sixteen specific criteria. http://www.npli.org/nsca/overview.html. Accessed 9-25-10.

Chapter 8

Systems, Structures, and a Spatula
Building a Community of Scholars

P.S. 42—Claremont Community School
Bronx, NY
Camille Wallin, Principal

When Camille Wallin was assigned to her position at P.S. 42–Claremont Community School in the Bronx, she couldn't imagine the disrepair she would find. Her background as a literacy coach at an early childhood school and K-1 teacher in Harlem grounded her instructionally, but it was her experience at the NYC Leadership Academy "intensive" and her mentor during the required year-long internship that gave her the turnaround leadership skills to accomplish her mission.

"When I think of turnaround," Principal Wallin reflected, "I think fast. . . . If you're that low performing that you need a turnaround leader, you need to show dramatic change in a few years. . . . You are running to the task, whether it's thinking or it's action. The expectation is that the ambulance doesn't take twenty minutes to get there, it takes three. That's why you have the lights, and that's why, at times, you can be creative with rules."

Principal Wallin felt a sense of urgency the moment she stepped into the school. Not only was the condition of the building hard to stomach, only about 20 percent of the more than 500 student population were performing on grade level when she arrived. She was replacing a short-term principal that was removed from the position. Unlike other turnaround schools, however, this school had a strong principal for a number of years. Sadly, during the last two principals' tenures, the school spiraled to underperformance.

The condition of the school was one major indication of the hard work that was ahead of her:

> The school environment was horrific. You walked in the building and it just screamed low expectations. . . . Classrooms were cluttered, broken furniture, bathrooms were filthy, hallways were not clean. . . . Students were not in their classrooms. There were teachers who were unable to manage their students, so there were a lot of classrooms out of control. And there were not the systems and structures for supporting those children or the teachers in those classrooms.

The low performance, a manifestation of low expectations, was the other.

> It was incredible. There were pockets where students were achieving and doing well, but it was really tiny pockets. There was a lot of *care* for the children. The staff members *loved* and *cared* for the kids, but it was almost as if that was all we had to offer, our love and care. We were not able to harness anything that would lead to higher expectations for student achievement.

P.S. 42–Claremont Community School was situated in a high-poverty neighborhood in the Bronx. According to 2000 census data,[1] the demographics of the area in which the school was located included a population that was 62 percent Hispanic or Latino, most of whom were either Puerto Rican (44 percent) or Dominican (26 percent).[2] Thirty-six percent of the population were identified as black or African American and 17 percent as white.

In addition to the Dominicans and Puerto Ricans, the principal reported they had an influx of immigrants over the years, including some from various countries in Africa. Thirty-one percent of the population were foreign born, compared with 11 percent for the United States overall, and not surprisingly, according to census data, over 60 percent of the population in that area spoke a language other than English in their homes.

With more than 40 percent of families living below the poverty level, the school served a number of homeless shelters as well. The school's student population was 42 percent African American and 55 percent Hispanic, and 96 percent of students were eligible for free or reduced lunch.[3]

Wallin knew that some parents worked around the clock making ends meet while in other homes grandparents cared for the children. Just half of the neighborhood population had high school diplomas and less than 7 percent had bachelor's degrees.[4] Wallin understood these factors might make it difficult for parents to be active members of the school community, and frankly, that wasn't her main concern.

Students were also underprepared when they arrived. Experiences were generally limited to the neighborhood and what they had around them at home, so pre-literacy, basic literacy, K-2 print awareness, and knowledge of books suffered as compared to other students in the city. Principal Wallin knew that their home lives may have been rich in many other ways, but academic attention, oral language development, and what Wallin referred to as "the stamina to succeed in a structured learning environment" were just a few of the challenges she faced.

Because the amount and quality of their pre-literacy skills varied, as a general rule of thumb, Principal Wallin brought significant effort and attention to early literacy and developing in students the drive to do well. "I imagine that our kids rely heavily on us to maintain the idea that . . . learning is cool. . . . You can do well. . . . It's important to do well. . . . Teaching our kids that stamina . . . that seems to be something our kids rely on us for," she explained.

Principal Wallin thought deeply about how best to instill the love of learning, the personal responsibility to take care of one's work and how to learn to be a "rigorous thinker," a "high achiever," "college bound" when chaos may be a normal way of life. A good bedtime may be 8 p.m. for most elementary school children, but for the majority of P.S. 42 kids 10 p.m. might be the norm. With moms working late or because of after school experiences, there were student attendance problems and many opportunities to lose books and not complete homework.

When Principal Wallin arrived, low expectations permeated the school.

> Our definition of "learn" was this sort of whatever the child is capable of. . . . I thought, "We don't even know what the child is capable of since we haven't even gotten in the game of teaching them." . . . We let them sit in classrooms with graffiti on the walls and the desks are dirty and the teacher has piles of papers all over and nasty file cabinets from the 1920s with the ditto that went with it. There was no conversation about what our goals were for our students.

PREPARING THE ENVIRONMENT

One of Principal Wallin's first tasks was to figure out the composition and drive of her teaching staff. Through observation and data, she determined that a core group of teachers had low morale but "didn't know any different." The Teach for America (TFA) teachers had particularly low morale and were overwhelmed by the discipline challenges. Then there was another group of teachers for whom the morale wasn't low, but expectations were low instead.

Here Principal Wallin found one of her greatest challenges. She had a strong community of adults that cared for each other like a family and put that energy into the students and themselves the best they could. Yet, they weren't focused on offering the best they could for students. Wallin concluded that they didn't expect that the students could achieve academically.

Principal Wallin's initial vision came from her experiences in the New York City Leadership Academy. She felt it was a privilege to be asked to lead a school and that the district believed she could make a difference. Now it was her job to believe in her students and staff. Wallin reflected, "I had a moral responsibility to do the job." She explained:

> I came in with belief in myself. But the vision of how that was going to be done, I didn't really make until I stepped foot in the building. It was in seconds that the vision to create a learning environment that is not only conducive to learning but . . . to create a learning environment that says we *believe* in you, we have high expectations for you, it goes without saying. . . . That your floors could be sat on, your auditorium has a sense of awe when you walk into it . . . that your classrooms are clean . . . and your books, you have plenty of them, and the paint job is warm and your artwork is displayed in a frame . . . and your name is typed . . . There is pride.

Cleaning House: Building a Student-Focused Team

It didn't take long for the majority of Wallin's staff to accept that they needed to change. They didn't want their students to accept the filth and grime, much less bathrooms that didn't work. "They knew the students were better than that," Wallin recalled. Believing in full transparency, she showed them the data upfront, so the teachers might learn quickly that what they were offering wasn't meeting the students' needs or potential.

Another of Principal Wallin's initial actions was to make sure everyone knew that the condition of the school reflected to the students (and themselves) that they were not good enough. By walking by the graffiti or ignoring the dirty bathrooms, they were sending the same message of tolerance. Fortunately, one member of her custodial staff was especially eager to meet her standards. He was Kenny Rollins, the school fireman, in charge of the boilers and repairs; "the fireman" was a fitting partner, as Principal Wallin brought new urgency to improving school conditions and creating a safe learning environment so that her students could focus and achieve academically.

It was clear from her approach to the building that dramatic change was imminent. As a leader, Principal Wallin knew that her actions would send an important message, so she personally cleaned the bathrooms, she cleaned the desks, and she removed graffiti. She walked around with a spatula in her back pocket, pulling it out to scrape gum off the wall, to show her custodial staff which conditions were just not acceptable.

While staff acceptance of change wasn't immediate, Principal Wallin's actions had an important effect. She ordered new desks, for instance, and soon teachers were offering to take the old ones out. Dumpster after dumpster was filled with old furniture, trash, and garbage. The staff became meticulous about lining trashcans, cleaning up paper, and keeping an orderly learning environment. Momentum was powerful, and the changes had a multiplier effect.

Wallin's ability to get things done was fueled by her status as a NYC Leadership Academy principal. The plant manager as well as members of the custodial team saw that things might finally be changing and were eager to assist. "They were right on point," Wallin recalled. They worked above and beyond to support the physical improvements to the building, even though a few custodians eventually chose to be reassigned.

Always raising standards, Wallin used her opportunity to get new floors to take the building to another level. After a four-year wait, it was finally P.S. 42's turn for the upgrade, and Wallin didn't want the usual black and white. She asked for something different and got shiny new blue and yellow tiles in the school's colors, and had them carefully patterned to brighten the school and emanate its pride.

Principal Wallin took immediate charge of her environment. "I had the keys to the building and knew it was my job to get it done," she said. Without asking permission to move out furniture or paint desks, Wallin took action. And with no extra incentives or funds as she took the job, she leveraged her general school funds to invest in the building improvements she knew would be essential to changing mindsets about teaching and learning.

The cleanup of the building was significant for Principal Wallin in that it raised expectations, gave the entire school community a shared purpose, and announced that change was happening, but Wallin knew it was just a necessary first step toward a laser-like focus on student achievement.

Parent Support

Principal Wallin found her parents largely receptive her first year and used every chance she had to demonstrate her commitment to them. For instance, during her first community meeting at the school, one parent asked her why she thought they were failing. In the midst of getting introduced, the lights kept flickering and the administrator went on about the importance of quality instruction.

When Principal Wallin started to speak, she made a joke about the lights and then told them that it was her goal to make the learning environment reflect high expectations for the students. She told them she was going to leave the room to call the custodian to get the lights fixed. Then she mentioned the chairs they were sitting in and the lack of technology and how she would address those as well. The parents that came applauded.

Principal Wallin also made it a priority to be present for the parents, teachers, and students, modeling high expectations and a focus on academic achievement. In the morning, she noticed that policies and procedures were not being followed correctly, parents were going in and out the wrong doors, and visitors weren't signing in properly.

In dealing with parents, Wallin knew she needed to have a presence and to explain the reasons for the changes. She did this by consistently emphasizing how they were ensuring students' safety and creating an environment so that the children could focus on learning. She concentrated on breaking the low expectations around teachers not being in the classroom teaching and kids "lollygagging" around.

She'd stand in the hallway encouraging purposeful movement of staff, students, and parents, thinking, "Quick, quick, fast, fast. The students have to learn." She took the criticism that she wasn't "parent friendly" because she was pushing them out the door. She knew it was her job to help parents realize that the teachers needed to focus on teaching. She knew she had to get them out so that she could bring them back in later to support the classrooms in a more meaningful way.

Building Shared Responsibility

Despite her petite frame, Principal Wallin demonstrated she had the will, perseverance, and physical strength to get things done at P.S. 42–Claremont. Though the Leadership Academy came with cachet, it did not afford her any specific degrees of freedom. Regardless, Principal Wallin felt that she had the authority to do what was necessary to turn the school around.

> I felt I had autonomy. I'm not sure if I really did, but I certainly *felt* I did. I felt that I was entrusted to do this job, to make decisions that were right for kids. I thought I was supposed to move out the furniture and throw it to the dumpster on behalf of the children. . . . Maybe I should write it down as obsolete equipment and someone should look up how to write off obsolete equipment but for now, [I] just put them in the closet [to] get them out of sight from the teacher and students who were trying to teach and learn.

Wallin's litmus test for her staff was for them to decide if it was good for their own children. "Would you let your daughter sit at that desk? Go to that bathroom?" she asked. If it was unacceptable for their own children, then it wasn't good enough for their students. These conversations and experiences around the physical plant built a sense of shared responsibility that led to a higher standard in their building and their work.

Assessing and developing staff was her next challenge. After careful observation, Wallin categorized staff either as "movers and shakers" leading change or cheerleaders for change. Wallin was lucky not to have a lot of resistance from the 60-person staff. While she was focused on the massive cleanup, a handful of teachers chose to move on, and Wallin appreciated the internal leaders that stepped up to have the difficult conversations that led to their departures.

Wallin created an "all hands on deck" urgency to get students into the classrooms and learning. Rather than finger pointing at teachers who were young or had classroom management challenges, she would take more experienced teachers into classrooms to help struggling teachers (some of whom were brought to tears at times) and showed them that no one should stand by and watch a struggling teacher. "You never walk by a teacher in crisis," she said.

Given the school's location and condition, Wallin appreciated having a group of Teach for America (TFA) teachers committed to the students. She found, however, that they were less confident and prepared to manage a classroom. By enlisting more experienced teacher leaders to help them acquire the classroom management skills they needed, Wallin found that those willing to do that hard work would be able to stay.

What TFA teachers lacked in classroom management, they made up for in embracing data-driven instruction. Recognizing this asset, Wallin forged a number of strategic partnerships between TFA and veteran teachers that would help them build a culture of high performance. One of Wallin's goals was to leverage skills and to maximize the talent she had in the building. Relying on talented leaders inside the school had many benefits, including accelerating teacher development, building trust among her staff, and providing students the support they needed to be successful.

Wallin recalled one moment when key staff members made a public display of support for her efforts in the building. To her, this signaled staff commitment. Sometimes incidents like these occurred in isolation, but the messages still permeated back to the rest of the staff.

> I remember approaching a group of over-age fifth graders, who were outside their classroom. I'll never forget the music teacher, an older gentleman, who was teaching in his classroom. He came out of his classroom to stand next to me when I addressed the students. I asked the children whose classroom they belonged in. They . . . did their thing, and the teacher said to them, "You are speaking to your new principal, and I think I heard her tell you [that] you were supposed to be in your classroom." And the kids grumbled but went to class.

- He could have ignored the situation; instead he chose to insure that the students understood and respected my authority as the principal.

Once she had the support of staff, they began to turn inward, rather than outward, for answers. At times, they turned down some of the central office tools available to them, finding confidence in their own strategies for reaching their students.

Principal Wallin had few disagreements with her Local Instructional Superintendent (LIS),[5] but early on, they diverged on whether to write up one underperforming teacher's lesson as unsatisfactory. The disagreement was a minor one compared to some of the other challenges on her plate, but Wallin sensed this decision might have reverberations well beyond this one staff member. While she understood the district's desire to document underperforming teachers, she thought there was a better strategy for this particular teacher in the context of her staff. "I knew that writing up that teacher at that time would have had a negative backlash and would stop some of the momentum I had," Wallin explained.

Wallin's initial read on the climate suggested to her that there would be a tremendous amount of resistance and collateral damage from writing up this teacher. So Wallin chose not to rate her lesson as unsatisfactory. Eventually, Wallin's resistance to following her supervisor's direction made its way to her staff in a way that benefited her. In fact, this decision ended up enhancing her credibility with the rest of the staff, and ultimately, the poor-performing teacher resigned on her own.

Wallin felt well prepared to address the performance challenges in her building. Her Leadership Academy training included specific exercises to teach the district's processes. The Academy also trained its principals to understand that there are many ways to go about building an excellent staff, and the strategies a principal decides to use must be carefully selected within the context. While she recognized that her choice in this case might have placed added responsibility on her hardest-working teachers, Wallin was confident her strategy fit the situation.

Principal Wallin was all about balance. Her strategy was to maximize the talents she had, while providing clear expectations about work habits and work products. Her bottom line was always student achievement. She wanted to see everyone working to his or her own potential, increasing the momentum.

As she relied on teacher leadership within her building for innovation, at times she found it difficult to recognize individuals while strengthening the team as a whole. She learned that they had to be true to the team, even if some might get their feelings hurt. If they found the answer "in the house," they all need to share responsibility for success. "Don't think the wheel is better than the handlebars," she said.

Even if many staff didn't outwardly resist the movement, Wallin acknowledged that they did experience loss, which she recognized was difficult. She explained, "Some leaders are no longer leaders. The adult community is no longer the most important. In fact, it was marginalized, and the students are the most important."

Wallin made it clear to her staff that she needed them to be instructionally driven, not contract driven. That meant that teachers covered lunches, used their preps[6] for the good of the school, and met with families before and after school. Some even chose to work with kids over their lunch break.

DEVELOPING THE EXECUTIVE

Wallin credits the NYC Leadership Academy with giving her a sense of how to be a better leader. The Academy helped participants understand that they could leverage talent and build capacity from within, which resonated with Wallin's own leadership style.

It was at the Leadership Academy that Wallin learned about putting in systems and structures that would benefit her students and conveying actions with the confidence her role demanded. She created a 90-minute weekly meeting for professional development, manipulating preps where needed and acting with surety that this was essential. They studied the principles of learning, read aloud, shared and guided reading, with special emphasis on the teaching side of the equation. Ultimately, though, it would be the evidence of the learning that was most important.

Principal Wallin created a cabinet (including the coaches, the assistant principal and the data managers) and as the professional development began, they started to see the results in the students' work, the notebooks, and classroom management. They could also discern which teachers were providing quality instruction and those that weren't. "Good teaching was now being defined by the learning and not just that teacher's control over the behavior of their students," she said.

Wallin's goal was to change the standard of excellence to student learning—the hardest challenge of her principalship. To do this, Principal Wallin focused on the quality of learning, both for students and for adults. She introduced protocols[7] to respect that as adult learners they needed a structure to ensure they were meeting their goals for learning.

The protocols ensured that the professional development opportunities and adult learning were focused and rigorous. They helped manage and minimize the distractions that might interrupt an engaged faculty. Professional meetings focused squarely on fulfilling their professional development goals, especially when colleagues were facilitating other colleagues. Wallin focused her team on the quality of learning and respecting professionals' time, which in turn raised their expectations of what adult learning looks like.

Principal Wallin also targeted her professional development based on what staff needed to make students successful. She and her team used data to help determine what to emphasize. She benefited from her TFA relationship by being able to leverage her tech-savvy teachers as well as any of the TFA teachers' many data analysis techniques.

"We've always been a 'design your own' school," Wallin said. This meant that instead of choosing from the Department of Education's menu of recommended assessments for math and English/Language Arts (ELA), Wallin's school applied for and was granted a "design your own" (DYO) status. With the assistance of a professional development consultant they were using to strengthen instruction, she and her staff designed predictive and interim assessments tailored to their own curriculum. This option was part of the Chancellor's focus on offering more autonomy to good leaders in the system. For Wallin and her team, the DYO status reinforced their entrepreneurial spirit and shored up their confidence in knowing that "the answer is in the house."

They tried a number of assessments and determined where they needed to pre-test, post-test and re-teach, based on the standards and units of the curriculum. She put staff together as grade level teams and encouraged use of "soft data" to understand the information they collected. Some assessments they created themselves; others they took directly from their curriculum resources. Most important was to find the combination of assessments that worked best for their school.

For ELA, they realized their assessments did not provide the data necessary to predict how students were going to perform on the state assessments. The assessments they used focused on reading level, reading behaviors, and some comprehension strategies. The running record data told them what to do with the students so they could differentiate for 20 different readers in the classroom. Relying on teacher skill and a one-on-one assessment made the relationship between the teacher and student especially important.

Principal Wallin was looking for something to more adequately identify where students needed support in comprehension strategies. She also was looking for a writing assessment that didn't just assess elements of a writing genre; they needed a better way to assess students for organization and clarity in writing. When she didn't find anything, they developed a protocol to look at what they had and determine what they wanted. Then they pulled from what they could get to create what they needed.

Wallin repeated this process many times over to continuously improve instruction. At times, Wallin wondered whether they over-assessed, but she was much more comfortable with too much data than not enough data. This was especially important as she developed a data-driven culture and emphasized strategic partnerships between staff members to support high achievement.

To build collaboration from within, Wallin worked on shared responsibility and the sharing of knowledge. "We shut down the attitude of 'this is my classroom,' and we focused our PD [professional development] on what we needed to do as a team," she explained. "There's always a core of teachers moving faster than others, pushing the envelope and setting a new bar for the rest of us."

FOCUSING ON EXECUTION

Especially troubling to Wallin was the low expectations she saw in the building. She carried with her a blinding sense of urgency that everything had to be about the children. No longer could the adult community take precedence. She knew her staff had thought that it was about the children, but the data told a different story.

In 2004, when Principal Wallin took the helm, the scores on the New York state accountability tests showed 40 percent of students (70 percent of special education and nearly 20 percent of general education) performing at Level 1,[8] an indication of no proficiency on state standardized tests.[9]

Only 30 percent of all third grade students (and just 42 percent of general education students) met or exceeded Level 3 or 4, indications of proficiency and advanced proficiency. In fifth grade, those ELA scores were at 47 percent and 55 percent for all students and general education students, respectively.

The picture wasn't much better in math, with just under half of all students meeting Level 3 or 4 proficiency and only one in 10 special education students meeting that level. In all grades and subject areas, special education students lagged their general education peers by as much as 50 percentage points.

Wallin knew that she had to work through these challenges. She relied on a few strong coaches who had been part of that adult community to help her lead through the sense of loss to a point where they could see that they wanted and needed to change. Once a few were on board, many others joined in. For Wallin and others, it was a long time coming but a welcome effort.

Wallin's training at the Leadership Academy developed her skills in creating conditions for teachers to reflect on and assess their areas for improvement, to take personal responsibility and to expose them to what they may not know. "It was my job to make it possible for the adults to openly learn and grow, so they could better serve their students and provide the right supports toward that learning and growth," Wallin explained.

Attending to Special Needs Students

One of Principal Wallin's greatest instructional challenges was addressing the special needs population. When Wallin arrived, the special education population topped 35 percent and most of these students were in self-contained classrooms. Wallin wanted to move the school toward a collaborative, inclusive model that she knew could further student growth and achievement.

Wallin used the "strategic pairing" of faculty members to accomplish this goal. One such pairing that had dramatic results was with Ms. Jeanette Foster, a 17-year veteran special educator, and Ms. Danielle Liebling, a "TFAer." She gave the teachers time to plan together, moving Ms. Foster from a self-contained special education classroom into a team teaching environment.

This move was a significant change for both teachers, and especially for Ms. Foster, who had decades of experience serving special needs children. Principal Wallin could see that Ms. Foster had a willingness and desire to improve herself, and she was also a teacher who would cheer the team on. She paired her with a young teacher who had strong content skills and who might benefit from Ms. Foster's specialized skills.

When Ms. Foster recognized that she needed to improve her math content knowledge so that she could better serve her students, for instance, Principal Wallin stepped in with the professional development and coaching support to help her become even more successful with such a critical population of students. Ms. Foster took the initiative to improve her own practice and embraced the collaborative teaching model, which led her, her co-teacher, and the students to be more successful.

Echoing in Wallin's mind was a comment someone relayed to her that an Individualized Education Plan (IEP) was not a ticket to college in New York City, but a ticket to jail. Wallin knew more had to be done. She began using Response to Intervention[10] and started to know students better. Her goal was to differentiate those students with true learning disabilities from students who presented like they couldn't learn because of circumstances or social/emotional issues.

When Wallin came to the school, most special needs students were treated the same. For instance, Wallin found that one MR (mentally retarded) girl and another little boy who lit a garbage can on fire were in the same classroom. Wallin was surprised to find there were no meaningful academic goals for the students and that they had the same placement on their IEP when clearly the students had different needs and required different services. She found that the teacher's expectations did not include their academic success, something Wallin knew she had to change.

As a result of Wallin's efforts, the special education children decreased to about 25 percent of the population, with nearly all moved out of self-contained classrooms. Wallin and her team embraced a pattern of services that included CTT, Collaborative Team Teaching (now ICT, Integrated Collaborative Teaching). With the evaluators' recommendations and the parents' consent, Wallin was able to move these students to less restrictive environments within this new model.

Wallin saw many benefits from bringing special needs students together with the general education population. Not only did it raise expectations for the students with disabilities but it also helped students in the general populations that may be struggling with similar issues. It spurred greater academic and social success for both groups.

Once Wallin began collaborative teaching, the teachers got a much better sense of how smart some of the special needs students were. One African American boy reached Level 4, advanced proficiency. He had been a special education student from kindergarten, had gotten in fights, and was generally disruptive. With his scores, he was able to apply to a better middle school. And with their continued support, he went on without an IEP.

"It's a big statement about which children get written off," Wallin admitted. "This was the school that received students that other schools were unwilling or unable to educate."

ICT, the collaborative teaching program, supported teachers with tools and techniques that helped them differentiate teaching. The program also emphasized how to leverage different backgrounds, see the different experiences, and teach the students how to function in the classroom and in the lunchroom. Before, the students were isolated from the rest of the community, and now someone visiting wouldn't be able to tell which kids in the school have special needs.

Mary Flores Camacho, the literacy coach, has been at P.S. 42 for nearly 25 years and was a strong contributor to the changes Ms. Wallin instituted at the school. She created a "book vault," a room for professional development sessions and the public display of data. It's a converted classroom filled with resources for the teachers. Ms. Flores Camacho could easily retire, but Ms. Wallin knows she's not leaving yet. They still have more work to do.

Ms. Flores Camacho has seen many changes at P.S. 42–Claremont over the last five years, the most important of which is a laser-like focus on the children and their needs. They now embody the New York City Department of Education's motto, "Children First. Always." "Before, it was like no one knew kids," Flores Camacho explained. "No one was telling [teachers] they had to collect data. They may have known their own kids but not the school. Kids are the number one priority. That's the biggest change, along with a clean building."

Providing a building students and parents could take pride in helped change mindsets. "Just because you are poor doesn't mean you sit on a desk that has graffiti on it. You don't sit in a broken chair," Flores Camacho said, echoing her principal's mantra.

Flores Camacho and Wallin remembered a time when students had no soap in the bathrooms, and so the teachers collected special soaps and placed them in the girls' rooms. The girls were so excited, the soap would be gone the next day, but that was okay with them. Like a hotel that expects soap to be taken as a souvenir, they just kept putting more there each day.

Preserving History and Building Community

There were so many changes at P.S. 42–Claremont under Wallin's leadership—building upgrades, raised expectations, data-driven staff development, instructional rigor, inclusive classrooms, and increased parent involvement, to name a few. While no one effort drove the turnaround, Wallin and her team's transformation of the 106-year-old auditorium was clearly one of her most significant accomplishments. It not only illustrated the transformation of a school building itself, but it also conveyed a fitting message about the beauty that lies beneath, a message that served as an apt metaphor of the type of expectations and rigor that Wallin helped infuse into her classrooms and learning community.

The auditorium was the dingy room in which Wallin was introduced to parents amid flickering lights. The floors were a mess, torn up in places, and the chairs were broken and some falling apart; it was hard to see beyond the dirt and grime.

Wallin met with the plant manager to explore her options for improving the auditorium. She was told there were only upgrade funds available, approximately $80,000 to fix chairs and repair tiles. Wallin knew simply repairing and continually fixing a run-down auditorium was not the solution.

This solution seemed entirely insufficient and so Principal Wallin consulted fireman Rollins, who suggested that they spend the entire amount on the floors so they could shine in their original hardwood. Then, he would "gut the place." Without additional funds, they had to improvise. Fireman Rollins painted the walls himself over a weekend and refinished a carved wooden doorway that framed the front of the room.

"He treated the auditorium as if it were his own home," Principal Wallin reflected. "He gutted it and painted it, and it was only after he did this that people could see the potential and started to pitch in." Carpenters from the Department of Education came in to help cover exposed pipes and others helped restore the original woodwork.

During the massive cleanup, one teacher found a set of artifacts that looked like frescos in her room. Wallin called the art director for the city and learned they were bas-reliefs with genuine artistic and historical significance. The Metropolitan Museum of Art visited and catalogued them, and the city had them redone. They now hang along the walls, and a refinished row of the original seating sits along the back wall.

"We transformed this room by sheer will," Wallin proclaimed during one visitor's tour. Rather than settle for the upgrade, she fought hard to get the upgrade funds for the hardwood floors. Fireman Rollins' willingness to do most of the upgrade work himself allowed for the remaining funds to be used for carpentry and detail work. The beauty of the restoration was remarkable.

It was highly unusual for principals to get that level of autonomy, but fortunately for Wallin, her request came at a time when the central office was changing too. She had the vision and secured the funds, working carefully to ensure they were used in the most beneficial way. Then she watched as her team and community pitched in.

"All credit [for the renovation] goes to the fireman," Wallin said. "Without him, we couldn't have seen what was possible, and we certainly couldn't have made it happen."

The transformation of the building and renewed staff commitment allowed Wallin and her team to demonstrate to the parents the possibilities that awaited their children academically and otherwise. Wallin saw a change in the engagement of parents, the majority of whom understood that they were now a part of a "good school."

Wallin took pride in the fact that they earned that reputation with their student achievement scores. Her school received an "A" grade from the NYC Department of Education, based on their Progress Report, which measures school environment, student performance, student progress, and closing the achievement gap.[11] P.S. 42–Claremont was named one of New York State's "Rapidly Improving Schools for 2008–2009."[12]

Each year, Wallin was required to submit a performance plan to the central office with targets for achievement. When she began, only 20 percent of students were reading on grade level and nearly half were meeting only Level 1 proficiency, well below standard.[13] Five years later, 87 percent of her fifth grade general education students (and 77% of all students) met proficiency (Level 3 or 4) in English/Language Arts.[14]

In math, 96 percent of fifth graders demonstrated proficiency, with nearly 40 percent meeting Level 4 advanced proficiency. Similarly for the third grade, 90 percent achieved at or above Level 3 proficiency.

Special education student scores are now the reverse of what they were back when the vast majority scored at Level 1.[15] Fifty-five percent of fifth grade students with disabilities scored at Levels 3 and 4 in English/Language Arts, 100 percent growth from the prior year. In fifth grade math, the movement forward for students is pronounced as well, with 87 percent at or exceeding proficiency, up from 56 percent in 2007–2008. Seventy-seven percent of third graders met proficiency in math, also up from 56 percent in 2007–2008. While grade 4 lagged behind the other grades, most areas continued to demonstrate progress.[16]

"It's significant improvement," Wallin said. She acknowledged that they mastered the tests but can't be sure all students are critical thinkers, readers, and writers. "We still have a ways to go."

Since many of her mean scores fall at the lower end of the range for proficiency, Wallin knows she and her team need to work harder to show that her students can perform beyond minimum standards. New state cutoffs for proficiency may affect how her school demonstrates progress in 2009–2010, but Wallin's approach remains the same: high expectations for every student and a relentless focus on quality instruction.

Her teachers rely more on assessments (pre, post, and re-teach) to analyze and improve instructions so that children get what they need to succeed. She continues to see a need to hone the system to include paying attention to the "soft data" around them and refining assessment tools that align with standards so that they can best target instruction.

If anything, Principal Wallin now feels like they over-assess, and some teachers worry about how to re-teach or regroup students who are continuing to struggle. But Wallin sees these concerns as exciting. "At least we're having the right kind of conversations," she says.

A Community of Scholars

"Good afternoon, scholars!" Ms. Wallin announces to an excited group of students awaiting dismissal for their spring break. "I want my friend to see what good learners you are. How scholarly you all are." She introduces her visitor, who is greeted with a chorus of friendly voices of students in uniform.

A third grade class fills their backpacks with books to read over break. Some students have one or two, but most have five or six books to read during their vacation. Principal Wallin encourages them to pack a few more.

A first grade teacher squeezes in one last lesson on money. "Cost," she says, asking them to visualize the word. "Cost," she repeats, then offers a sentence to illuminate the meaning of the word, "This pencil costs a dollar."

A few kids scramble by Principal Wallin as she walks the halls bidding farewell to her students for the break. "Excuse me," she bellows to them. "Excuse me. I *know* you are not running." The students slow to a walk, taking her admonishment.

Wallin is proud of the accomplishments at P.S. 42–Claremont. She likes to say they are "out of the weeds, but barely." She sees a long road ahead to ensuring her students can go to college and be successful if all the other barriers in their lives stay the same.

Wallin places a high value on bringing in talented teachers. Her partnership with Teach for America stands out for all the new ideas their teachers have brought. They also set a college-bound tone in the building, naming tables for schools like Harvard, Brown, and Stanford and making test taking like a college bowl game.

Her only regret about her TFA partnership is that their teachers leave the school after two or three years. Still, she takes pride in preparing these leaders, for she knows they may one day be principals or other leaders that will hopefully transform others schools and neighborhoods.

Wallin focuses now on recruiting and developing teachers so that she not only has her "starting players" but also her "back bench." She seeks teachers that have high expectations and understand the importance of developing productive community members, those that will be able to "fully participate in society." This is especially important in a school with a large special needs population.

Wallin looks for reflective teachers, who use data, who are willing to take risks, and who learn and are up on the latest. Math content knowledge and understanding how to ensure a year's growth out of each child are two skill areas of particular interest. She continues to build a staff that knows developmentally where a child is, can break instruction down so the child moves forward, and can integrate professional development for teachers around getting there. Wallin hopes she can help her staff reach those high levels.

Yet, Principal Wallin also considers her eventual succession. She trusts that the systems and structures they have put in place will afford any new leader the opportunity to move the school to the next level and avoid sliding back into dysfunction. She has taken time to identify and develop a few internal candidates.

With a staff capable of following through on the systems they now have in place to plan instruction, use data, and collaborate in and out of the classroom, Wallin thinks they have what's needed to ensure "consistency and coherency in the curriculum and a safe and orderly environment."

The adult community is squarely focused on the students, and the community they had for each other is secondary. "There's not one person on this staff that I would ask to go above and beyond and they say no. If it is good for the kids they'll do it. . . . And the give back is that you try to create a culture of mutual respect," Wallin said, noting she tries to provide flexibility for doctor's appointments, family needs, and school wherever possible as a demonstration of that respect.

Still, Wallin admits that while she knows the changes were essential, she struggles with the sense of loss those changes brought to the school community. She explains:

> You always feel like you want to make people feel good about who they are and what they have to offer. There are so many people on this team who were part of bringing us to where we are. They lost a great deal under my leadership— they lost maybe their status as a leader, they lost how much P.S. 42 was a place that they socialized and had very rich and meaningful adult relationships. . . . It was an important community of support for many adults, but one that seemed to dictate the day rather than it's 8:30 and you are now at work, and you need to be in the classroom and you need to have your lesson plan. And if you are not able to work today it's better that you didn't come to work . . . than you come to work to get what you need from all these other adults. . . . All these other adults need to be with their children.

Wallin stays focused on her mission that at the end of the day, the role of the school is to educate the students. Even after five years of constant change, Wallin sees much room for improvement, especially in the area of writing. Her students may not have a vibrant vocabulary or use academic English at home, and so when writing or editing a passage, they struggle with knowing what's wrong in the passage.

Wallin has begun a new push herself and with staff to correct spoken language, with its broken phrases and fragments, to reinforce what students need. "How many of us are not careful or correct with our language? We just need to try a little harder, make a conscious effort to raise the standard for how we communicate," she says.

Wallin knows that after five years, including the building transformation and dramatic improvements in student achievement, her turnaround is nearing completion. The problems she tackles now are important but, for her, are certainly not as energizing as those days when she was walking around with a spatula in her back pocket doing the hard work of turnaround.

In a way, she acknowledges that the issues have become thorny. It's not just about removing clutter from classrooms or energizing teams; with other things in order, she has to tackle parts of the job that are less enjoyable and

may take longer, like the removal of a tenured teacher. It's still important, crucial work, and work for which the NYC Leadership Academy prepared her well, but not what Wallin finds most rewarding.
Wallin thrives on the speed and challenge of leading the turnaround.

> The number one priority was—all hands on deck. You row. Bail the water. On the count of three, pull it up. . . . It's very much [work where] you have to grab it, embrace it, [and] be comfortable with the saying you ask forgiveness not permission. You do what's right and get it done. And as you do it, it's replicable to someone else. You're breaking, fixing, and building the bicycle while you're in the race.

NOTES

1. U.S. Census Bureau, Summary File 1 [SF 1] and Summary File 3 [SF 3]. *Fact Sheet: Zip Code Tabulation Area 10457.* Accessed 6-10-10. (U.S. population figures of those three groups were 12.5 percent, 12.3 percent, and 75 percent, respectively).

2. U.S. Census Bureau, Census 2000 Summary File 1 [SF 1], *Matrix PCT11. QT-P9. Hispanic or Latino by Type: 2000.* Accessed 6-10-10.

3. http://schools.nyc.gov/SchoolPortals/09/X042/AboutUs/Statistics/register.htm. Accessed 6-2-10.

4. U.S. Census Bureau, *Zip Code Tabulation Data, 10456, Fact Sheet. Census 2000 Demographic Profile Highlights.* http://factfinder.census.gov/servlet. Accessed 6-3-10.

5. The Local Instructional Superintendent oversaw a network of 10–12 primary and secondary schools.

6. Time allotted to teachers during the school day for lesson preparation.

7. See http://www.nsrfharmony.org/protocol/learning_texts.html for more information.

8. Schools are assigned Performance Indices (PIs) ranging from 0 to 200, based on the performance of continuously enrolled tested students at the elementary and middle levels and cohort members at the secondary level on state tests. Student scores on the tests are converted to four achievement levels, from Level 1 (indicating no proficiency) to Level 4 (indicating advanced proficiency). Schools are given partial credit for students scoring at Level 2 and full credit for students scoring at Level 3 or Level 4. They receive no credit for students scoring at Level 1. Schools improve their PI by decreasing the percentage of students scoring at Level 1 and increasing the percentages scoring at Levels 3 and 4. http://www.emsc.nysed.gov/repcrd2005/information/elementary/guide.shtml. Accessed 6-7-10.

9. P.S. 42–Claremont Community School. Standardized test scores and reports for P.S. 42–Claremont 2000–2009.

10. The National Center on Response to Intervention (RTI) uses this definition: Response to intervention integrates assessment and intervention within a multi-

level prevention system to maximize student achievement and to reduce behavioral problems. With RTI, schools use data to identify students at risk for poor learning outcomes, monitor student progress, provide evidence-based interventions and adjust the intensity and nature of those interventions depending on a student's responsiveness, and identify students with learning disabilities or other disabilities. http://www.rti4success.org/index.php?option=com_frontpage&Itemid=1. Accessed 11-7-10.

11. http://schools.nyc.gov/OA/SchoolReports/2008-09/Progress_Report_2009_EMS_X042.pdf. Accessed 8-17-10. P.S. 42–Claremont received an overall score of 85.8 in 2008–2009, placing it in the 65th percentile of all city elementary schools. Schools with overall scores between 68 and 100 receive a letter grade of A. According to this site, Progress Reports measures student year-to-year progress, compares the school to peer schools, and rewards success in moving all children forward, especially children with highest needs.

12. http://www.emsc.nysed.gov/irts/accountability/highPerform/2009/RI_2008-09.pdf. Accessed 8-17-10.

13. P.S. 42–Claremont Community School. (2010, March 23). *Standardized test scores and reports for P.S. 42–Claremont 2000–2009.*

14. The New York State School Report Card: Accountability and Overview Report 2008–2009. P.S. 42 Claremont. https://www.nystart.gov/publicweb-rc/2009/1e/AOR-2009-320900010042.pdf. Accessed 8-17-10.

15. P.S. 42–Claremont Community School. *Standardized test scores and reports for P.S. 42–Claremont 2000–2009.*

16. The New York State School Report Card: Accountability and Overview Report 2008–2009. P.S. 42 Claremont. https://www.nystart.gov/publicweb-rc/2009/1e/AOR-2009-320900010042.pdf. Accessed 8-17-10.

Chapter 9

Walking in a Turnaround Leader's Shoes

Believing Is Achieving

Fred M. Lynn Middle School
Woodbridge, VA
J. Harrison Coleman, Principal

Students called it "The Lynn." Located on "the other side" of Prince William County, Fred M. Lynn Middle School was among the lowest-performing schools in the district just a few years ago. Predominantly Hispanic (56 percent) and African American (22 percent), it was a stark contrast to the schools on the other side of the county, west of Interstate 95, which is a well-known divider between the less affluent, more diverse east from the wealthier schools west of the highway.

Lynn Middle School serves about 850 students and is located in Woodbridge, a diverse community along Route 1, just 25 miles south of Washington, D.C. U.S. Census data (2000)[1] show a difference of more than $40,000 in median family income between the area in which Lynn is located (at $53,000) and Manassas, the community rival Benton Middle School serves (at $95,000).

According to these census data, more than 40 percent of families live in rental units around Lynn, versus just 5 percent of their cross-county peers, and the poverty rate is double that of Manassas. Whereas 40 percent of Benton-area residents hold at least a bachelor's degree, that percentage drops to 18 in the Lynn neighborhoods. And those figures don't account for the potential numbers of illegal immigrants in the area.[2]

The two parts of Prince William County couldn't be more different, with strip malls and a trailer park abutting the Lynn campus. In Manassas, upscale shops and restaurants serve the largely white population (88 percent). Lynn occupies a former high school, a low-lying brick structure built in 1964, whereas Benton Middle School came to occupy its facility in 2000.[3]

PREPARED FOR THE CHALLENGE

When J. Harrison Coleman became the principal of Fred M. Lynn Middle School in 2007, she understood immediately what "The Lynn" meant. Students, staff, and even community members viewed it as a school in "the hood," one less valued than its peers. As a Virginia School Turnaround Specialist, however, she had seen a version of this story before. This was her fifth turnaround assignment as a principal, and while she expected to find new challenges, she was confident that her skills as a turnaround leader would be well utilized in her new community.

When Harrison Coleman joined the first cohort of Governor Warner's Virginia School Turnaround Specialist Program, she had already turned around a school in Charleston, South Carolina and another in Portsmouth, Virginia. In 1999, Harrison Coleman arrived at Mt. Zion Elementary School, and the school was graded a D–. Two years later, she moved the school up to a B+, achieving Palmetto Silver, a state distinction for schools achieving significant results.[4]

Harrison Coleman returned to Virginia in 2001 to be with her ailing parents and accepted another turnaround assignment, this time at Emily Spong Elementary School in Portsmouth. The school was among the lowest-performing schools in the division, and Harrison Coleman's first challenge was to wrest the school away from parents and "return it to a place of learning."

While working on instruction, she also brought in uniforms and implemented single-gender classrooms to bring order and focus to the students. She even connected with the naval presence in the area and had officers come in to inspect the students in uniform. The school improved steadily until it made AYP (adequate yearly progress) and received full accreditation.

Harrison Coleman felt honored to be chosen for the Governor's program at the University of Virginia in 2004. She especially resonated with his notion of developing turnaround specialists that could be deployed to struggling schools. She had done this twice already and was soon to get her third assignment at Stephen H. Clarke Academy.

In those days, however, this urban elementary school was known as "the forbidden place," according to Harrison Coleman. Her superintendent was impressed by her ability to work outside the box and get results at Spong, and she remembered him saying as she took the challenge, "What you did at Spong, you can do at Clarke."

Harrison Coleman led Clarke's turnaround while she was in the Governor's program, restoring order, cleanliness, and confidence to the staff and students inside.[5]

> I went into Clarke and Clarke was the first time I had any glimpse of what autonomy could be. I could call the director of human resources . . . and she'd say, "Tell them to meet me in my office before the office closes today." And in two or three days, they'd be gone [from the school]. I was building this culture with a group of people who wanted to work, because you have to want to work. That's what it's all about.

Part of the culture change at Clarke came when Harrison Coleman taught the staff, students, and parents to value the school's name. She began calling it "Stephen H. Clarke" and educated people regarding its namesake.

Harrison Coleman turned the school into "The Gifted Place," a message that she placed on its marquee. It signified her belief that, as a former gifted teacher, all students are gifted. "[The school] was in the dirt and it moved. They believed it because I believed it, and I encouraged my teachers to believe it because if you didn't believe it you had to go," she recalled.

PREPARING THE ENVIRONMENT

When Harrison Coleman arrived at Fred M. Lynn Middle School, the outside of the school looked "cluttered" and "unkept." It wasn't in the kind of disrepair that she had dealt with before, but it was definitely in need of a facelift.

Her predecessor had been there for six or seven years before she came, and she had heard only positive descriptions of him. "I heard things like, 'he's a really nice man' or 'we really like him.'" Harrison Coleman recalled.

Principal Harrison Coleman started her journey there with a Friday meeting that her associate superintendent invited her to attend. When Harrison Coleman walked in, the tension was palpable and the questions started flying. "What does a turnaround specialist do? Why are you here? What changes will you bring?" she recalled. Harrison Coleman tried to answer as many questions as she could, but she also knew they would soon learn how different she was from the leader they had liked so much.

Andy Grupp, a science teacher at the school, remembered Harrison Coleman's arrival.

> Before [Ms. Harrison Coleman] arrived, everything was kind of going with the flow. Whatever was going just kept on going from the year before. [There] wasn't a lot of updating and reevaluating your plans and what you were doing.

What happened just kept going and going for years and years. The energy was level, with everyone just going as they had done before. There was a "We're all in this together" kind of attitude. It was positive but there was a sense that if [you] can't get this kid to pass this kid is never going to pass. It was like, well, he's one of those. We have a lot of those . . . those that are going to sink.

Grupp remembered his former principal reassuring him, "Well, Mr. Grupp, you can only do your best."

Rebecca Abbott, a newly minted math teacher, came to the school two years before Principal Harrison Coleman and remembered her first year at Lynn. "After my first month, they congratulated me for making it a month because they all thought I would be gone."

Thomas Dwight, a science teacher from England, arrived the year after Principal Harrison Coleman. Before he met anyone at the school, he was in a supermarket and his accent led to a conversation about why he was in Virginia. "I said, 'I was here to teach,' and she said, 'That's fantastic.' And then she asked about my school assignment and I said, 'Fred M. Lynn.' She then put her hand on my shoulder and said, 'Oh dear, love. You're in for trouble.'"

Harrison Coleman saw the challenges immediately. "When I walked into the school, it was in the red financially and test scores were almost nonexistent. They were pitiful," Harrison Coleman recalled. She told them, as she always did in her school, that "things were going to change." She began telling staff what they could not purchase, what they could not afford to fund, what they weren't going to do, like putting through a collection of $80,000 in purchase orders with $8,000 dedicated to the cheerleading squad.

"Thus started the war. I told someone, 'I'm not buying your cheerleading stuff.' I told someone, 'I'm not signing for a transfer.' It was the beginning of the end for them," she explained.

Harrison Coleman was aware that her decisive actions would and did alienate many on her staff. One staff member responded to her early actions by placing a five-page letter on her desk, critiquing everyone in the school, except herself. It detailed what they did and didn't do, what they were accused of doing. For Harrison Coleman, this took away "the newness of it," her opportunity to examine and assess the situation for herself. Others acted out in faculty meetings, speaking out or cutting her off when she was trying to do staff development. Still others wrote the superintendent seeking her removal.

Harrison Coleman was most disappointed in what was happening—or not happening—inside the classrooms. Teachers were not used to turning in lesson plans or assessing students. "Even though I was showing the teachers the data, that just one in 10 [students] were performing at the basic level, they believed they were teaching well," Harrison Coleman said.

Of 110 on the faculty and staff, 42 people put in for transfers during Harrison Coleman's first year at Fred M. Lynn. This was nearly 40 percent of the school's employees and didn't include the ones that had left before she got there. "A lot of people didn't make it that first year," English teacher Meghan Morse explained. "There was a lot of bucking up against changing. 'We've always done it this way and now I'm being told I have to do it this way.'"

Morse admitted to having issues with some of her new principal's initiatives at first.

> I wasn't a first year teacher. But I quickly learned to give some of the things she said a chance and if it didn't work, go to her about why it wasn't working. . . . If she [was] hard on you, it [was] because there [was] something you [weren't] doing. Her expectations [were] high, very high, especially for the teachers *she* hired.

Part of Harrison Coleman's strategy was to offer the kind of structures and supports for teachers and students that set high standards that were consistently applied. She required that all teachers turn in lesson plans, which she read, and she shared strategies for ensuring they were teaching what they intended to teach. One teacher handed in the same lesson plan three weeks in a row, which Harrison Coleman eventually caught and handled.

Principal Harrison Coleman required them to "plan with the end in mind." She asked them to design their own assessments and then write the lesson plan. "They started doing that and it was, 'I don't like her, I don't care for her. She's working us to death.' . . . But I never stopped telling them, 'You're doing a great job. I can see kids moving.'"

DEVELOPING THE EXECUTIVE

Principal Harrison Coleman devoted the majority of her faculty meetings to staff development. Her teachers needed to understand how data could "reform and transform" instruction, and how to design benchmark assessments that could show what students were and were not learning. At first, she implemented her own benchmark tests to show them that her students were not learning. "They were failing one subject area after the other," Harrison Coleman recalled.

> They didn't like me, and they didn't like me *telling* them. They didn't like me walking in and telling them what they needed to do. And while they didn't like

me, they had to respect my *ability* to know what I was doing and to know what they needed to be doing. They acquired a mindset of competition. One grade level against the other. One classroom against the other. One teacher against the other. One team against the other.

While Harrison Coleman found faculty retreats to be important development opportunities, as a rule, she kept a healthy distance between herself and her team in order to get the hard work of turnaround done. "I'm not their friend, I am the person in charge of their school. I don't drink with them. They won't have a good time if I'm there," she explained.

During the turnaround process, Harrison Coleman used a combination of observation, real-time feedback and staff development to move her teachers to consistently deliver high-quality instruction with exceedingly high expectations. Harrison Coleman described her approach.

> I did a lot of assessing the quality of what happens in the classroom. When I look at your lesson plan, when I hear your voice, when I look at your rapport with your students, the knowledge of your content. [Are you] building [an] environment . . . that is conducive to learning, and is it safe?

To further develop staff and identify potential leaders, Harrison Coleman employed a strategy that worked well in her turnaround at Clarke, a program she called "Walking in J's Shoes." Anyone could apply to do it, and Harrison Coleman would cover their classes while they fulfilled her administrative duties.

Harrison Coleman found that this initiative allowed her to get things done in ways that, in some instances, were better than she could do herself. She would give the person a problem and "they didn't stop until they got it done." The program had the important side benefit of showing them the challenges the principal might be tackling while they focused on instruction.

These opportunities were especially important since Harrison Coleman never let up on her efforts to ensure her faculty believed and proved that students could achieve. "I'm always on you. I never stop. I bring you in as a group. I help you plan," she said. Harrison Coleman described early feedback on staff surveys as "awful." Still, she brushed off criticism, especially when she was certain it was "the right thing to do."

Harrison Coleman took an especially hard hit on her surveys when she decided to make test scores public at a faculty meeting. She put the pie chart of their pass rates in black and gold, the school colors, on the table inside the library then talked about the range of scores and engaged them in conversation about what they needed to do to improve. She replayed those meetings.

I'd say, "We've got a problem here. Johnny. Mary, can you help Johnny with this problem because we've got to work on this?" And then Johnny states, "Mary can't help me with that problem. I don't need help. It's the kids." Johnny is asked to reflect and remove the obstacle. "Can you share what are you doing in your class, Mary, to get the results you have?" And you know what happens? Johnny starts getting better. And if Johnny doesn't get any better, Johnny's kids are going to be with Mary because I don't have time to let you fail them.

There was constant change for that major period of growth, but Harrison Coleman viewed this as part of what turnarounds were all about.

Staying Fresh to Stay the Course

Through continued reading, Harrison Coleman has kept herself fresh and prepared herself to "stay the course" through the difficult work of turnaround. She conducted book studies with her faculty as well. She has had to pay particular attention to what is going on at the state level, given the constant changes, new policies, and opportunities for invention, support, and funding. She has found over time that this technical knowledge is critical and uses her networks from 11 years of turnaround work to ask questions and clarify policies.

She also tried to tweak what has worked for her in other turnaround situations and implement new ideas for new challenges. "I'm always interested in learning what are the programs and processes you can do to move struggling children," she said.

From her experience in the Virginia School Turnaround Specialist Program, Harrison Coleman developed as an executive and refined her leadership skills.

> I see myself as a CEO. I see myself as in charge of this company, and I see that my kids are going to go out and be productive academically as well as socially. I have learned . . . how to delegate. I have learned how to put my vision out there and give the book, the magazine, the article, the training and have [the teachers] go with it.
>
> I have learned to organize my team so there is a "go to" person between the classroom teacher and me. But you can always come to me, too. I may have to go to someone else before I can give you an answer because it's broken in a way that I need more information to answer.
>
> As hard-core as I am, I have learned how to humble myself. I have learned to say, "I haven't always done it quite right. I hope you can forgive me. I didn't quite understand. I hope you can understand me."

For Harrison Coleman, though, the bottom line is that she is responsible for the school. "I have to be in charge of my ship. Some people might not like the fact that you can't go around me. You can go over me, but it's going to come right back to me," she explained.

Harrison Coleman's bold leadership style could be off-putting to some, and she didn't always mind politics, especially when student needs were at stake. She admitted that being a turnaround specialist was not an easy job; sometimes she's felt like "the most hated person around."

During one difficult period with her staff, she remembered her superintendent saying, "'They do more for you when they like you.'" Harrison Coleman responded, "But sometimes, you don't have time for them to like you. You've got a job to do."

FOCUSING ON EXECUTION

Harrison Coleman knew that she needed to send a strong message to the community as a whole that Fred M. Lynn Middle School mattered. When she came, she couldn't get the Parent-Teacher Association (PTA) off the ground, so she implemented what she knew worked: HAS (Home-and-School Connection) meetings.

The impetus behind the meetings was that Harrison Coleman thought parents wanted to be engaged but may not have the time or resources. HAS meetings became a proxy for the PTA. Harrison Coleman knew she could get them to come in to see their children's work, and they'd end up spending $20 on hot dogs, drinks, and chips, which would help and support the school, too.

At the beginning of the school year, they'd invite the entire community to an open house, with printed invitations. Seventh-grade history teacher Mark Marchinetti described it as "an absolute blowout," then qualified its overall purpose. "At the same time, we're giving parents information on the SOLs right off the bat, what our students will be learning and after-school opportunities. We have our Hispanic translators and liaisons there." Over 2,000 people attended, including parents and business community members. Monthly HAS meetings have drawn about 500 people each time, and Harrison Coleman has begun to secure parking at a nearby church to accommodate the crowds.

"*Every* child does something so *every* parent has to come," Harrison Coleman explained. One month, for instance, they had Young Authors' Night, where each student wrote a book and then brought as many family members, as possible to sign the book that night. Another month was History Day, where every child completed a history project that was on display that night.

Teachers have embraced and extended this "open door policy" to enhance the home-school connection. They've become especially sensitive to some of the Hispanic parents, who may have been afraid to come to the school for a variety of reasons, including language barriers or immigration status. They all have smartphones to contact parents anytime and have used bilingual staff members to help translate phone calls.

Changing the culture from "The Lynn" to one that students and families could take pride in required not only a facelift outside but a shift from the low expectations that ruled the day inside the school. In effect, the school needed an image boost as well. Harrison Coleman knew from past experience that uniforms would go a long way toward showing the community, and the students, that Fred M. Lynn Middle School was a serious place for learning.

"I remember one person telling me years back that kids don't get in trouble on picture day," Harrison Coleman said. Since then, Harrison Coleman has implemented uniforms in every school in which she had been a turnaround specialist except one. "It's not competitive. It takes away the 'You have and I don't,' and it helps us a lot in identifying our kids. . . . It sends the message that we're different. We look different. We act different. We're an oasis." And it cuts down on gang members communicating through colors.

Harrison Coleman's approach had always been to try and work through the proper channels, but when she believed in something and didn't get the support she needed, she didn't hesitate to make her case to the next level above. She had to navigate through some sticky politics to get the uniform policy implemented, but the results were worth the effort. Keith King, a former high school teacher and football coach who is now the athletic coordinator at Fred M. Lynn, explained. He had been a coach at a nearby high school and for years struggled to keep the students from Lynn eligible to play after one year. Mr. King explained.

> It was like pulling teeth. But . . . I've noticed a huge change. The dress policy provides a structure that students need. As much as some [students] complain, I think every kid wants structure in their life. From their home, the school, they want structure. They may act like they don't . . . but they want someone to tell them what's right and what's wrong. Ms. Harrison Coleman does a good job of doing that.

The teachers noticed the uniforms not only improved the image in the community and within the building, but also have helped discipline.

As teachers started to understand Harrison Coleman and her vision, they began to take more ownership of their instruction and student success. While her first year led to a "mass exodus," in her second year only twenty-four put in for transfer. Harrison Coleman didn't feel she could give the teachers voice during that first year of negativity, or "they'd just tear the whole place up and it would be a mess," she explained.

As a result, she conducted meetings at 6:45 a.m. each week in that first year. By the second year, she only needed them once every two weeks. Her third year, it was every payday. The early hour is daunting, especially for those with a long commute, but Harrison Coleman chose a time when she knew the teachers wouldn't have to be excused for a doctor's appointment.

Harrison Coleman always had the desire to move to a faculty-led meeting, but waited to make sure they were on the same page. As Harrison Coleman began to see the culture change, she started to send faculty to places to visit and watched them grow. In one instance, they applied to be among the first schools to pilot the implementation of the district's new evaluation tool, the PPP (Professional Performance Process).

In addition, Harrison Coleman observed them, not just in the classroom, and then gave them the opportunity to present. She had roles for the meetings and protocols for making them successful. Again, Harrison Coleman drew on what worked for her in other schools, and she saw it work at Fred M. Lynn, too.

Faculty began to share strategies, and a professional learning community started to develop. They put in a system of assessment that ensured they could understand what their students were grasping well and what they may need to re-teach. Still, literacy was a significant challenge. They had gone to full inclusion for special needs students, with a co-teaching model of special education/English for Speaker of Other Languages (ESOL) and general education teachers, which helped.

But with a 45 percent ESOL population, they have had to work differently than peer schools. Michelle Knowlton, reading teacher, explained.

> It's extremely difficult. You can't expect all students to come into sixth grade and expect them to read on grade level, because they don't. . . . The bottom line is that everyone in this school is a reading teacher.

Vice Principal Mary Jane Boynton noted that they have worked heavily on strategies that distinguish which students may be just "getting by" from those that comprehend well. Boynton noted the plan for ESOL students in particular, given their large representation.

> We have our stronger content area teachers teaching our ESOL students, where their expectation is that [the students] will be successful. They have been allowed to fail for so long that [these students] expect to fail. So providing them with teachers that expect the best from all of them, no matter who they are, has made a huge difference.

The presence of a highly qualified, motivated teacher has been essential, according to Boynton. "They're unmotivated and lethargic and they don't see what [failing] is going to do to them later on. We've had some amazing gains just moving teachers." She noted one student whose scores jumped 40 points in one nine-week period just because they changed his teacher.

Motivating Faculty and Moving Student Achievement

By the third year of her tenure, Harrison Coleman's turnaround strategies were in full motion. She had only a small handful of transfers, and her leadership team fully embraced the work of turnaround. In many ways it was a new school; between retirements, resignations, transfers, and other departures, only 13 members of the faculty were at Fred M. Lynn when she arrived.

Coupling high-quality instruction with strong assessments made a tremendous difference at Fred M. Lynn. Interim benchmarks were essential, and teachers disaggregated the data to pull out the exact strands, by child, to find out strengths and weak areas. Targeting instruction to individual needs became standard practice.

To further gauge student learning, Harrison Coleman's teachers developed and implemented "the WRAP." Every week teachers designed five questions, four multiple-choice and one with higher-developed thinking, to get a quick read of how the students were doing. If students failed the WRAP, they had to take it again. It not only allowed the teachers to see where the students were, but the students also could take responsibility for their results.

Harrison Coleman and her leadership team liked the fact that teachers had to own when their students didn't learn. "If I see the WRAP and they missed two questions," Mr. Marchinetti said, "I ask myself, what did *I* do wrong."

To ensure their Standards of Learning (SOL) tests were taken seriously, they started to administer them in "arena-style" seating for all students, except those with accommodations. The content area teacher administered the tests, since they had direct ownership of the results.

A newcomer to Fred M. Lynn, King has appreciated being in a school where the principal "surrounded herself with teachers . . . that truly care about the kids and not about themselves." Putting student needs first has been an important change in mindset. "You can know everything, but if you can't teach about what you know, then you're not very smart," King said.

King explained that the community surrounding Fred M. Lynn needed their support.

> This isn't like teaching at Benton. Those kids go home to a . . . family where their parents sit down with them at the table and do their homework with them.

These kids don't get that. We *are* that support. That's why I think [Principal Harrison Coleman] is so hard on her teachers, to make sure that you have given them every ounce of support you can give because when they leave here, that may be it until they're back the next day.

To provide that individual support, Harrison Coleman has kept small cards with each student's data on them. Those that fail must meet with the principal and agree on goals that are then noted on the card. The teachers and Harrison Coleman have tried to provide support to every student, making teaching and learning a personal process, building relationships with the students and their families while offering every expectation of success and support—whether tutoring, Saturday school, or something else—to ensure they achieve.

Harrison Coleman has taken particular pride in the plan they completed for mathematics. She was required to submit a state plan because they had been in year 3 of School Improvement. She fought to use a program she knew well, and when the district told her she couldn't buy it, she used its unique teaching method instead. "Teach this, make sure they understand it, do a WRAP for it. Teach this, pick up part of that, and make sure they understand it." The students came through.

SOL performance in sixth grade mathematics jumped over 30 percentage points from 2006–2007 to 2008–2009. Results were even more dramatic for students with disabilities, who were passing at a rate of only 23 percent and reached nearly 80 percent in 2008–2009. Achievement of Limited English Proficient (LEP) students, a significant population at Fred M. Lynn, more than doubled, from 29 to 72 percent.[6]

Similarly, reading achievement rose in all grades in those two years. Pass rates that hovered in the mid-60s and low 70s reached 84, 87, and 90 percent for all students in grades 6, 7, and 8, respectively. The school's lowest pass rate in reading was 77 percent for sixth grade LEP students; two years before, none of the reading pass rates for targeted subgroups had reached even 75 percent.[7]

Discipline was another area that they had to tackle head on. Harrison Coleman decided to offer leadership roles—department chairs and deans for each grade level. While she couldn't offer any monetary incentives, she could send them to conferences wherever possible and give them latitude to address instructional and building-level challenges.

Harrison Coleman didn't necessarily choose her most experienced teachers for the jobs, but she did choose trusted leaders within the building. For sixth grade dean she chose Kimberly Cort, a nine-year teaching veteran who transferred into Fred M. Lynn just before Harrison Coleman's arrival; she had high school experience and taught civics and economics at Fred M. Lynn. Mr. Grupp, a newer teacher but one that had been at the school long enough to see the old and new cultures, became seventh grade dean.

For eighth grade, Harrison Coleman selected Mr. Marchinetti, a veteran of Operation Iraqi Freedom and a teacher that chose to come to Fred M. Lynn because it was in transition. Marchinetti said, "[I] liked the idea that we were going to change things around, move students in the right direction." He turned down another position to hold out for this challenge.

Marchinetti explained that the deans were taking what he called a "boots on the ground" approach—to make sure students were where they need to be. They've taken a proactive approach, building relationships by talking through issues to stem future conflict and moving students into classrooms because, as Marchinetti put it, "if they're not in the classroom, they're not learning."

Principal Harrison Coleman reported that in a year's time, from April 14th of 2009 to April 14th of 2010, discipline referrals went from 723 to 88. "The deans are doing their jobs," she relayed proudly.

Inside the classrooms, department chairs have monitored instruction and honed the lesson planning process. To Harrison Coleman, the lesson plan has been her most important instructional tool. Now she can rely on her team to ensure that plans are turned in weekly and reviewed. They also have developed many tools themselves. When in doubt, Harrison Coleman has gone back to what has worked for her in other, similar settings.

Harrison Coleman has used a turnaround plan in other schools. At Fred M. Lynn, she worked with the state on a specific plan for math in her first year, given that they were in year three of School Improvement in that subject. The state Department of Education liked her format so much that they asked if they could use if with other schools. This year Harrison Coleman started using the balanced scorecard, a tool the district has implemented also.

Wherever possible, Harrison Coleman and her team have embraced technology to improve communication, hasten analysis, and reach and motivate more students. They have implemented School Fusion on their website, which has allowed teachers to post homework, lessons, and grades; parents can come into the school and pull it up on computers with a password if they don't have access at home.

Harrison Coleman worked hard to bring Smartboards to the classrooms, often having to raise her own funds where other schools were already equipped. Next year, in order to get a Smartboard, she will have teachers sign a "promissory note" that commits them to creating a "smart notebook" for posting lesson plans.

Making Students Shine

These days, teachers at Fred M. Lynn Middle School take pride in the fact that they are a school in which students are now more consistently achieving. They see their students take pride in their work and the parents and community trusting that the teachers will work their hardest on behalf of the students. VP Boynton recognizes what Harrison Coleman also knows, that the teachers are the heart of the school.

> Because Ms. Harrison Coleman's expectations are so high, the teachers go above and beyond the call of duty. That's part of how a lot of the children are being assisted. . . . We have teachers who work with kids before school. We have teachers who work every day with kids after school. We have teachers that come in for Saturday School. We have teachers that are making sure that everything that child needs to know is being taught within that 90 minutes because the expectation is that they may not have that opportunity to do it when they get home. Our teachers are the real spearhead as far as meeting the needs of the populations. . . . Many of them are the mother and the father for our kids, as far as academics.

Under Harrison Coleman's leadership, teachers have ensured that Fred M. Lynn students can access higher-level math courses. If the teachers say a child is ready for geometry or Algebra I, then parents will agree. The results speak for themselves.

"This year, Fred M. Lynn Middle School has 19 students taking geometry," Harrison Coleman explained. "We're the only school [in the county] that has 56 students going to high school with Algebra credits." Principal Harrison Coleman and her team beamed with the news that 100 percent had passed the geometry SOL and 14 made "pass advance" in a course they only began offering two years ago. In addition, 49 seventh graders (100 percent) passed Algebra I.[8]

Pushing their students to achieve is critical, according to Harrison Coleman. "I believe that children don't always get what they need because there is no one back there pushing them." Now, the geometry students will take four credits to high school and Algebra I students will take three.

Teachers are at the center of the turnaround at Fred M. Lynn, and Harrison Coleman has worked hard to assemble and develop a faculty she knows puts students first. She has "volunteered" teachers for leadership roles that allow them to further their own development while supporting colleagues and strengthening the overall teaching corps.

History chair Cory Cox, who came to Fred M. Lynn the same year as Harrison Coleman, has enjoyed working with the new teachers that have come to the school to share his experiences. Cox was an early supporter of the changes Harrison Coleman was trying to implement and now can see the results.

The biggest change I've seen in the past three years is that people are actually getting on the same page, going in the same direction. Whereas, my first year here you had a lot of opposition with what we wanted to do, people who were negative and wanted to stay with the old way. . . . It's really filtered out into a faculty that's going in the same direction.

District Support

Harrison Coleman acknowledges that her passion and commitment can sometimes get her into hot water with supervisors. Superintendent Stephen Walts has smoothed the way for her to bring her turnaround skills to Fred M. Lynn and has tapped her as a resource for other schools when needed. When Harrison Coleman has clashed with more direct supervisors or other administrators, she has benefited by Walts' support.

Harrison Coleman's first year at Fred M. Lynn brought her a stipend from the Virginia program Governor Mark Warner had started. Since that program ended, Harrison Coleman and her team do the work because of what she refers to as their "commitment to the students, the commitment to change, the commitment to show that these kids really can make it."

Even though she may not have the autonomy herself, Harrison Coleman has nurtured and developed as many people as she could to fight for the students of Fred M. Lynn. "They will have the quality of knowing what it takes to move the school." Harrison Coleman also knows that developing a successor is a critical part of her job.

"The worth of a good principal is that we have people that move in behind us to keep the school moving," said Harrison Coleman. She is confident that vice principal Boynton is a strong candidate, and she has focused her efforts on strengthening the entire administrative team as well. Her summer retreat will focus on Edward Murrow's (2009) *This I Believe*[9]. Staff, including teachers, the custodial staff, the cafeteria workers, and others, will write their own *This We Believe*.

Every year, Harrison Coleman invites the entire staff to the faculty/staff retreat. Harrison Coleman feels it is critical to nurture an inclusive school community, from the teachers to custodians to bus drivers and teaching assistants; everyone must support student achievement. Last year, one person didn't arrive until Sunday. "She didn't know what to wear," Harrison Coleman remembered. "But to be included, that meant something. It was like giving her a check for two or three thousand dollars."

Despite Harrison Coleman's tough, no-nonsense exterior, and criticism that she takes too much of the credit, she reveals that she has tempered herself over the years. Principal Harrison Coleman admits that some days she doesn't even get into her car before she starts crying. The work of turnaround can be painful.

Harrison Coleman explains what turnaround leadership means to her.

> I think it is the fact of not being afraid and that strong sense of belief. Not being afraid of failure, not being afraid to take risks. Not being afraid to stand by yourself, because sometimes you know you will be. Turnaround has to be an embodiment of "against all odds." You can do this. You've got to have that commitment yourself that you can make a difference. And [believe] that children can do. Given the opportunity, given quality, they can do. They may not all do it at the same time, but they *can* do.

Harrison Coleman and her team continue to face down naysayers who think they know better for Fred M. Lynn students. When Harrison Coleman ran into some opposition for her summer program, she persevered until she came away with a Prep Academy for incoming sixth graders. The program went so well last year that other schools are implementing it this year.

Harrison Coleman also requested a summer school program at Fred M. Lynn. "My kids don't need to be home during the summer," she argued. Now Fred M. Lynn runs its own site-based summer school.

Now that Fred M. Lynn is fully accredited and no longer in School Improvement, Harrison Coleman and her teachers continue to upgrade the school's image. Harrison Coleman talked with the county public relations department to find ways to showcase her students. Harrison Coleman wrote a grant to support a drum line, and recently the drum line performed at a $100-a-plate dinner. "What school was that?" Harrison Coleman was asked by one of the guests. "That was Fred M. Lynn Middle School," she responded proudly.

BELIEVING IS ACHIEVING

Student work lines the wall of Fred M. Lynn, which is not seen often in middle schools. The 600 Club lists students that have made a perfect score on an SOL test. The uniform policy is posted as well. Fred M. Lynn was originally a high school, so the 850-plus students have plenty of room, separate hallways by grade, a greenhouse, athletic fields, and an auxiliary auditorium, among other features.

Each classroom is unique in content, but each has a word wall. Outside each room hangs the teacher's mission statement of what the teacher believes for students in his/her subject area. There is a consistency of approach, a structure binding instruction and assessment.

As Principal Harrison Coleman walks by the classrooms, she listens for the DASH-BYE. "They all do DASH-BYEs," Harrison Coleman explains. "The Date, the Assignment, the SOL, and the Homework, and the bye is your closure. The way you end it—Before You Exit. They all start the class with a DASH and end with a BYE." Just one more way Harrison Coleman creates consistency.

Such structures assure Principal Harrison Coleman that the turnaround will be sustained when she moves on. In just three years, Fred M. Lynn Middle School English performance has surpassed district and state pass rate averages for every reported subpopulation. In sixth grade, African American students are now passing at 91 percent, LEP students at 90 percent, economically disadvantaged students at 93 percent, and students with disabilities at 83 percent. During Harrison Coleman's tenure, eighth grade pass rates have doubled for LEP students and students with disabilities, going from 40 percent passing to 80 percent passing.

Mathematics continues to be a challenge, but gains are clear. In addition to the students earning high school credits for higher-level courses—which opens opportunities for more advanced-level classes in high school—pass rates for all students have gone from a low of 32 percent in seventh grade in 2006–2007 to 81, 63, and 86 percent for sixth, seventh, and eighth grades, respectively, in 2009–2010. Still, the school did not make AYP (a 2010–2011 designation) due to the math performance of students with disabilities. While pass rates for eighth grade students with disabilities moved from 50 percent in 2006–2007 to 91 percent, sixth grade scores retreated to 59 percent in 2009–2010 from a high of 68 percent the year before. Considering that for students with disabilities only 23 percent of sixth graders and 14 percent of seventh graders were passing four years ago, and now 59 and 69 percent, respectively, are passing, the school's achievement record remains impressive.

Harrison Coleman and her team are building a community, what Harrison Coleman calls "a family that truly wants to be here." She knows that some teachers see Fred M. Lynn as a steppingstone to a school in the west end of the county. "We're not going to stop until we flesh out the ones that don't want to be here out because that's what our students deserve," Harrison Coleman says.

It's that mental toughness and perseverance that earns Harrison Coleman her reputation as Fred M. Lynn's Patton. "She has a different personality and she makes no bones about it. She's down to business," Ms. Knowlton explains. But her team sees the benefits in that approach. Knowlton finds each day "fabulously challenging," a phrase that draws laughter and agreement from her peers.

"She's helped me become better at what I do. Because of the things she puts down in the classroom and the expectations she has in the classroom. She's helped us all get better," says Mr. Dwight.

180   *Chapter 9*

As the school day ends, Mr. Marchinetti leads the Drill Team outside to take down the flag. They fold it military style, with all the proper cuts and folds, and perform the cadences their leader instructs. No one would know that these students "made" the team because they had gotten three or more referrals last year. With a focus on self-discipline, Harrison Coleman says it has made a difference. "They aren't the ones giving us problems."

Principal Harrison Coleman takes heart in having built another successful turnaround team. "They see the success in the children and the confidence that they can achieve. They see it on their faces and know how important it is."

NOTES

1. U.S. Census Bureau, Summary File 1 [SF1] and Summary File 3 [SF3]. *Zip Code Tabulation Area 22191 and 20112.*

2. The Pew Hispanic Center reported over 500,000 unauthorized immigrants in the District of Columbia, Virginia, and Maryland in 2009. http://pewhispanic.org/unauthorized-immigration. Accessed 11-8-10.

3. Prince William County Schools. *Fred M. Lynn Middle School 2008–2009 School Profile.* http://www.pwcs.edu/Departments/accountability/Profiles/Documents/FredLynn.pdf. Accessed 6-15-10; *Benton Middle School, 2008–2009 School Profile.* http://www.pwcs.edu/Departments/accountability/Profiles/Documents/Benton.pdf. Accessed 6-15-10.

4. South Carolina Department of Education, Education Oversight Committee, Division of Accountability. (2001). *Criteria and procedures for Palmetto Gold and Silver program. State Statute 59-18-1100.* Award program based upon "improved performance on longitudinally matched student data and may include such additional criteria as: student attendance; teacher attendance; student dropout rates; and any other factors promoting or maintaining high levels of achievement and performance." p.1.

5. See Burbach, H., Kelly, D., and West, J. (2005) *Stephen H. Clarke Academy (A).* Darden Business Publishing. UVA-OB-0857. Case study depicts Harrison Coleman's turnaround at Clarke.

6. Virginia Department of Education. *Fred M. Lynn Middle, Prince William County. Virginia Assessment Results for 2006–2007.* Customized Report. Accessed 8-25-10; *School Level Report Card.* Accessed 8-20-10.

7. Ibid.

8. Interview with J. Harrison Coleman 5-24-10 and *Virginia Department of Education Fred M. Lynn Middle School Report Card 2009–2010.* https://p1pe.doe.virginia.gov/reportcard/report.do?division=75&schoolName=820. Accessed 8-20-10.

9. Gediman, D., Gregory, J., and Gediman, M. (Eds.). (2009). *Edward R. Murrow's This I Believe: Selections from the 1950s radio series.* BookSurge Publishing.

Chapter 10

Inspiring Success through Student and Teacher Empowerment

High School for Violin and Dance
Bronx, New York
Tanya John, Principal

A "landscape of hopelessness"—"burnt-out apartments, boarded windows, vacant lot upon garbage-strewn vacant lot"—surrounds the school. Statistics tell us, says the [*New York Times*], that the South Bronx is "the poorest congressional district in the United States." But statistics cannot tell us "what it means to a child to leave his often hellish home and go to a school—his hope for a transcendent future—that is literally falling apart."

The head of school facilities for the Board of Education speaks of classrooms unrepaired years after having been destroyed by fire. "What's really sad," she notes, "is that so many kids come from places that look as bad as our schools—and we have nothing better to offer them."

A year later, when I visit Morris High School, most of these conditions are unchanged. Water still cascades down the stairs. Plaster is still falling from the walls. Female students tell me that they shower after school to wash the plaster from their hair. Entering ninth grade children at the school, I'm told, read about four years behind grade level.

From the street, the school looks like a medieval castle; its turreted tower rises high above the devastated lots below. A plaque in the principal's office tells a visitor that this is the oldest high school in the Bronx.

—Jonathan Kozol, *Savage Inequalities,* 1991, p. 100.[1]

By the time Tanya John became principal of the High School for Violin and Dance (HSVD) and its 218 students in 2005, the Morris high school campus had come a long way from those desperate days when it rained inside the guidance office, stairwells had gaping holes, and blackboards were so cracked they were too dangerous to write on.[2]

Part of the New York City initiative to create smaller schools, HSVD was one of four specialized high schools now occupying the massive medieval-looking structure. The building had been transformed inside to house schools that focused on the arts, international studies and global issues, science and the environment, and leadership. Though the outside seemed to be in a perpetual state of renovation, with scaffolding covering the main entrance, inside the school buzzed with learning activity.

John took the helm of HSVD after being trained in the inaugural class of the New York City Leadership Academy. She came to the Academy by way of Lehman High School, located in the Throggs Neck area of the Bronx, where she taught math to some of its 4,000 students. It wasn't until her principal Robert Leder gave her the opportunity to be program chair for the implementation of an innovative scheduling system that she began to consider seriously the impact she could have as a school leader, especially when you have a committed and talented team.

John and her team's success with the scheduling implementation led to her appointment as assistant principal for programming and testing at Lehman. It also afforded her a chance meeting with a woman who encouraged her to pursue the new Academy. The connection with Kathryn Briger was brief but for John it would mean an opportunity of a lifetime and a lasting relationship.

John entered the first cohort of the New York City Leadership Academy in 2004, signing a contract that, after her training and internship, committed her to a turnaround school for the next five years. The ultimate goal: complete transformation. In those days, the laptop they provided her alone would be incentive to take the opportunity, but the Leadership Academy offered a principal's salary for the year she was in training as well. John felt lucky to have been selected.

Before Morris was divided into small schools, only one in four students on the massive campus graduated. When John arrived, two years later, the other three schools were well on their way to becoming orderly and academically focused. HSVD was the "black sheep" of the Morris campus.

The task was significant, and John knew she was up for the challenge. Born and raised in the Bronx herself, she understood the struggles her students faced. She also knew she needed a complement to her hard-charging leadership style. She questioned everything, and her filter was not necessarily to do what she was told, but what was in the best interest of the students and the school.

John immediately knew who her assistant principal needed to be. She had met Franklin Sim, a fellow math teacher, at Hunter College's Teacher

Opportunity Program a few years earlier. The two hit it off right away, exchanging teaching strategies and innovative techniques. When Principal John got into the Academy, she encouraged Sim to secure his administrator's license so that once she had a school she might bring him on as an assistant principal (AP).

In their first month at HSVD, Principal John and AP Sim witnessed eight egregious fights, complete with hair pulling and requiring major adult intervention. They also noticed that the head of security exacerbated rather than quelled student outbursts and aggression. During morning scanning through the mandatory metal detectors, the security agent provoked students who might already be having a difficult day. He sought immediate and excessive sanctions (like suspension) when students mouthed off. Witnessing the fights and this poor treatment, John and Sim knew that handling discipline was a top priority.

The school was in its third year when Principal John arrived. With a student population that is nearly 100 percent Hispanic and African American, and at least 9 out of 10 students eligible for free lunch, she looked to the staff first for answers. The staff was nearly all white, and many commuted in from other boroughs or Westchester County to get to the Morris campus. Staff diversity would have been secondary had John and Sim found students engaged in rigorous work. "You walked in a class and you'd see kids doing handouts . . . of a very low caliber," Sim said.

"Technology was absent. . . . There were no SMART boards . . . no graphing calculators, which as math people was crazy to us. . . . The focus was on making sure every student had a violin or a leotard," John remembers. After all, the former principal was the founder, who had a vision for violin and brought in a dance teacher who served as his co-administrator. John could appreciate their primary focus was on the arts, but could see that they weren't working on the work of academics. "They were building artists, not academic success," she reflected.

The culture was steeped in demoralizing experiences from the security entrance to the classroom. Some teachers blamed the students for their underperformance, never observing each other or considering what they might do to improve their own instruction. Instead of just failing a student, some teachers would give the actual percentage on the report card, even if it was a mere 10 percent.

Student attendance was a constant challenge, which AP Sim knew contributed to the poor grades and discipline problems. Sim remembered research suggesting that students lose two instructional days for every day missed, so he figured they were missing more than half of the lessons given over a 10-day period. Later, he would use these data on home visits.

Staff absences were another red flag for John and Sim. Certainly not all teachers were cause for concern, but the chronic absences of a small handful were especially troubling and led a few to be "U-rated."[3] Teacher absences and student absences didn't necessarily coincide either, which had to amount to even more lost instruction.

John and Sim looked at the low attendance, disruptive disciplinary problems, and low expectations; it was no wonder that half of the 9th grade didn't have enough credits to move on to the 10th. To make matters worse, half of the 11th grade were still in 10th and half of the 10th were still in 9th. With this trend, John and Sim realized that a 50 percent graduation rate would be the best they could hope for, unless they were able to offer more time for instruction and help students to make up the credits.

On top of all this, John noticed that students had no voice. "There was no student empowerment," Sim recalled. "I remember the first day I arrived, I found [Principal John] in the gym, sitting in a circle with a group of students. They were engaged in an ice breaker so she could get to know them." John probed the students for their thoughts and ideas, what was good and not so good, and from there pieced together the culture.

John initially acted as a bystander. "Not coming in and pushing your agenda, your MO, but coming in and getting a feel, getting to know the culture . . . inquiring. Then slowly making the moves you need to make"—this was John's approach to the turnaround she faced.

PREPARING THE ENVIRONMENT

"A huge criteria for me was that you have to *love* the kids," John explained. One of the immediate needs of the students, John knew she could fill. They wanted to have a dance, and so John and Sim set out to fulfill that need.

She and Sim began regular classroom observations, which were not something teachers had experienced. This produced some pushback and a lot of discomfort because teachers were used to teaching in isolation.

Examining the prior year's data, the year before she became principal, John noticed that students performed better in science, and so she called the teacher, Matthew Paterakis, in to talk. "He knew exactly what the school needed," John said. "He laid it down for me and said, 'We need you in the classrooms.'" This teacher and a few others helped confirm for John that instruction had to change. John had hoped the science teacher would help lead the changes, but unrelated personal circumstances required that he move away.

Principal John and AP Sim continued their observations, sorting teachers into a number of categories. There were "venomous" teachers that had to go.

The "bare minimalists," those that came in at 8 a.m. and left at 3 p.m. and wanted to be left alone, also weren't a good fit for the culture they were trying to build. Others fell into the "invested but not positive" category, a group that thought they had the best interest of kids in mind, but many times didn't. A small handful of teachers had "the heart for the work" even if they were struggling. And then there were the "screamers." Sim remembered those days.

> We had quite a number of staff who were screamers. Yelling at kids . . . a poor example for adults and children. We had one school [instructional] aide who was a body in the hallway . . . often sleeping on the job. We were seen as the evil empire.

John found this aspect of the job extremely challenging. She reflected:

> I was trained to build culture. . . . I thought my interpersonal skills were great . . . but when I walked in here, I had problems with everyone and everything . . . very quickly, I noticed that when a culture is really toxic, you just have to cut. You have to clean house.

Rather than "U-rate" as "unsatisfactory" all those who were not aligned and performing toward the new vision, she'd bring them in individually for a conversation, something she had learned from her mentor principal in the Academy training. "I'd bring them in and say, 'You're not happy, let's be honest. Our philosophies are not aligned. And if you're not happy, the kids aren't happy.'"

By having conversations with teachers, John found teachers would make the choice to leave, especially if they weren't going to be a good fit or may have been misguided. She only needed to U-rate one teacher; some actually left the teaching profession, and the rest she hoped to work with.

John could see that it was easy for some teachers to become misguided. She knew it took time for some people's philosophies to change, and so she fed them research studies and data to help them see what they needed to consider. She was trying to shift the culture to open communication, learning, and collaboration so teachers could offer more to their students.

To build understanding about the students and their differing backgrounds, for instance, John asked her staff to read *A Framework for Understanding Poverty* (2005) by Ruby Payne. This book gave John a means to begin a conversation about expectations and helped her staff to discuss the cultural, racial, and economic differences that may have spawned concerns about safety, achievement, or abilities.

At the same time, the district was changing too, offering resources John knew could help. She received coaches from the National Academy for

Excellent Teaching (NAFET) at Columbia's Teacher's College, a resource provided by the district so they could focus on professional development. With coaching support from Sherrish Holloman and Keely Ball, they began "learning walks," visiting teachers in the classrooms. The short write-ups about their instruction that followed these visits created a healthy discomfort John knew her teachers needed. The work was so helpful that John and her team continued to use NAFET for five years.

"Teachers saw a slow shift," John recalled. "They were not used to anything more than verbal conversations, and mostly about the kids, not them." But John's vision was to create self-sustaining professional development that was teacher-led and based on needs they identified. She would need five years of coaching support from NAFET to realize this vision.

Behind the scenes, John and Sim struggled with a budget that amounted to approximately $3,000 per student.[4] John credits her mother's frugality, giving her only $1 a day for lunch, for her strong budgeting and financial survival skills.

John knew that to survive she had to occasionally blur the lines of what was appropriate. She had to figure out how to utilize the staff and resources she had to meet requirements while moving her own vision for student achievement forward. Without money for supplies, she used her networks to get donations and asked to use General Electric's Crotonville facility for weekend professional development retreats. There was absolutely no money for overtime. She and Sim made do, stretching to make the school and everyone inside work.

DEVELOPING THE EXECUTIVE

John's training in the Leadership Academy exposed her to a number of prominent executive leaders, including Jack Welch, Mayor Michael Bloomberg, Chancellor Joel Klein, and Carmen Farina, then Deputy Chancellor. The Chancellor would come and talk to the principals. "He instilled [in us] that you needed to do what's right for your community. . . . Even if there's pushback, in the end, [he] will support you," John explained.

While no official autonomy came with her new post, John felt a strong sense of support and commitment from the top. "I didn't have freedom initially, but I had the *thought* that I had the freedom."

She remembered one visit from Jack Welch, in particular.

> I remember him saying, "You have to get out of your building. And the reason for that is that how are you going to know what other people are doing and

what's working if you're in your own building rut." . . . But as a first year [principal], I wouldn't leave and so we started visiting other people in the building because there were a lot of good things going on right here.

Principal John knew that her "models of speaking" came from the Bronx. With the support of her peers from the Leadership Academy, she improved her speaking, writing, and vocabulary so that she was ready for the leadership role she was preparing to take on.

The Academy assigned her to a team and together they analyzed and responded to various problems or simulations they might face as principals. "It was boot camp," John noted. "The days went from 8. a.m. to at least 5, sometimes 8 p.m. I'd wake up at 3. a.m. and read and prepare and do it all over again."

"My thoughts were being challenged; the way I was thinking was being challenged. I could see myself changing," John said of the Leadership Academy experience, "I had many epiphanies throughout my time [there]."

During her year-long internship, John was assigned to a small, innovative school—Mott Haven Village Preparatory High School, where the principal, Ana Maldonado, focused on professional development and where she learned more about how to work with constituencies and build community. It was a small school, much different from her experience at Lehman High School, which she thought had a great school culture and leadership, although established years ago.

Here they were building a culture from the ground up and John had a front row seat. It was at this school that she learned the advantages of the smaller school environment and, most important to John, that students would not fall through the cracks. John was grateful for this placement and could see how the Leadership Academy was working strategically to prepare her to take on a school of any size and type.

In her culminating leadership presentation, John talked about one of her Lehman students who left one exam shy of graduating. She had a math class to finish and John wanted to ensure she would make it. But one day, the student disappeared.

> I didn't know any of her friends. The Rolodex had the wrong number in it. I sent letters home. . . . It didn't matter. I didn't want that little girl to give up and not have her diploma. But I couldn't find her. Didn't know where to look, didn't know who to talk to to find her. She was a dropout. That was it. . . . In the school I did my internship in, that would have never happened.

This internship, with its community-oriented, professional development–rich environment, helped to anchor Principal John's leadership at HSVD. She and Sim focused on providing their staff with the tools necessary to succeed, encouraging them to share best practices and reach out to the community. Once the initial exodus had occurred, Principal John and AP Sim were ready to take staff to the next level.

One first-year teacher, Sophia Pentoliros—or "Ms. P," as they called her—NYU educated and eager, was among those who embraced John and Sim's hands-on development. They pushed special education students by forming collaboratively taught classes that served all students. Then they began analyzing data from benchmark tests they used.

Ms. P was one of the collaborative special education teachers. Mr. Sim taught her how to give and use a diagnostic assessment and how to focus in on the skills she wanted to teach first, something she never learned in her NYU training. He taught her how to focus in on what she wanted to teach, create assessments for those skills only, look for patterns for what the students got right, identify common mistakes, and decide what she needed to re-teach. When Ms. P took the class over in February, all of the students had failed the math Regents[5] exam; by June, 87 percent of her students had passed.

Ms. P began to look deeper into the mathematics data from the eighth grade and found students were performing at the lowest level (Level 1). She moved those students to Level 3 (a 65–84 percent passing range). Ms. P gained confidence by being strategic about planning instruction, using data, giving assessments, and analyzing her data to learn what to re-teach so that she could help students to succeed. She saw the professional growth she and her peers experienced in analyzing and using data to improve instruction as a turnaround in itself.

FOCUSING ON EXECUTION

Methodical and consistent, Principal John knew that as she entered her second year, she needed a simple way to focus her staff and students on what was most important. The first year had been tumultuous for the staff, students, and administrators. John resonated with her corporate speakers and especially liked Carmen Farina's use of the 3Es in a speech she heard. So, John came up with an acronym of her own, the 3Ps.

Based on what she heard from the executives that visited the Leadership Academy and the corporate books she read, John realized long-term success for companies was based on positive outlooks, and so her first P was "Positivity." This was especially important after the first difficult year. John wanted to stem complaints and have her community engage optimistically.

John knew that the students at HSVD needed first and foremost "to feel loved by their teachers." As a result, part of this P included ensuring that all staff cared deeply for the students because John knew that students needed special support to remain positive about school and their ability to achieve. Many were faced with a family history of failure in school and a personal feeling of inadequacy around academic performance. Students didn't lack for esteem in many areas, but motivation to achieve academically suffered and so teachers that were well liked often were able to help students overcome their academic fears. As important to their achievement was the feeling that their teachers like *them* as well.

The second P was "Planning Collaboratively." John knew that her team needed to work together, with open doors and classrooms, to share knowledge and talk together. She and Sim used teams and programs to change the way teachers and students were engaging. They looked for ways to infuse what they thought was important into the schedule, making time for content team planning, and soon moving to such topics as cross-functional collaboration, attendance, teacher leader/administrator, student empowerment, and curriculum teams.

"Providing Opportunities" was the third P. This had to be done on both the leadership and student levels, John thought. For teachers and staff it focused on building leadership capacity, and for students it meant providing Saturday school, clubs, and other opportunities to learn beyond the classroom.

The budget at HSVD continued to be a significant barrier, but this allowed John and Sim to leverage their resources and get creative with what they had. They reached out to the other principals in the building and found many willing collaborators. They secured resources including a part-time social worker, professional development from other building teachers, Princeton Review classes, chemistry connections, and the United Federation of Teachers' Teacher Center.

But Principal John also learned the limits to collaboration when she had to face powerful constituents. "I learned that I wasn't really the principal," John noted, referring to the realization that a title is never enough to move the work or motivate people. She thought it could happen *because* she was the principal. She learned that when she tried to use the power of her position, it created more disharmony than unity.

She used political mapping, a technique she learned in the Leadership Academy, and her strategic planning skills to assess the situation, realizing that the union leadership was one of her most important stakeholders. If she didn't get that right, John knew they wouldn't be able to do what they needed to for the students. So Principal John worked hard at that relationship, providing her union rep with heads-up on the issues, seeking his feedback on a new initiative during the planning phase, and respecting his opinions and feedback.

The 37½-Minute Dilemma

Along with the long hours, creative financing, and difficult conversations, and even with her union leader's support, John learned in her second year that there were limits to what she could do. She came face-to-face with the challenges of working within a large bureaucracy with a set chain of command and a tense set of constituents when she tried an alternative delivery of "37½ minutes," a district-funded program that provided tutoring time four days a week to the students most in need. It had come out in John's first year, and in her second, she used it after school, but no one came. Teachers were paid for the extra time, but they had no student takers.

At the same time, John was battling her students about going to lunch. Teachers were having problems getting students to go to the lunchroom. HSVD was located in "the tower," an elevator ride (or several flights of stairs) away from the basement-level cafeteria. With students skipping lunch and the after-school tutoring underutilized, John figured they could leverage the time better by having students bring lunch up to their classrooms to eat it and give the 37½ minutes to every student that needed help (not just those that qualified) while offering other enrichment.

The change they needed was a "school based option," a legal alteration that required many approvals, which John and her team began to pursue. She talked with her union chapter head and garnered his support. All the teachers liked the idea. She needed signatures from the principal, UFT head, district head, and LIS (local instructional superintendent), as well as the Chancellor's office.

John and her team secured all the necessary signatures, except for the union leadership and the LIS. The union didn't want teachers giving up lunch to work with the students, and the LIS was concerned about union tensions. Principal John remembered the Chancellor's promise to be there when needed, and she knew she didn't reach out her entire first, difficult year. She decided to e-mail him.

Within minutes, Chancellor Klein responded and asked her to explain the situation. He said he'd look into it and get back with her. The next day his call came during a morning of greetings. It was Principal John's birthday. At first, she didn't recognize him when he referred to himself as "Joel," and she greeted him in the same manner she did her other birthday calls. Getting down to business, he told her he had spoken to the UFT President, then Randi Weingarten, and had gotten it approved. Principal John had gotten the support she needed to do what was right for her school. John and her boss shared a laugh about her birthday before they hung up.

Focus on Empowerment

At the end of her second year, Principal John got the opportunity to lead an "Empowerment School."[6] John signed a contract that, among other things, called for her removal if the school got three consecutive "C" ratings or one "F." In addition to the conditions, John got $100,000 of financial assistance, a significant windfall for her struggling school.

As the system decentralized, John continued to benefit. As a result of this increased autonomy, she had the opportunity to "shop for a boss," which allowed her to find a supervisor that fit her vision. She selected Joel DiBartolomeo, who supported them with data, including Assessment for Learning that gave them summative, six-week, and on-the-spot assessments. John and Sim employed this with their teachers, who in turn could get immediate and relevant feedback from students.

Building Community and Engaging Parents

Parent engagement was one of the most challenging objectives for John's team. As in many impoverished communities, parents were encumbered with many responsibilities just to provide essentials for their children. Initially, Principal John let this go, when the instructional challenges consumed her. She adopted a mindset that the school had to be able to educate their students without the parents, many of whom were in survival mode.

Principal John's attendance team put parent engagement back on the table. They wanted to build rapport with the parents, and so they decided they (and not others) needed to go out into the community and visit families. Initially, however, teachers and staff weren't comfortable with going out into a community in which most of them didn't live. They talked about how to dress so they wouldn't seem too formal or institutional, like a visit they might have had from child services.

They also talked through questions like, where do I park my soft-top convertible? Or how do I know where to go when I'm not from here? Finally, they included information they thought could sway parents about the importance of attendance, like the information AP Sim had gathered about the impact of missed classes. Talking through these details was essential to building parents' confidence upfront and ensuring that the parents had a good experience the first time.

John and her team incorporated a number of structures that helped them to focus and create safer, smaller environments for discussion. "We developed a culture, with the help of protocols, so it forces everybody to go through what we call a whip or a turn. You may not speak in the first turn, you don't have to . . . but in the second turn, after you've heard concerns expressed . . . now [you] should feel safe to share," Sim explained.

The protocol structure allowed them to change the dynamic of how teachers were engaging the work. With support from Steven Strull, their LIS at that time, they embraced protocols that helped them create adult professional learning communities, collaborating to troubleshoot and solve problems. They looked to the National School Reform Faculty[7] website for sample protocols, adapted them, and eventually created their own when they didn't find what they needed.

For attendance, the team set up a system of home visits to check in with parents more regularly. Sim explained:

> We're like foot soldiers. We go out [with partners] on Saturdays once a month. We select five homes based off the data. Sometimes the parent or guardian prefers, because it's a Saturday morning, that we call in advance. We show up at their door. We have some data saying this is where your child's at. We always use the "glows-grows" approach. We tell them something shining about their student, and then we tell them this is where we need them to go and this is what we're looking at right now.

The team finishes the visit with a dialogue about what they can do to better support that student. In one parent's case, getting the child back to school meant giving her an elevator pass because she's asthmatic, but the parent couldn't provide the documentation at that point.

Another parent had a hard time getting her child up and out to school, so now a staff member living nearby their Yankee Stadium neighborhood swings by to get him. To Sim and others, these are easy fixes once they know the problem, and the benefits once that relationship and trust are built are exponential for the child.

From 3Ps to 3Ss

It took John and her team three years to master the 3Ps. They became so ingrained in the culture that new hires don't even get trained in them. Now, John focuses on the 3Ss: Strategic Planning, Self-Empowerment, and Student Empowerment. Strategic planning has them focusing on getting the most from their team, working with data, planning and giving and receiving regular feedback.

Every Friday, the curriculum team meets to plan for professional development the following week. The entire teacher team then meets every Monday for two hours, when the students are otherwise engaged in a grant-funded character-building program with guidance counselors. They look at the data, analyze it, share best practices, review videos they take of each other's classes, create protocols, and support each other with feedback using the "glows-grows" approach.

When they learned they didn't have strong teaching strategies for English Language Learners (ELLs), for instance, the team developed protocols and strategies that every teacher could use. They even included a Spanish-speaking parent coordinator who also provides tutoring.

As leader of an Empowerment School, John felt her best work could be done engaging her team to collectively take responsibility and solve problems collaboratively. The teams, protocols, and data analysis skills allow the faculty to become self-empowered—the second S. Parents as well as students are included in Saturday retreats, mock site reviews, and planning meetings so that they feel empowered to contribute.

Teacher leadership is central to HSVD's continuous improvement. John found three teachers to lead the expansion of a program targeted at middle performers. This funded program, AVID (Advancement through Individual Determination) helps students become organized for success through standards and benchmarks. Mr. Julio Lopez, Ms. Pentoliros, and Mr. Daniel Rubin took strategies such as binder checks and tutoring from AVID and created DIVA (Dreams Inspire Victory and Achievement) and VIDA (Vast Initiative for Diligence and Accomplishment), respectively, to reach more students struggling in reading and math.

A physical education teacher turned data czar, Mr. Lopez is a master at managing classrooms. This year he is a dean focusing on the structures and consequences to help create a better culture. "The data tells me that those teachers that have the least connections with their students are the ones that struggle the most with them. The ones that have more experience, that know how to talk with them properly, communicate with them, have more patience, they are the ones that can move the students," he explained.

Mr. Sim used a connection with a friend from church to bring i-Mentor to the students. This program carefully matches students with a mentor who will e-mail and support them for at least a year.[8] While he learned about i-Mentor in his first year at HSVD, he had to wait until they had tackled other pressing issues before he could ensure their commitment. Now, they are focusing on having an i-Mentor for every ninth grade student, following the student for all four years.

Principal John's favorite area, however, is the third S, Student Empowerment. Inspired by a volunteer from another school in the building who told John she didn't understand why the schools weren't developing students as leaders, John remembered how integral student empowerment was to her Leadership Academy experience, where interns helped facilitate professional development and contributed valuable insights into leadership and school development. As a result, John began to find ways to incorporate students into every aspect of the school. The focus is not on the higher-level students but on all kids, especially those needing an extra push to succeed. Students are on teams, are present during reviews, give professional development, do peer tutoring, go on site visits, and a few are even on payroll.

John's team has seen the school transformed by student empowerment and teachers reap the benefits of an engaged student body. Moreover, she's preparing them to work in the business world. John explained:

> My vision initially had to be "create a culture that supported kids to graduate 'by hook or by crook.'" . . . There was so much in place that they couldn't fail . . . we got kids to graduate but I was sad because when we turned them out into the world, I felt like I failed them because we supported them too much. We didn't give them a sense of how to survive on their own. I had to switch my thinking. . . . It changed to "you have such a high sense of self-esteem and self-efficacy that you have the tools to be able to 'fish' . . . to hold the job *and* to finish school simultaneously," because our kids have to do that. *I* had to do that. That's how you're going to change the history of this community and your neighborhood.

Planning for Success and Succession

Walking in to the High School for Violin and Dance today, students are greeted professionally and respond respectfully. Girls are able to drop their babies at the LYFE Center (Living for the Young Family through Education) on campus so they can finish their high school education. Students are so engaged at HSVD, the days when they needed a school-sponsored dance are over. Students are busy co-leading meetings, preparing for state-level assessments, participating in mock Quality Reviews, and engaging in other school activities.

Test scores have shown dramatic growth since John took over the school in 2004. According to Datacation software reports that John and her team generate on demand, Global History Regents scores have risen from 115 on the Performance Index to 183; American History regents reached 186, up from 131. English Language Arts moved from 141 to 186, while Math regents are now at 191, up from 131 in 2006. Science improved nearly 40 points, from 133 to 171.[9]

There was a time in recent memory when Principal John and AP Sim held their breath when visitors came to their school. In those days they knew people weren't going to see good things. That pressure helped them improve, and now they are the ones being visited. They have built a relationship-driven performance culture that assures them that students and teachers will perform consistently, reaching for the highest of standards.

John and her team have seen first hand what can come from hard work and an unwavering commitment to student achievement. On the 2005–2006 Progress Report they received from the NYC Department of Education, Principal Tanya Lippold (John's maiden name) received a percentile rank of 38.7 percent among all high schools.[10] In HSVD's 2008–2009 Progress Report, John and her team received a total score of 98.9 out of 100, placing the school in the 98th percentile of all high schools citywide.[11]

The disclaimer at the bottom of the 2008–2009 Progress Report explains the purpose of the report.

> The Progress Report is a key component of Mayor Michael R. Bloomberg's and Chancellor Joel I. Klein's Children First reforms. The Progress Report is designed to assist administrators, principals and teachers in accelerating the learning of all students. The Progress Report also enables students, parents and the public to hold the NYC Department of Education and its schools accountable for student achievement and improvement and for ensuring a high quality education for every student in NYC's public schools.[12]

Rating the schools against peers and citywide on three categories (school environment, student performance, and student progress) and offering additional credit for a school's strides toward closing the achievement gap, Principal John's team earned a solid A overall. Forty-five percent of city schools received A's, with scores ranging from 70.0 to 105.3. The only B on their 2008–2009 report was in the category of school environment.

Above and beyond these major categories and peer comparisons, HSVD also earned 7 (out of 16 possible) "additional credit" points for showing exemplary gains with high-need students. For instance, 76 and 45 percent of Hispanic and Black students, respectively, in the lowest third citywide made "exemplary proficiency gains." Fifty percent received a Regents Diploma,[13] with more rigorous requirements than the Local Diploma, which was a dramatic increase from the 13 percent back in 2005–2006.

Student progress, a category that makes up 60 percent of the overall score, has changed significantly under Principal John's leadership. Whereas in 2005–2006 only 35 percent of students earned 10 or more credits after their first year, the 2008–2009 report shows that percentage is now at 81 percent. The city now tracks this through the third year, where 82 percent of John's students earned 10 or more credits; this percentile was not only better than all schools in HSVD's "peer horizon," but also better than 73 percent of the "city horizon."[14]

Principal John and Assistant Principal Sim would say that in those first years there was a lot of "cleanup work" to do to improve the school environment, culture and especially instruction. Scores relative to peers now show HSVD at the top of its peer group in nearly all measures. They still struggle to get more students achieving beyond minimum proficiency and into the Level 4 measure of advanced achievement, but they continue to make progress.

They also know that their attendance rate, at just over 80 percent, is not where they need to be to further accelerate academic achievement (in this category for 2008–2009, HSVD ranked better than only 56 percent of the peer horizon). John and Sim are counting on their home visits and their student engagement strategies to help move the needle.

On a recent day, just before spring break, one student intern brought a stack of awards for Mr. Sim to sign. This young man is among a few selected interns that help administrators, teachers, and staff to make the school run smoothly. He politely interrupted, greeting the visitor with a strong handshake and eye contact. "I got here this year and so far I have close relationships with the teachers," he remarked when asked about the school.

This young man is one of the many HSVD students engaged in the Student Empowerment initiative. At first, John and Sim limited interns to student role models, those high performers with social and emotional confidence. The program expanded so that everyone could be a part of Student Empowerment, as long as they were committed and showed progress. With guidance, students even developed a rubric to gauge their progress. "We extended it to all students," John explained, "because, as long as you choose it, it doesn't matter how you come in. It matters how you progress."

As Principal John completes her sixth year, she knows it's almost time for her next challenge. She recommended Mr. Sim for the NYC Leadership Academy's Leadership Excellence Apprenticeship Program (LEAP), a leadership development program that gives him the "boot camp" and network while he's in his current assignment. Together, they are nurturing two more teachers at HSVD, Mr. Lopez and Ms. Pentoliros, who have been accepted into the LEAP program for the coming year.

According to Sim, the administrator's license he received prior can't compare to the rigor of the Leadership Academy. "The stretching of the mind, the body, the soul, it was just grueling. That experience helped inform me of what the principalship would be like, the reality of the day to day," he said.

Now, Sim has a teachable point of view that he shares readily. "Every student deserves and can learn. My heart pangs for students, thinking of my own son, could I place him in this situation? Every child in the classroom becomes my own child."

Relationships are fundamental to the way John and Sim operate. They are so aligned that at times they finish each other's sentences. And they are mindful that one day, they will have to move on. Mr. Sim may be the best successor for now, but he, too, knows the Leadership Academy is training them to transform *any* school, a process that can take three or four years. Until that time, though, they plan for summer school, their next self-financed strategic planning retreat (with staff and students) to Florida, and the next set of home visits.

John sees her students and staff working collaboratively and knows how important that is to her own success—and to theirs. She remembers her childhood and adolescent experiences with an organization called Youth for a United World, which focused on "making yourself one with others." Here, John developed "a mental framework and idealism to really believe that we can be a united community," she said. The NYC Leadership Academy helped her cement this belief in building community and culture through collaboration. For John, that was essential to transforming schools and communities.

In order to actualize this ideal at the High School for Violin and Dance, John had to work with the founding principal. Together, they formed a partnership to marry an academic drive with the artistic focus of the school. The founder continues to contribute to the school community today by providing mentoring relationships with the performing arts teachers, investment that John values greatly.

Principal John sees turnaround leadership as courageous work, "sticking with what you know to be good and right in your heart." She explains the essence of her work:

> You have to be able to take a lot of punches and get back up. . . . Nothing can stand in your way. The self-empowerment has to be there. What you're able to do and capable of doing, it has to be inspirational. . . . I speak to their hearts [using] stories of real life that speak to me, that made me change my views, and help people see why things have to happen, why it's urgent. People have to understand this is life or death.

NOTES

1. Kozol, J. (1991). *Savage inequalities.* New York: Crown Publishers, Inc. Kozol's overview of Morris High School was drawn from interviews at the school in February 1990 and a *New York Times* article, December 10, 1988.

2. Ibid., pp. 100–103.

3. The term "U-rated" refers to an "unsatisfactory" rating on an evaluation or performance report.

4. The average per-pupil expenditure for New York City in 2005–2006 was $14,961. U.S. Dept. of Commerce, Bureau of the Census. (2008). *Public*

education finances 2006. U.S. Census Bureau. Table 17. http://www2.census.gov/govs/school/06f33pub.pdf. Accessed 11-7-10.

5. High school students in New York State take Regents Exams to assess their mastery of New York State Learning Standards. In order to graduate from high school, students must pass exams in five subjects: English, mathematics, science, global history, and U.S. history and government. Students may also earn an Advanced Regents diploma if they pass additional exams in math, science, and a foreign language. New York City Department of Education. http://schools.nyc.gov/Accountability/resources/testing/default.htm#CT%20Regents. Accessed 11-4-10.

6. http://schools.nyc.gov/offices/empowerment/default.htm. Accessed 5-28-10.

7. http://www.nsrfharmony.org/. Accessed 6-1-10.

8. http://www.imentor.org/about-imentor. Accessed 6-1-10.

9. High School for Violin and Dance. (2010). *School Comparison Report by subject for 2006–2009.*

10. High School for Violin and Dance. *New York City Department of Education 2005–2006 Progress Report (Draft): High School for Violin and Dance.* Principal John noted that this was a preliminary report provided to the newly formed Empowerment Schools and not made public by the NYC Department of Education.

11. High School for Violin and Dance. *New York City Department of Education 2008–2009 Progress Report: High School for Violin and Dance.*

12. Ibid.

13. Effective for the class entering ninth grade in 2008, Local Diplomas will not be an option for General Education Students. Students must pass all required regents exams with a score of 65 in order to obtain a Regents or Advanced Regents Diploma. http://schools.nyc.gov/documents/offices/GT/TL/2009_GenEd_Grad_Card_FINAL.pdf. Accessed 11-7-10.

14. High School for Violin and Dance. *New York City 2008–2009 Progress Report: High School for Violin and Dance.* The report notes that peer and city ranges are based on the outcomes of schools from 2005–2008.

Section IV

Policy Essentials for Turnaround Leaders

Chapter 11

Policy Imperatives to Bring Turnarounds to Scale

Turnaround leaders are fixing schools all across the country. Greeted by academic and social deficits, they build strengths and demand excellence. Faced with catastrophic circumstances of Mother Nature or urban blight, they find opportunity and develop confident learners. These leaders transform buildings that symbolize failure into academic showpieces, defying statistics and expectations.

They are an elite group with a tough exterior and the knowledge and fortitude to get the job done. Yet, they also shed tears, endure painful and often public critiques, and sometimes sacrifice their own health and family balance for the urgent work of turnaround. Leadership can be lonely, but the mission is vital.

Consider Camille Wallin, the principal in New York City whose spatula in her back pocket came to represent intolerance for mediocrity and disrepair. Her spatula represented more than a clean building; it scraped off the grime that clouded judgment and dulled expectations. The transformation of her auditorium is a lasting and visible symbol of the beauty that lies beneath. With "all hands on deck," she and her team built a school that reinforces in students, staff, and parents a culture of high performance. It ensures students know they not only can do more, but also deserve better.

Aretha Eldridge-Williams in Louisiana met the devastation brought on by Hurricane Katrina with a spirit of hope and promise. The storm only exacerbated the academic challenges she already was facing; she had to rebuild the school as well as the instructional program and offer her students a different path. With a "hug and a handshake," she established a new way at her school—the Kate Middleton Way—and demanded of her staff nothing less than she expected of herself. Every program, walk-through, and meeting reinforces their commitment to educate, to seek answers, to use data, to make certain every student can read, to ask for the community's help, and to leave no stone unturned when it comes to supporting student achievement.

J. Harrison Coleman approaches turnarounds with an exacting and critical mind that dissects failure and with the care of a surgeon reassembles a school to one of achievement. She extinguishes every low expectation and demands consistent and accountable instructional excellence. Earnest and confident, she holds students and staff to standards that eradicate failure and showcase learning.

To J. Harrison Coleman, names mean something. After the death of her uncle and before her own father's passing, she gave her dad a birthday gift. In order to carry on her family name, she began using only her first initial, proudly displaying her maiden name as part of her first name and alongside her husband's last name. To Harrison Coleman names are purposeful. The name of her school, in this case Fred M. Lynn Middle School, symbolizes its history, identity, and the pride students take in it. By using its full name, she broke from its image as "The Lynn," projecting its transformation into a school, which protects and honors a learning environment that fosters student achievement.

To Tanya John, turnaround leadership emanates from love. Her analytical skills, instructional know-how, and creativity abound, but it is not just that she cares but *how* she cares that makes a difference for her students. She feels the pain of their circumstances, the demoralization of past failures, and she embraces "positivity" and accompanies students and teachers on the path to achievement. She practices "tough love" that ensures her students will not only succeed in high school and college, but also in life. She and her team empower students, instilling them with the experiences and confidence necessary to quiet fears and defy expectations. Her leadership fosters her students' love of school, community, and most of all, themselves.

These leaders didn't turnaround schools on their own. They created environments where success and achievement could prevail. When that meant teaching staff, students, parents, and those in the community a new way, they did that. When that meant helping some out of the school and replacing them with like-minded others, they tackled that challenge. When that meant driving home the need for consistent, data-driven instruction, they did that too. When that meant making everyone a reading teacher, they did that as well.

Alongside these leaders stand a set of talented teachers and coworkers that ensure the learning environment is rigorous and supportive for all students. They are in critical lead roles on the front lines of the transformation. Behind these leaders is a set of administrators, school board members, union representatives, community, and other partners that know how to facilitate rather than impede the hard work they must do to transform a struggling school into one that consistently succeeds.

It is here, with these supportive yet influential players, where policies that can make the difference for turnarounds originate.

IN PURSUIT OF COHERENT POLICY

Policies are at the crux of this new turnaround movement. They are what will validate, sustain, and institutionalize this work. They can drive how problems get solved, how gaps are closed. In many ways, policies direct the work of a principal while staying well in the background. Most turnaround principals and teachers don't have the time to be involved in the most significant policy changes; their immediate work is much more pressing. Yet, policies undergird the work of turnaround, often determining the ability of and speed by which leaders can accelerate improvement.

The domain of policy is multi-leveled and multi-layered. Some policies result from federal or state regulations, while others stem from a firm's values and ethics. In the private sector, management and employees develop, administer, and carry out policies, while the board of directors safeguards them. A legal team stands ready to defend against noncompliance or malfeasance.

Public sector policy making serves the purpose of facilitating more efficient or effective practices, albeit in the realm of a multi-level government system. Public policy serves as a quasi-agent for those whose interests may not otherwise be served. Similar to the private sector, incentives do not necessarily encourage cross-level or cross-organizational collaboration. Just as every problem cannot be categorized into one agency, policies cannot be discretely developed and implemented within each governmental unit. A child with special needs, for instance, may require support from the schools, but may also need medical assistance and social services support, depending on the circumstances.

In the complex arena of public policy making, policy actors convene formally and informally to further interests that serve a desired outcome. Differing perspectives must be managed to achieve an intended purpose. Stakeholders, usually of varying means, wield influence in a process that examines evidence and churns out a set of conditions, a compromise that, with determination and likely a bit of luck, becomes policy.

Education policy is as imperfect a discipline as any other public policy domain. Complex interests compete for attention and scarce financial resources. The bully pulpit—often the president, governor, or mayor—attempts to use voice to create sway when the teeth of real accountability cannot legally be mandated. Influential partners, advocates, and critics do research, analyze data, and shape messages to have an impact.

Various levels of the system weigh in, supporting or refuting the data that drive the issue at hand. In such a complex system, good intentions may go awry, electoral realities tend to encourage short-term thinking, underfunded mandates build frustration, and unintended consequences may create the need for more policy action. Staying in tune to what really matters for teachers and students and aligning rather than adding on policies can be especially difficult.

Education researchers like Richard Elmore and Susan Furhman and their colleagues at the Center for Policy Research in Education (CPRE) have long studied policy fragmentation, arguing for more coherent policy in support of systemic reform.[1] A decade after *A Nation at Risk* was released, numerous policy initiatives, from heightened emphasis on homework to increased math and science requirements for graduation from high school, attempted to address the harsh realities depicted in the report.

CPRE, among others, argued that systemic reform would not take hold without coherence in policy making. At that time, for instance, Elmore wondered whether a more coherent high-level policy could trigger a constructive district response to affect change that ultimately would improve student performance.[2]

More than 10 years later, Elmore, Fuhrman, and colleagues (2004)[3] continued their pursuit of coherent policy making through the lens of accountability systems. The *No Child Left Behind (NCLB)* law had just brought performance-based accountability to the fore of the federal education policy agenda. Through accountability came ever-increasing stakes to improve performance—sanctions and rewards designed to call out poor performance and drive change. Elmore argued, "When stakes are applied to educators . . . They can and do engage in political action to shape and mitigate the impact of policies on them (p. 287)."

This mutual shaping of policy can be a delicate negotiation or an aggressive debate that policy actors engage in pursuit of actions that will further their interests. What one hopes is that the outcome builds capacity for improving student performance. Yet, without coherence within and across the system, and without meaningful stakeholder engagement, the chance that policy will have its intended impact becomes slimmer. Coherent policy requires a system-stakeholder approach.

In the political arena, trade-offs that may either enhance or weaken policy actions targeted at shoring up real reform are inevitable. Ultimately, when faced with a choice of no policy versus compromise, most choose the latter in hopes that some movement toward a desired outcome is better than the status quo. As Frederick Hess and Michael Petrilli pointed out after the close of President George W. Bush's term, "On education-reform legislation, compromise trumped conservatism."[4] Bush's original proposal for NCLB included a number of conservative-minded reforms (such as more parental choice and greater state and local flexibility) that were negotiated out of the final bill.

Trade-offs are inevitable and may thwart efforts to do what is necessary in favor of what is more politically expedient. Rarely do enough stakeholder groups embrace the boldest of actions to produce revolutionary change. And sometimes even the notion of policy change is so polarizing that protests result.

Beyond the challenges of compromise, policies inevitably bring about a set of unintended consequences, some positive, others likely negative. One way to mitigate the impact of the unexpected is to engage in scenario planning.[5] This process of creating sets of possible futures based on the policy at hand offers the opportunity to think through consequences (intended and unintended) of the desired outcome—improved student achievement—as well as the stakeholders engaged in the policy. It's the kind of scenario building that is used on the battlefield or in business strategy, though found less frequently in education.

Policy actions are essential to the changing landscape of education and especially to those of turnaround. Policies drive needed change, and policy actions necessitate further change. Policies can be important responses to a set of external conditions—international competitiveness indicators, assessment scores, graduation rates—and policies can unstick entrenched problems. Policies also can spur innovation—like charter schools—and can uphold civil rights as in desegregation efforts or the hard work of closing achievement gaps. Strategically pursued, policy establishes the framework for solving problems.

POLICY MAKING TO FACILITATE SCHOOL TURNAROUNDS

In the time-bound context of turnaround, policy support is essential. As noted earlier, school improvement has been pursued for decades, including targeted efforts at persistently low-performing schools. Yet, achievement gaps that were closing in the 1960s, 70s, and 80s widened in the 90s and early 21st century. "Drop out factories" have been exposed and policies rewarding ineffective teaching revealed. With an estimated 5,000[6] schools to fix, policy action is not just necessary, it's urgent.

In a new era of accountability, NCLB may have resulted in many unintended consequences during implementation, but one legacy is clear. The law created a level of transparency across school data that had largely eluded (or to the more cynical, had been ignored by) policy makers, administrators, parents, and even teachers. The vast achievement gaps and the need for turnaround on a larger scale has become readily apparent from the subpopulation data now regularly reported and tracked.

Some schools may prefer such results be left undiscussed and gaps in achievement addressed locally. However, the pressure of such accountability has created unparalleled transparency to fuel the urgency for change. No longer can schools hide behind the majority of students making minimal standards. No longer can schools mask student attrition throughout high school. Historically, schools were allowed to report drop out rates that dubiously conveyed the percentage of students that completed 12th grade rather than the full cohort—sometimes twice the size—that began in ninth grade.

Policy action is an especially prudent support mechanism for turnaround leaders. Policy changes are particularly important initially as leaders throughout the system—from turnaround principal to district leaders to state and federal officials–build supports that facilitate and sustain student achievement gains. Memoranda of Understanding (MOUs) between districts, principals, and states that have turnaround programs clarify goals and expectations but also can offer essential political cover for the turnaround leader in action.

Policies also can facilitate needed focus on sustaining results once the turnaround is complete. Turnarounds occur at the school level, with students in communities that may not have the financial resources or social capital to sustain results. Without policy supports to buttress the practices that a turnaround leader puts in place, a turnaround can be undone.

A charismatic, skilled, and committed turnaround leader's efforts can achieve turnaround but may not be able to sustain it. Turnarounds require the will and action by those with political capital at the state, district, and community levels not just during the exciting phase of turnaround but well beyond. Policy changes may not be able to guarantee continuous improvement, but they can address the obstacles that impede turnaround success, and they can ensure that the post-turnaround path is cleared for continued growth.

Turnaround Policy Accelerators

In the hard work of turning around chronically underperforming schools, time is an especially precious commodity. Turnaround leaders are working tirelessly to change the tide of low expectations, low morale, and low performance. They are making change happen even in the face of numerous obstacles. They are recognizing opportunity under the filth, capability inside the classroom, and promise in the eyes of students.

Often, turnaround leaders are surpassing expectations by working around a broken system, finding ways around policies that don't strengthen teaching and learning. Rarely does a turnaround specialist have the time to fix district policies or advocate for changes to policies that don't make sense; they and their teachers are busy keeping the school going, especially in the first year or two. They are making sense out of chaos, with or without policies that support them. They are bending rules to ensure students come first.

In some turnaround situations, policy after policy, intervention after intervention has been tried to little or no avail. If the school is not suffering from neglect, programs and resources may have been layered on so thick that a clear instructional vision and core program is missing. Policies that may work for some schools don't work in these underperforming schools, often leading to more sanctions and greater oversight. More time is required to keep up with audits, paperwork, school improvement plans, and other federal, state, and district interventions. The cost to students and teachers is rarely considered.

Imagine if instead of overburdening schools with more audits and program solutions that districts and states used resources to streamline processes and refashion policies. Rather than bureaucratic overlay, more states and districts would reexamine and reinvent how they supported school leaders.

To bring turnaround efforts to more schools, more effective coordination of services and policies is essential. This is especially important at the district and state levels. The PELP Coherence Framework[7] developed by Harvard's Public Education Leadership Project, for instance, is one resource districts can use to identify and integrate elements of an improvement strategy that can support turnaround.

The Turnaround Readiness Sequence, which the authors developed for the Louisiana Department of Education, is another resource for states, districts, and schools building capacity to lead turnarounds. This readiness sequence analyzes each stakeholder's responsibilities and articulates considerations—necessary actions and policy changes—that might expedite the design and execution of a robust turnaround program at the state level.

In this sequence, stakeholders are categorized as "turnaround partners" supporting "turnaround professionals" that are enabling achievement. Using the 3Es as an organizing framework the Turnaround Readiness Sequence guides stakeholders through the elements that should be considered and "readiness indicators" that facilitate turnaround success. (A Turnaround Readiness Sequence Template is Provided in Appendix H.) Policy change can have important influences on all aspects of the turnaround, from preparing the environment, to developing executive talent, to focusing on execution. Using the 3Es as an organizing framework, here are some compelling examples of policy changes that can accelerate turnarounds.

Preparing the Environment for Turnaround

The passage of *NCLB* in 2002, with its accountability goals and metrics, may have "prepared the environment" for turnaround in the Obama Administration, which has made turning around failing schools a centerpiece of its agenda. The bully pulpit wields influence—and resources—providing incentives to states and districts ready to address the urgency at scale. School Improvement funds, Race to the Top incentives, i3 innovation grants, Title I funds, and the reauthorization of the Elementary and Secondary Schools Education Act (ESEA) all articulate funds, policies, and incentives related to chronic underperformance in schools.

With an unprecedented amount of federal investment at stake, the federal policy agenda includes competitive grants that are causing reform-minded states and districts to adopt charter-friendly policies, address teacher contracts, and revise performance standards and rewards and evaluation systems. This agenda is also motivating states and districts to close or turnaround schools that have persistently failed students.

By offering incentives for adopting conditions conducive to turnaround, the federal government has made it clear what it thinks will facilitate turnarounds on a larger scale. If the Race to the Top fund is any indicator of how to prepare the environment, 41 states applied for some of the $4 billion available to the states that have "ambitious yet achievable plans for implementing coherent, compelling, and comprehensive education reform."[8]

Even without federal monies at stake, some states have made adjustments to create a fertile ground for policies targeting turnarounds. For instance, when Governor Mark Warner in Virginia wanted to develop a cadre of turnaround specialists and purpose them throughout the Commonwealth of Virginia, he went to the legislature for program funding, which included incentives for the principals and schools willing to engage in the arduous work of turnaround.

Taking a cue from private sector performance bonuses, the legislature approved funding for the following incentive system: $5,000 upon completion of the training and development of a turnaround plan, $50 per student to address the conditions and needs of the school, and a salary differential of $8,000 in the first year and $15,000 in the next two years if they met turnaround targets.[9] Such incentives can be a powerful tool in recruiting leaders willing to take on the challenge of turnaround.

At the district level, New Haven's teacher contract has been hailed[10] as a game-changing strategy for supporting chronically underperforming schools. The District of Columbia teacher's union contract also was completed with hard fought concessions from both sides—as well as unprecedented funding commitments from philanthropic sources.[11]

With the urgent need for reform and the determination to change current policy, district leadership and union officials acted courageously in support of students. Yet, the question remains whether and how such contracts will be implemented, especially as political tides change.

Developing Turnaround Executives

Innovative policies can also help to build the necessary human capital to lead turnarounds. Whether providing incentives to colleges or universities to create partnerships that forge research or develop curriculum for struggling schools, or working with district superintendents to design processes to ensure that strong teachers and principals will work in these often rural or urban, high-poverty environments, policies can influence the talent that joins this growing field.

Louisiana is one state that has embraced a portfolio approach to building educational leaders capable of affecting turnarounds. The Louisiana Educational Leaders Network,[12] for instance, is an online resource for all Louisiana school leaders that also offers specific resources targeted at struggling schools.

Louisiana's School Turnaround Specialist Program (LSTS),[13] Educational Leader Alternate Programs,[14] and its Turnaround Leadership Endorsement[15] are three examples of state policies that build capacity for turnaround. Starting with a commitment to develop principals for the difficult task of turnarounds, Louisiana created a regional provider approach seeking university partners to train and support turnaround specialists in a two-year program, with coordinating support from the Department of Education. Faculty from education and business schools in universities across the state are working to implement the state's executive leadership program, serving more than 60 principals in chronically underperforming schools.

Demonstrating a commitment to developing and maintaining strong education leaders in Louisiana, the state Board of Elementary and Secondary Education (BESE) created an alternative certification process for administrators. The Educational Leader Alternate Program provides links to program providers. One of the benefits of expanding certification beyond traditional means was to be able to attract New Leaders for New Schools to Greater New Orleans. This was especially important post-Katrina when the Recovery School District assumed responsibility for reviving New Orleans schools.

Through this alternative process, New Leaders New Orleans has provided 24 leaders serving nearly 5,000 students in the New Orleans area.[16] Advance Innovation Education, an organization in the state's capital, also has leveraged this policy change in its work with East Baton Rouge schools.

Under State Superintendent Paul Pastorek's leadership and with BESE's support, Louisiana has been pursuing multiple strategies to build a larger and stronger bench of talent. Department staff examined policies that support turnaround specialist principals, and even before their program was underway, established a performance-based Turnaround Specialist Endorsement, the first in the nation.

Recognizing the specialized skills of a turnaround specialist, Louisiana offers the endorsement to principals completing the Louisiana School Turnaround Specialist Program and successfully meeting student achievement goals. By definition, the turnaround must be completed for the endorsement to be conveyed. While the Virginia program conveyed a performance-based credential along with the program certificate, Louisiana took the added step of changing state policy to recognize the impact turnaround leaders could have on the state's public education system.

The leadership development program, alternate certification route, and the endorsement have created a broader path for principals and superintendents leading chronically underperforming schools out of decline. They offer incentives—knowledge and credentials—to principals seeking the turnaround challenge. They present opportunities for innovators like New Leaders for New Schools to come to Louisiana. As important, they provide a clear strategy through which philanthropic and other supportive players can productively contribute, making the opportunity to achieve real and lasting reform even stronger.

These programs also extend into higher education as they combine university faculty from business schools and colleges of education. In doing so, they recognize the importance of cross-sector experiences and a multi-discipline approach to educational leadership. As faculty work with turnaround practitioners, they gain insights for their own classrooms. The involvement of colleges and universities as regional providers then increases the probability that coursework for aspiring administrators will place increased emphasis on school improvement strategies and instructional leadership that specifically target school turnarounds.

Louisiana based its approach on Virginia's now national model, yet sought a customized solution. Its program reflects its context and the influence of policy makers seeking to offer a portfolio of options including charters and state takeover for improving student performance. The development and implementation of the LSTS was supported and approved by BESE[17] and has garnered assistance from the Wallace Foundation and the Louisiana Board of Regents, Louisiana's governing body for public higher education. These and other entities are all working together to facilitate the capacity building and policies necessary to support turnaround leaders.

Turning around low-performing schools is arduous work. It requires the vital support of states, districts, and other key stakeholders so that leaders can create a platform for turnaround. With a regional approach and state-run program that includes an endorsement, Louisiana is one state that is on a path to building its own network of specialists who can learn from and visit each other to consistently improve the prospects for Louisiana's students.

Focusing on Execution

In 1997, Mel Riddile, then principal of JEB Stuart High School, took on the challenge of turning around a high school in Fairfax County, Virginia, one of the wealthiest counties in the United States where over 75 percent of high school graduates go on to some form of postsecondary education. JEB Stuart High School, an outlier among its Fairfax peers, has 59 percent of students qualifying for free and reduced-price lunch and over 35 percent of students classified as English Language Learners.[18] With only one quarter of incoming students reading on grade level, Riddile and his team set out to embed literacy in every classroom. Literacy coaches and new library books geared toward teenagers but offered at levels appropriate for struggling readers were among Riddile's strategies to drive student performance.

Riddile and his staff believed that, given sufficient time, all students could learn at high levels. Said Riddile, "There's really no magic in the approach. Research has shown that if we have more instructional time with students, performance improves. It's really common sense."[19] Thus, they developed a year-round calendar that would increase the academic year from 180 to 242 days. The change required support from 80 percent of the teachers and community. With school board approval, Riddile sought a waiver from the State Board of Education. Following his testimony, the Board approved a five-year waiver for Riddile's innovative program.

Focusing on execution for Riddile meant removing all roadblocks, including policies that stood in the way of furthering student achievement. Executing a comprehensive strategy to move students from nonreaders to achievers, Riddile's leadership and policy makers' support offered the opportunity for turnaround to take hold at JEB Stuart.

Stuart High School, as it is known today, continues to make AYP and meet state accreditation requirements. While data show that students with disabilities and Limited English Proficient students still lag their peers, other achievement gaps are closing. Accreditation adjusted pass rates in the four main subject areas range from 85 to 91 percent and the performance gaps for black, Hispanic, and disadvantaged students are closing in on those averages.[20] In this case, the turnaround has been sustained.

Executing turnarounds necessitates taking on policies that no longer make sense for the time or the context. It requires leaders at the local, state, and federal levels willing to question what heretofore had gone unnoticed and those able to create a pathway toward achievement. Rosalind Taylor, principal of Woodville Elementary School in Richmond, who attended the first cohort of the Virginia School Turnaround Specialist Program, understands this well.

Leading a 600-student elementary school in which approximately 95 percent qualify for free or reduced-priced lunch, Taylor embarked on a turnaround and has maintained achievement for over five years. Her turnaround plan included engaging volunteers that could offer extra support to needy students. Through what she calls "distributed accountability,"[21] Taylor and her team demonstrated that turnaround strategies and turnaround leadership can be successful even in the most difficult neighborhoods.

For many turnaround leaders, however, policies that support turnaround are already clear—human resource autonomy, uniforms, streamlined audits and coordinated improvement plans, more time, to name a few. Each of the principals leading the schools profiled in this text pursued policy changes or exemptions so they could best serve the needs of their students. They used high-level advocates and influential stakeholders as well as old-fashioned communication with parents to make their case for changes that would further student achievement.

Entities like Mass Insight, New Leaders for New Schools, the New York City Leadership Academy and others are assembling knowledge about what works. Turnarounds at scale, however, will require wholesale acknowledgement that systems and policies must change so that turnaround leaders aren't spending precious time and energy on onerous paperwork or district or state policy impediments, time they could be devoting to students and teachers.

UNTANGLING RACE AND POVERTY

One complexity of turnaround seems to be the comingling of race and poverty. While there are plenty of schools in rural areas with largely white and poor students failing to be served well, there are a disproportionate number of African-American or minority students, also poor, who are equally underserved in urban and rural contexts.

One question that has fueled debate is whether desegregation should play a more prominent role in turnarounds. Large proportions of chronically underperforming schools serve overwhelmingly minority populations, and researchers like Gary Orfield, a professor at the UCLA Graduate School of Education and Codirector of the Civil Rights Project stress that the answer lies in more integrated environments, such as those produced by magnet schools.[22]

While few would argue against the continued pursuit of Martin Luther King's dream and the many social and educational benefits of integrated classrooms, the question is open as to whether desegregation efforts measurably help to improve failing schools, especially in the short-term. KIPP schools, for instance, often do very well with all African-American populations, making significant gains for students years behind grade level. Yet, charter schools have been criticized for contributing to, rather than ameliorating, segregation in schools, and rates of isolation are particularly high for African Americans.[23] For parents seeking a rigorous and supportive learning environment for their children, the choice, if there is one, may be difficult.

A 2010 study[24] by Mathematica Policy Research, Inc. reported, "For the vast majority of KIPP schools studied, impacts on students' state assessment scores in mathematics and reading are positive, statistically significant, and educationally substantial" (p. xi). Similarly, turnaround specialists in Virginia like Deloris Crews in Danville, Rosalind Taylor in Richmond, and J. Harrison Coleman in Prince William County have shown that student performance can increase significantly in schools that lack diversity.

For some turnarounds, the goal of desegregation adds another obstacle to hurdle. In Louisiana, for instance, the Dandridge Desegregation Order had an adverse impact on principal Aretha Eldridge-Williams' ability to hire her own teachers. A principal in another part of the state dealt with similar challenges when his school with nearly all African-American students was required to maintain a certain racial balance of staff. Legal desegregation orders trump local policy measures such that compliance with the law, however just, may come in conflict with what others—and sometimes turnaround principals—see as best for a school.

When faced with chronic underperformance, the question of how best to allocate students and staff is a critical one. Are students and therefore resources like Title I funds better concentrated, or will integration be "the rising tide that lifts all boats?" One state's experience suggests yes, and no.

A 1970s-era voluntary desegregation program in Connecticut dispersed a group of urban, minority students to suburban, majority white schools. Chosen by lottery with the option of riding a bus out to the suburbs, a busload of students left their underperforming high school in pursuit of a better education. While the program stopped in the 1980s, researchers from Yale followed the students and found that those students that were part of "Project Concern" did seem to have better outcomes as far as job attainment. Desegregated students worked in white collar or professional jobs more than their control group peers.[25]

Voucher programs and magnet schools are among the alternatives that can offer desegregation options for underserved students. Charter schools may also offer greater prospects for similar students. Yet the numbers of failing students is too great to ignore the public schools serving so many students today, and thus turnaround leaders are needed to jump in and defy statistics. Options must not be *either/or,* but *both/and.*

It may be argued that desegregation policies both facilitate and hamper turnarounds. Segregation occurs within even the most diverse schools. Gifted programs and achievement groupings create enclaves—schools within schools—that many times are noticeably racially segregated. Playgrounds and lunch tables follow suit, at least in part due to residential segregation. Only time and additional research will help determine how best to meet Dr. King's goals and those of an equitable society while also serving students and families most effectively.

Consider the following. Who weighs the intended positive effect of targeting instruction to black students clustered in lower achievement groups against the potential accompanying social stigma of academic inferiority? What do these groupings, however helpful, say to these students about who achieves? Likewise, what do the white students in higher achievement groups learn about who can and can't achieve? And how do these groupings impact confidence and achievement in the longer term?

While such questions may be beyond the scope of this book, policy makers and educational leaders should engage in dialogue and examine data that tackles these and other questions. Most urgent, perhaps, are the glaring statistics about black male achievement that must be carefully considered in the realm of turnarounds. The Council of the Great City Schools (CGCS) in its 2010 report *A Call for Change: The Social and Educational Factors Contributing to the Outcomes of Black Males in Urban Schools* presents a set of sobering statistics that indicate achievement gaps in urban settings extend beyond class distinctions. Some highlights include:

- Between 2003 and 2009, the percentage of large city (LC) fourth-grade black males performing at or above Proficient in reading improved from 8 to 11 points, but remained at least 27 percentage points lower than the percentage of white males in national public schools (NP) scoring at or above Proficient levels. (Figure 2.5, p. 26)
- In 2009, the average reading scale score of large city (LC) fourth-grade black males who were not eligible for free or reduced-price lunch (Non-FRPL) increased significantly (+11 points) since 2003, but was one point lower than the score of white males in national public schools (NP) who were eligible for free or reduced-price lunch (FRPL). (Figure 2.6, p. 28)
- In 2009, the percentage of large city (LC) fourth-grade black males performing at or above Proficient in reading who were not eligible for free or reduced-price lunch (Non-FRPL) was similar to the percentage of white males in national public schools (NP) who were performing at or above Proficient levels and were eligible for free or reduced-price lunch (FRPL). (Figure 2.7, p. 29).

Education reformers and others have called closing the black–white achievement gap the "civil rights issue of our time." At the heart of this issue lie especially difficult realities in a world of scarce resources—how to appropriately level the playing field so that all students have adequate books, clean facilities, safe conditions, and strong and talented teachers; how to build confident learners of all races, ethnicities, abilities and genders in schools that exude high expectations for every student; how to engage adults in the difficult conversations about race and class that are necessary to move forward; and how to devote the time necessary to accelerate achievement.

Integrating schools is a noble pursuit, especially in a highly diverse society and interconnected world. However, residential segregation is a stubborn problem that often means some students must travel further to get to a "good" school. Which ones should ride the bus longer? Which group should be "other"? What schools must close? If integration means that students gain social capital offerings of well-resourced schools but don't get the interventions necessary to overcome the achievement gap, then the problem remains, just more dispersed. Moreover, the need for turnaround may be obscured.

Understanding poverty requires thoughtful discussions that at least include socioeconomic conditions, sometimes hidden advantages, and social capital. Appreciating and seeing the role that race continues to play in school life is another matter altogether. While the two are often connected, stereotypes and racial legacies in some communities extend well beyond economic realities. Leaders need to develop the skills to talk openly and honestly about how poverty and race affect expectations, interactions, and achievement.

Turnaround leaders confront the troubling legacies of racial and economic inequalities with the vision of eradicating achievement gaps and ensuring all children have equal opportunities to achieve wherever they go to school. Leaders at all levels cannot shy away from the difficult conversations about race and poverty that will ensure high expectations for all students. Whether in integrated or less integrated, well-resourced or under-resourced settings, all students deserve to have teachers and other supporters that recognize their potential and make sure they know they can get there.

ENVISIONING TURNAROUNDS AT SCALE: SOME POLICY RECOMMENDATIONS

Among the greatest challenges of education reform is replicating what works across varying school environments. The education sector seems especially susceptible to fads or "cookie cutter" approaches that may promise elusive results for students. These pursuits can end in accusations of "dumbing down" instruction, simplifying curriculum, or an excessive focus on assessment. Finding "what works" is often more complicated than replicating a program or pursuing an intervention. Leadership and context matter; together they can mean the difference between successful and failed implementation.

Policies that facilitate turnaround may have less connection to the invention itself than the context and support given to the leadership. Turnaround leaders seek capacity-building initiatives that improve instruction and cement high expectations for all students. In the pressurized world of turnaround, they are looking for research-based interventions that increase student achievement, ones that they can then customize to their own environments. They value efforts to remove excessive paperwork requirements, audits, duplicative planning documents, or imposed interventions that take time away from core instruction.

When considering policies that reinforce the innovative work of turnaround leaders, a return to the 2-S Systems-Stakeholders approach (presented in chapter 4) may be helpful. Turnaround starts with understanding the system in which the struggling school operates. It is a system that starts locally but extends upward to state and federal policy levels and outward to feeder schools, community organizations, businesses, churches, and neighborhoods.

Principals are the building-level leaders carrying out policies that sometimes strengthen and other times detract from the necessary and dramatic change they are charged with bringing. Such policies may be district-based or the result of state or federal mandates. Whatever their origin, principals sometimes need the flexibility, authority, and political cover to do what's right for students, rather than what's required for compliance.

Stakeholders can serve an especially important role in supporting policies that facilitate the turnaround. Stakeholders span unions, school boards, leadership associations, universities, employers, churches, and community groups, just to name a few. In a politically charged environment, stakeholders can either accelerate or impede leaders' efforts. As policies flow across the levels of the system, multiple stakeholder groups weigh in on them, strengthening a leader's confidence to move forward or causing concern that may stymie necessary changes.

Policies to Facilitate School Renewal

In the essential work of turnaround, policies can and do make an important difference for the principals and teachers working on school renewal. If turnarounds are to be a viable and sustainable education strategy and discipline, policy makers must consider how to solidify leadership competencies, shore up consistent training, leverage resources across multiple agencies and efforts, and learn from the work that is already being done. To meet this challenge, here are a few capacity-building policy recommendations and how they can be facilitated at the federal, state, and local levels:

Defining Turnarounds

As the nomenclature of school turnarounds becomes well-known, the need to specifically define what constitutes a turnaround is essential. Some programs have used Adequate Yearly Progress and "safe harbor"[26] or state accountability lists to define the sought-after changes. Others look at discipline, graduation rates, and student growth or a combination of indicators as the marks of improvement. Still others take a more holistic approach to turnaround, adding measures of the organization's health, culture, teacher retention, and satisfaction into the mix.

With unprecedented amounts of federal dollars targeted toward chronically underperforming schools, a common definition of success is important. Even if states continue to use their own systems of accountability, when national funds flow to turnaround, what constitutes a turnaround—or at least some general guidelines for assessing the success of a turnaround—becomes a federal policy matter.

National Clearinghouse on School Turnarounds

Many organizations, from consulting firms to multinational corporations, use knowledge-management systems to catalog and utilize the intellectual assets of the organization to solve problems more efficiently and effectively. In the still nascent arena of school turnarounds, federal policy could support the creation of a national clearinghouse on turnaround leadership. Such a system would have stringent criteria by which turnaround successes—and failures—are assessed.

Like the Effective Practices Incentive Community[27] developed by New Leaders for New Schools through the Teacher Incentive Fund grants, such a national system would catalog consistently the practices and cases of documented turnarounds. Multimedia case studies, protocols, techniques, and practices would be catalogued and become readily available to educators.

Professional development modules could offer opportunities for in-service learning sessions on practices or cases most relevant to a school or district's challenges. Practices might be nominated at the local level, validated at the state level, and coordinated federally into a set of tools that could be accessed easily through social networking technologies for real-time support and implementation.

A national effort, designed with support from industry experts who do it best, could be a shared resource, available to turnaround professionals. Rather than a competitive or closed marketplace among a set of strong suppliers, stakeholders involved in school turnarounds might ask themselves whether this urgent work and the students at these underperforming schools deserve a comprehensive and collaborative effort that brings together the knowledge of major philanthropic entities, venture funds, national nonprofits, consulting firms, universities, and other organizations engaged in this work. Can the pressing work of turnaround cause collaboration and drive innovation?

National Turnaround Curriculum Framework

A natural companion to a national clearinghouse on effective turnaround practices would be a body of knowledge on school turnarounds. Based on a set of leadership competencies on turnaround leadership, this framework would guide curricula for credentialing specialists in this field.

The New York City Leadership Academy's Leadership Performance Planning Worksheet might provide a starting point for competency-based curriculum development. The private sector version from the Turnaround Management Association also might offer guidance for such an endeavor, as might the work of the Rainwater Leadership Alliance (RLA), which recently released lessons learned from convening a set of leaders from innovative principal preparation programs.[28]

States like Louisiana are developing curriculum to be used by regional higher education providers. Louisiana's Board of Regents, with support from the Wallace Foundation, is developing curriculum materials including case studies of turnaround schools written by university researchers for its turnaround program. Universities such as University of Virginia and Harvard also have developed case studies and programs that address turnarounds and system-level coherence-building strategies across multiple stakeholder groups.

Nonprofits like KIPP, New Leaders for New Schools, and NYC Leadership Academy and Broad Superintendent's Academy have invested in developing curriculum, simulations, and case studies and other instructional tools that build a competitive advantage for their participants or schools. Mass Insight and the Wallace Foundation continue to tackle district and state impediments to affecting turnarounds. Moreover, the U.S. Department of Education website offers numerous resources, including video segments of successful turnarounds, to spread knowledge and further capacity building.

Taken together, these organizations and others have a collective body of knowledge and leadership development materials that could dramatically accelerate turnaround leadership at the school, district, and state levels. Given the urgency and vastness of chronic underperformance, along with the demand for strong teachers and leaders to take on the challenge of turnaround, the need for such a body of knowledge is clear.

Now is not the time to hoard insights or leave the work to localities to reinvent the wheel. The mission is too urgent and what works can be adapted, validated, and shared in learning communities. Rather than taking the "plant a thousand flowers" strategy, policy makers could support more efforts, like the Rainwater Leadership Alliance (RLA), to bring these talented and committed organizations together to share knowledge. Moreover, they could provide incentives for universities and their respective colleges of education (business and public policy) to work with innovative leadership development organizations to ensure a thoughtful body of knowledge for turnaround leadership is developed and employed in the broader field of education administration. Now is the time to develop turnaround as a legitimate discipline within educational leadership.

National Board Certification

In the private sector, the Turnaround Management Association (TMA) provides programs, testing, and certification for those seeking to become turnaround operators. Courses are offered and materials can be purchased to prepare for an examination that leads to a credential of Certified Turnaround Professional (CTP) on the well-established body of knowledge (written by researchers) on corporate turnarounds. In education, a national board certification process for turnaround leadership could be incorporated into state licensure regulations to recognize those who have demonstrated knowledge and practice in the school turnaround arena.

At the local level, districts may offer recognition and incentives in the form of "distinguished" or "executive" principal or other leadership positions to those who have obtained advanced licensure. At the state level, existing endorsements like Louisiana's could serve as a model to develop tiered licensure systems with appropriate pay differentials based on performance. An association or national certification would allow turnaround operators in education to be purposed across the nation. Whatever the level, a certification or endorsement of the turnaround field brings rigor, accountability, and legitimacy to those demonstrating a skill set that is vital to the well-being of many communities.

PROVIDING INCENTIVES FOR SUSTAINABILITY

In an era of accountability, formulas bring scores and grades that flag schools in distress, bringing sanctions and support to those most in need. Yet, one unintended consequence of the *NCLB* policies was the loss of funds once schools improved. Struggling schools find their way onto a list that brings with it many challenges—audits, choice, and public humiliation among them.

Money for interventions, consultants, and programs can provide precious resources to support instruction.

While getting off "the list" should hail success, in some cases there are disincentives built into the system when schools receiving resources to help facilitate turnarounds lose eligibility because of their improvements. The school leader moves on, and with that principal go the resources that helped reverse the decline. With a positive trajectory come fewer—not more—supports that may have been vital to turnaround. In the worst case, the school's resources decline, and a few years later, scores slide back and underperformance again rules the day.

Given the immense challenges of turnaround, policy makers must strike a careful balance between offering enough resources to facilitate improvement while rewarding results. Resources and interventions must be streamlined and leadership succession thoughtfully considered so that sustainability of results is ensured. Too often, however, a school finds itself broken again; sapped of resources and hurdling obstacles over again. With policies directed at sustaining success, the need for turnaround should lessen and the path to long-term growth should be cleared.

Turning around low-performing schools means that policy makers must grapple with how to apportion scarce resources to best facilitate and sustain improvements in student achievement. Where and how to target these resources and policy actions is challenging, especially as policy actors are often bringing needed voice to schools that otherwise might remain silent. How to spur innovation as well as collaboration takes political will and perseverance. Balancing a federal role with state and local control and sorting through multiple layers of bureaucracies to develop policies that bring out intended results is extremely complicated.

What policy makers and engaged stakeholders must focus on is that chronic underperformance is unacceptable; "the equal treatment of unequals" may not be equal at all; tools and resources facilitate but more is not always better; with autonomy, flexibility and permission to act boldly—and with support—turnaround leaders can help students make dramatic gains; and ensuring success for all students will ensure economic security and prosperity in the future.

IN PURSUIT OF TURNAROUND: LESSONS FROM AN EMERGING FIELD

Stakeholders pursuing the difficult work of turning around schools have a number of interacting elements to consider. There are lessons from history, lessons from policy initiatives, lessons from research, and lessons from those tireless leaders building schools with high expectations and achievement for all students.

This book has attempted to illustrate the importance of turnaround as a subspecialty of educational leadership. It offers stakeholders a 2-S approach and the 3Es organizing framework (Preparing the Environment, Developing the Executive, Focusing on Execution, presented in chapter 5) around which to consider turnaround. It demonstrates a number of tools that can be effective supports for the turnaround leader in action.

As the field develops and turnaround leaders are equipped with the necessary skills to tackle distressed conditions effectively, these lessons may offer insight to stakeholders engaging in this important work.

- Turnaround leaders are born *and* made. Selection and training around the environment, executive, and execution are essential. Part of turnarounds is about getting the right leader. Another part is about ensuring they have the skills and networks to succeed. This field is not for everyone. Turnaround leaders must have the passion, knowledge, and tools to move schools forward.
- Turnaround leaders must be unleashed to get the job done. Once leaders are specially trained, they must have some leeway in which to take risks, succeed, and fail. This includes providing district "cover," advocacy, autonomy, and incentives.
- Turnaround leaders provide instructional and operational strategies that move student achievement. Each case study echoes this point. While structures and processes and even tools may be different for different schools, they must be put in place. Along with a 90-day Plan, each turnaround specialist can implement his or her own Turnaround Value Chain, addressing the influences and influencers that will make a difference for students. Whatever the toolset chosen, turnaround operators determine the critical path to dramatic improvement and take the actions necessary to achieve those gains.
- Turnaround leaders understand that the student, school, district, and larger community are all interconnected. They see the "big picture" and know how to maintain a laser-like focus on student achievement. They integrate and eliminate in pursuit of a cohesive and coherent vision for their schools and communities.
- Turnaround leaders *believe*. These may be leaders at all levels that create and sustain the highest of expectations. They recognize and are able to address stereotypes, implicit biases, and assumptions of those whose expectations are too low. They demand the most of students and extract anything and anyone that doesn't do the same. They believe and also deliver results.

- Turnaround leaders develop successors to sustain improvements. These leaders engage stakeholders and create systems and processes that work. They build successful structures that should be sustained. Most are short-term leaders that like to do this work (and must do this work) over and over again. They are an elite group that thrives in the turnaround environment. Districts must prioritize sustainability so that successors can play an equally important role in furthering student achievement in the post-turnaround context.

Three Game-Changing Imperatives

With so much at stake for so many communities, the questions that lie ahead are many. Turnarounds in schools are happening, but the need continues to outpace the supply of leaders ready to meet the challenge. Unprecedented federal funds are available, and yet the turnaround field is still incubating.

How will the funds be used expeditiously yet effectively to improve the thousands of struggling schools across the nation? How will the turnaround field in education evolve? How will enough turnaround leaders be created to consistently improve schools, and how will those changes be sustained so that this conversation isn't happening again in five or ten years?

There are many answers presented in this book to inform educators and key stakeholders about how to facilitate and support turnarounds at scale. Turnarounds are not about one school; they involve a system. They are not driven by a single inspirational leader but by a team of stakeholders. Turnarounds require planning, developing, and executing with commitment and compassion, transparency, and teamwork. Turnaround leaders have the highest of expectations for every student and never give up on them.

The good news for underserved students is that those weighing in on the work of school turnaround is growing. Major entities including Mass Insight, McKinsey, FSG Social Impact Advisors, NewSchools Venture Fund, the Wallace Foundation, and the Council for Great City Schools to name a few, along with various charter management organizations, innovative nonprofits like Teacher for America, universities, most state departments of education, many districts, the U.S. Department of Education, and many others are urgently and seriously invested in eradicating chronic student underperformance.

For turnaround leadership to have the dramatic success required in struggling schools and for the students they serve, those involved in this work might consider these game-changing imperatives.

1. Establish turnaround leadership as a legitimate subspecialty of the principalship. The emergent nature of the field is clear, but its path as a research discipline in education is less apparent. What is needed is a coordinated

effort to define and refine this specialized field and for universities and others to recognize it as a specialized endorsement within the administrative preparation programs and to identify and develop interdisciplinary faculty and partners best able to support it.
2. Invest in turnaround *successors* as well as turnaround *specialists*. For all the focus on school turnarounds and turnaround leadership, the post-turnaround environment has largely been overlooked. Yet, if significant investments are made in the turnaround itself, then ignoring the succession planning necessary to sustain turnaround will serve only to undercut the legitimacy and long-term success of turnaround strategies and the field itself.

    Succession planning is not in the repertoire of many school systems, and most organizations preparing turnaround leaders provide little if any focus toward sustaining and improving on turnaround results. Turnaround specialists need turnaround successors to carry on their work, and successors need to understand turnaround so they support and grow, rather than recreate anew, when they take over.
3. Engage in meaningful and open dialogue about race and its impact on expectations and student achievement in schools, particularly low-performing ones. For all the focus on achievement gaps, the field guides to turnaround, and the sobering statistics available that show race matters in education, the mention of race, racial stereotypes, implicit racial bias, racial histories and legacies, and racial identity development in children seems noticeably absent.

    Like the challenge of racial bias itself, the problem may be the elephant in the room, yet it remains invisible. Even in CGCS's alarming report on black males, no recommendation addressed the possible effects of teacher expectations, implicit bias, or years of racial legacies and stereotyping on student achievement.

    To be sure, these conversations are difficult. Taboo even. Yet, when policy makers, educators, and those that seem to care so deeply about student success overlook this critical topic, how can solutions be thoughtfully developed? Perhaps it is an honest, painful dialogue about the trade-offs in education and the economy and how our blind spots play into them that can unlock a missing link to student achievement.

CONCLUSION

Courageous leaders are working in schools now, but not enough of them exist, and the scalability of charters and other nontraditional approaches cannot meet the demand for turnarounds in public schools today. Now, it is incumbent on those support players—the leaders outside the classroom—to have the courageous conversations necessary to establish turnaround as a legitimate subspecialty of the principalship.

Such conversations mean addressing legacies of race and income inequalities that plague our communities and our nation. It means convening leaders across organizations and working across states and districts to change systems that impede student achievement. It means analyzing and reporting data with fidelity and reporting on gaps, wherever they are found and no matter how stubborn they may be. It means crossing service boundaries and building capacity within neighborhoods to not only change schools, but parents, businesses, and local opportunities, as well.

It means adapting tools from other fields like management that facilitate strategic conversations and provide critical paths that guide leaders. It means building succession plans that free up turnaround leaders to continue their work while providing skilled successors to further growth. It means accepting that change takes time, more time than the 24-hour news cycle can report with the necessary depth to understand root causes and solutions; more time than a two-year or even four-year election cycle can deliver.

Turnarounds in education can and must deliver thunderous change. But to get there, leaders need others to help them find more time, deliver more direct conversations, and bring greater levels of transparency to the problems they see. They need others to have more heart and to bring more help. A turnaround mindset can transform schools, and high achievement will become a reality for all of our young people.

NOTES

1. Fuhrman, S. (1993). "The Politics of Coherence." In S. Fuhrman (Ed.) *Designing coherent education policy: Improving the system* (1–34). San Francisco: Jossey-Bass.

2. Elmore, R.F. (1990). *Restructuring schools: The next generation of educational reform.* San Francisco: Jossey-Bass.

3. Elmore, R.F. (2004). "Conclusion: The problem of stakes in performance-based accountability systems" in *Redesigning accountability systems for education.* (274–296). Fuhrman, S.H. & Elmore, R.F. (Eds.) New York: Teachers College Press.

4. Hess, Frederick M. & Petrilli, Michael J. (2008, December 23) "Bush the Hall Monitor," National Review Online. http://www.nationalreview.com/articles/226594/bush-hall-monitor/frederick-m-hess. Accessed 11-8-10.

5. See Schwartz, P. (1991). *The art of the long view: paths to the future in an uncertain world.* New York: Currency Doubleday.

6. Five thousand underperforming schools is about 5 percent of the nearly 100,000 public elementary and secondary schools in the U.S. National Center for Education Statistics, *Fast Facts. 2007–2008.* http://nces.ed.gov/fastfacts/display.asp?id=84. Accessed 11-8-10.

7. Childress, S., Elmore, R., Grossman, A., and King, C. (2007) *Note on the PELP Coherence Framework.* Public Education Leadership Project at Harvard University. PEL-010. This framework focuses on connecting the instructional core with a district-wide improvement strategy and considers the elements and interdependences and environment forces impacting that strategy.

8. http://www2.ed.gov/programs/racetothetop/index.html. Accessed 6-27-10.

9. http://www.nasbe.org/leadership/information by state/virginia/state-profile/case-study. Accessed 6-26-10.

10. Zuckerman, E. (2010, January 27) "School reform still evolving in New Haven." *Yale Daily News.* http://www.yaledailynews.com/news/city-news/2010/01/27/school-reform-still-evolving-new-haven. Accessed 6-27-10.

11. Turque, B. (2010, June 3). "D.C. teachers' union ratifies contract, basing pay on results, not seniority." *The Washington Post.* http://www.washingtonpost.com/wp-dyn/content/article/2010/06/02/AR2010060202762.html?sid=ST2010060202812. Accessed 6-26-10.

12. http://www.leadlouisiana.net/index.asp. Accessed 6-27-10.

13. http://www.leadlouisiana.net/la_state_turnaround_specialist_program.asp. Accessed 6-27-10.

14. Ibid.

15. Bulletin 746. Item 710 HISTORICAL NOTE: Promulgated by the Board of Elementary and Secondary Education, LR 35:645 (April 2009).

16. http://www.nlns.org/Locations_NewOrleans.jsp#results. Accessed 6-27-10.

17. BESE provided funding for the LSTS through what is known as 8-G funding, a set of discretionary funds resulting from a mineral settlement that Louisiana voters chose to target to education, which is at the disposal of BESE. http://www.louisianaschools.net/LDE/bese/1081.html. Accessed 3-19-10.

18. Fairfax County Public Schools. School Profiles. 2009–2010. http://schoolprofiles.fcps.edu/schlprfl/f?p=108:13:163087688262752::::P0_CURRENT_SCHOOL_ID:100. Accessed 11-8-10.

19. Liedtke, J., Fairchild, T., and Kelly, D. (2005). J.E.B. Stuart High School. Darden Case Collection. Charlottesville, VA: Darden Business Publishing. UVA-OB-0853. Quotation as cited in case from Benning, Victoria, *The Washington Post,* "Fairfax to Build Up Failing High Schools; Extra Resources Tied to Improvement." February 18, 2000.

20. https://p1pe.doe.virginia.gov/reportcard/report.do?division=29&schoolName=1369. Accessed 6-26-10.

21. Reid, Zachary. (2009, February 2). "School thrives under principal's firm hand," *Richmond Times Dispatch.*

22. Orfield, G. (2001). *Schools more separate: Consequences of a decade of resegregation.* Cambridge, MA: Civil Rights Project, Harvard University.

23. A study by The Civil Rights Project at UCLA found black students in charters schools to have even more isolated experiences than their traditional public school counterparts. Frankenberg, E., Siegel-Hawley, G., and Wang, J. (2010, February). *Choice without equity: Charter school segregation and the need for civil rights standards.* Los Angeles: Civil Rights Project / Proyecto Derechos Civiles. http://civilrightsproject.ucla.edu/research/k-12-education/integration-and-diversity. Accessed 11-10-10.

24. Tuttle, C.C., Teh, B., Nichols-Barrer, I., Gill, B.P., and Gleason, P. (2010). *Student characteristics and achievement in 22 KIPP middle schools.* Washington, DC: Mathematica Policy Research, Inc. http://www.mathematica-mpr.com/publications/pdfs/education/KIPP_fnlrpt.pdf. Accessed 6-26-10.

25. Crain, R.L., and Strauss, J. (1985) *School desegregation and Black occupational attainment: Results from a long-term experiment.* Johns Hopkins University, Washington, D.C.: Center for Social Organization of School for the National Institute of Education.

26. Safe harbor provisions under NCLB allow schools an alternate means to demonstrate Adequate Yearly Progress (generally by reducing the failure rate in English Language Arts or mathematics by 10 percent).

27. http://www.nlns.org/epic.jsp. Accessed 6-27-10.

28. Rainwater Leadership Alliance (2010). *A New Approach to Principal Preparation: Innovative Programs Share Their Practices and Lessons Learned.* Fort Worth, TX: Cheney G. R., Davis, J., Garrett, K., and Holleran, J.

Appendix A

A NATION AT RISK: FACTORS FOR URGENCY

The National Commission on Excellence in Education cited the following factors as evidence of the urgency for action:

- International comparisons of student achievement, completed a decade ago, reveal that on nineteen academic tests American students were never first or second and, in comparison with other industrialized nations, were last seven times.
- Some 23 million American adults are functionally illiterate by the simplest tests of everyday reading, writing, and comprehension.
- About 13 percent of all seventeen-year-olds in the United States can be considered functionally illiterate. Functional illiteracy among minority youth may run as high as 40 percent.
- Average achievement of high school students on most standardized tests is now lower than twenty-six years ago when Sputnik was launched.
- Over half the population of gifted students do not match their tested ability with comparable achievement in school.
- The College Board's Scholastic Aptitude Tests (SAT) demonstrate a virtually unbroken decline from 1963 to 1980. Average verbal scores fell over fifty points, and average mathematics scores dropped nearly forty points.
- College Board achievement tests also reveal consistent declines in recent years in such subjects as physics and English.
- Both the number and proportion of students demonstrating superior achievement on the SATs (i.e., those with scores of 650 or higher) have also dramatically declined.

- Many seventeen-year-olds do not possess the "higher order" intellectual skills we should expect of them. Nearly 40 percent cannot draw inferences from written material; only one-fifth can write a persuasive essay; and only one-third can solve a mathematics problem requiring several steps.
- There was a steady decline in science achievement scores of U.S. seventeen-year-olds as measured by national assessments of science in 1969, 1973, and 1977.
- Between 1975 and 1980, remedial mathematics courses in public four-year colleges increased by 72 percent and now constitute one-quarter of all mathematics courses taught in those institutions.
- Average tested achievement of students graduating from college is also lower.
- Business and military leaders complain that they are required to spend millions of dollars on costly remedial education and training programs in such basic skills as reading, writing, spelling, and computation. The Department of the Navy, for example, reported to the Commission that one-quarter of its recent recruits cannot read at the ninth grade level, the minimum needed simply to understand written safety instructions. Without remedial work, they cannot even begin, much less complete, the sophisticated training essential in much of the modern military.

Source: The National Commission on Excellence in Education (1983). *A Nation At Risk: The Imperative for Educational Reform.* Pp. 8–9. U.S. Department of Education.

Appendix B

RESOURCES ON SCHOOL TURNAROUNDS

For a more detailed review of the scholarship, the authors suggest:

Murphy, J.F., and Meyers, C.V. (2008). *Turning around failing schools: Leadership lessons from the organizational sciences.* Thousand Oaks, CA: Corwin Press.

For additional insights and frameworks, the authors suggest the following major reports that are shaping how turnarounds are being pursued in schools.

Herman, R., Dawson, P., Dee, T., Greene, J., Maynard, R., Redding, S., and Darwin, M. "Turning Around Chronically Low-Performing Schools: A Practice Guide." National Center for Education Evaluation and Regional Assistance, Institute of Education Sciences, U.S. Department of Education, 2008.

Kowal, J. M., Hassel, E.A. and Hassel, B.C. (2009, September 15). "Issue Brief: Successful School Turnarounds: Seven Steps for District Leaders." Center for Comprehensive School Reform and Innovation.

Kutash, J., Nico. (2010). School Turnaround Field Guide FSG Social Impact Advisors.

Mass Insight Education. (2007). "The Turnaround Challenge" and "The Turnaround Challenge: Supplement to the Main Report."

New Leaders for New Schools. (2009). Principal Effectiveness: A New Principalship to Drive Student Achievement, Teacher Effectiveness, and School Turnaround with Key Insights from UEF.™ New York: New Leaders for New Schools.

Public Impact. (2008a, June). *School turnaround leaders: Competencies for success. Part of the Turnaround Collection from Public Impact.* Public Impact for the Chicago Public Education Fund. Chapel Hill, NC: Steiner, L. M., Hassel, E. A., Hassel, B., and Valsing, E. http://www.publicimpact.com/publications/Turnaround_Leader_Selection_Toolkit.pdf. Accessed 10-15-10.

Public Impact. (2008b, June). *School turnaround Leaders: Selection toolkit. Part of the Turnaround Collection from Public Impact.* Public Impact for the Chicago Public Education Fund. Chapel Hill, NC: Steiner, L. M., Hassel, E. A., Hassel, B., Valsing, E., and Crittenden, S. http://www.publicimpact.com/publications/Turnaround_Leader_Selection_Toolkit.pdf. Accessed 10-15-10.

Rainwater Leadership Alliance. (2010). A New Approach to Principal Preparation: Innovative Programs Share Their Practices and Lessons Learned. Fort Worth, TX: Cheney, G. R., Davis, J., Garrett, K., and Holleran, J.

Scott, C. (2009). "Improving Low-Performing Schools: Lessons from Five Years of Studying School Restructuring Under No Child Left Behind," Center on Education Policy.

Appendix C

MEMORANDUM OF UNDERSTANDING

Types may include:

- MOU between district and turnaround principal
- MOU between turnaround partner and district
- MOU between state, turnaround partner, district, and/or principal

SAMPLE MOU BETWEEN DISTRICT AND SCHOOL

(administered by turnaround partner)

This Memorandum of Understanding (the "Agreement"), dated as of _____, _____ (the "Commencement Date"), by and between the _____ (the "School District") and _____ (the "Principal").

RECITALS

WHEREAS, "Turnaround Partner Name" and the "State Name or other Partner" have jointly developed the "Turnaround Specialist Program Name" the Principal has completed (or will complete) Turnaround Program (T/A Program). The School District now wishes to employ the Principal at the _____ school (the "School") to apply the methods of the T/A program to the School.

NOW, THEREFORE, the parties hereby agree as follows:

1.0 DUTIES OF SCHOOL

1.1 The School District will employ the Principal for a minimum of _____ years. The School District will offer the Principal the salary, benefits, and performance-based incentives set forth on <u>Exhibit A</u>.

1.2 The School District will cooperate with the Principal and Turnaround Partners in implementing the school turnaround plan devised for the School by the Principal and the T/A program. The School District hereby promises to use its best efforts to allocate the resources and personnel requested by the Principal or the T/A program to develop, implement, and administer the school turnaround plan. These efforts will include providing sufficient time and funding to the Principal to attend any follow-up training or additional meetings related to the T/A Program as requested.

1.3 The School District shall use the performance criteria and goals set forth in <u>Exhibit B</u> to evaluate the performance of the Principal.

1.4 The School District shall ensure that the Principal shall have the following [**List *specific* items, amounts, and powers:** Examples Include: The School District shall provide additional funds to the School to be used at the Principal's discretion for the purchase of instructional materials, technology for staff/students, and staff development or other items deemed necessary by the Principal for the improvement of the School. The School District shall provide additional funds to support staff development/training needs unique to the School. The School District shall provide teachers at the School with an additional stipend for classroom materials. The School District shall provide the Principal with increased autonomy in the area of recruitment and hiring of needed teachers and support staff to help implement the turnaround plan for the School.

1.5 The School District shall also use its best efforts to provide the Principal with the following [**List more generalized items and powers:** Examples Include: The School District shall provide funding, personnel, and planning assistance in the focus areas established by the Principal through the use of the School District's resources, grants, partners, mentors, coaches, or other interested parties. The Principal shall designate the kinds of required assistance in these focus areas needed by the School in accordance with the School's improvement plan or the Principal's interaction with the Turnaround Partner. The School District shall provide similar support of Principal in efforts to improve discipline (such as with school-wide student behavior plans, uniforms, or other methods), improve attendance, reduce truancy, improve time on task, implement alternative instructional grouping strategies, remediation programs, or other long-term School improvement goals. The School District shall provide funds for additional staffing needs unique to the School (such as in-school suspension monitors, instructional aides, after-school program instructors, technology support, grade level team leader, or improved clerical support). The School District shall provide the School with increased funds to ensure reduced pupil-teacher ratio (at critical designated grade levels). The School District shall provide the Principal with any requested support technology (such as a laptop, blackberry, PDA, or other educational technology).

2.0 TERM
The initial term of this Agreement shall begin as of the Commencement Date and shall continue in force for a period of three (3) years from the Commencement Date. This Agreement shall be renewed for successive renewal terms of one (1) year, as long as neither party provides written notice to the contrary up to thirty (30) days prior to the termination of the initial term or at any time during a renewal term.

3.0 REPRESENTATIONS AND WARRANTIES
Each party hereto hereby warrants and represents that it has the right to enter into this Agreement and to grant the rights herein granted and that it has not and will not assign, pledge, or encumber such rights.

4.0 ASSIGNMENT
This Agreement may not be assigned by School District without the Principal's prior written consent. This Agreement may not be assigned by the Principal without the School District's prior written consent. This Agreement shall be binding upon and inure to the benefit of the successors and permitted assigns of the parties.

5.0 SURVIVAL
The warranties, representations, and covenants herein contained shall survive the expiration or earlier termination of this Agreement for a period of one year.

6.0 WAIVER
A waiver of any breach of this Agreement, or of any of the terms or conditions by either party, shall not be deemed a waiver of any repetition of such breach or in any way affect any other terms or conditions hereof. No waiver shall be valid or binding unless it shall be in writing and signed by the parties.

7.0 GOVERNING LAW

This Agreement is subject to and will be construed in accordance with the laws of the [STATE] applicable to agreements wholly to be performed therein, and the parties hereby agree that any legal action hereunder shall be instituted within the [STATE].

8.0 ENTIRE AGREEMENT

This Agreement evidences the complete understanding and agreement of the parties with respect to the subject matter hereof and supersedes and merges all previous proposals, contracts, communications, representations, understandings and agreements, whether oral or written, between the parties with respect to the subject matter hereof. This Agreement may not be modified except in writing executed by authorized representatives of both parties.

9.0 COUNTERPARTS

This Agreement may be executed in any number of counterparts and may be executed with a facsimile signature.

IN WITNESS WHEREOF, the parties have duly executed this Memorandum of Understanding.

The School District
By: _____(signature, title & date)

The Principal
By: _____(signature, title & date)

EXHIBIT A

Salary, Benefits, and Performance Incentives

<u>Salary:</u> Principal shall be paid $ _____ per (year/month).

<u>Benefits:</u> Principal shall receive the following benefits (such as: medical/dental/life insurance/short-term disability/long-term disability/pension/401(K) or 403(B) retirement plan/tuition assistance/vacation/sick leave/personal leave).

<u>Professional development assistance:</u> such as subscriptions to professional educational journals or memberships to professional educational organizations. Provide funding and the appropriate time for the Principal's

continuing professional development to attend state or national educational conferences.

Menu of Possible Incentives:

Participate in the defined contribution plan (as set forth in Virginia HB 576) for the Principal with payment from the School District of $_____ per year.

Full Payment of insurance benefit costs for (medical / dental / life insurance / short-term disability / long-term disability) by the School District.

Initial signing bonus of $ _____.

Provide pay differential of $_____ or annual stipend of $_____ per year.

Housing assistance of $ _____ per (year/month).

Relocation expenses of $ _____.

Payment of Retirement Plan (such as a 403(B) plan) contribution for the Principal by the School District of $_____ per year (or the then current maximum allowed contribution by federal tax year per year). Vesting would be immediate.

Matching of the Principal's contribution to the Retirement Plan (such as a 403(B) plan), and a ratio of [2 to 1, in which the School District contributes two dollars for every one paid in by the Principal] up to $_____ per year (or until the account reaches the then current maximum allowed contribution by federal tax year per year). Vesting of both Principal and School District contributions would be immediate.

School District could fund a Roth IRA account in the name of the Principal at $_____ per year (or until the account reaches the then current maximum allowed contribution by federal tax year per year).

Payment of commuting costs of $_____ per (year/month). Or the payment of a vehicle allowance of $_____ per year. Or the use of a city/county vehicle. Or a combination of these benefits as appropriate.

Specific Bonuses for achievement of predetermined performance goals such as: _____.

Subsidized (or free child care) of $ _____ per (year/month).

Reimbursement for cell phone use or provision of a School District–paid cell phone.

Annual reimbursement for unused annual/sick leave at a per diem rate of $_____ per _____.

EXHIBIT B

Performance Criteria and Goals

Examples Include:

- Existing Achievement Data
- Goals & Targets by Subject, Subpopulation
- Timeframe to Achieve

Appendix D

Turnaround Specialist Endorsement

STATE OF LOUISIANA

§710. Turnaround Specialist Endorsement (Optional)
A. The Louisiana School Turnaround Specialist Program (LSTS) is a leadership development program designed to strengthen the organizational and instructional leadership skills of currently certified and experienced principals to prepare them to lead low-performing schools to higher student achievement. This endorsement is valid for five years and is renewable based upon successful completion and verification of required continuing learning units.

1. To receive a Turnaround Specialist Endorsement the individual must meet all of the following requirements:
   a. hold a valid Level 2, Level 3, Type B, Type A, or out-of-state (OS) certificate with three years of teaching in the certified area and certification as an elementary/secondary principal, principal, or educational leader;
   b. successfully complete the LSTS Program;
   c. meet all achievement targets which are a part of the LSTS program;
   d. receive the recommendation of the Louisiana employing authority.

2. Renewal Requirements. For the purpose of maintaining a valid endorsement, holders of the Turnaround Specialist Endorsement are required to complete 150 continuing learning units (CLUs) of professional development consistent with the Individual Professional Growth Plan (IPGP).

a. If an individual holds a Louisiana Level 2 or 3 teaching certificate, then the renewal date is tied to the renewal date on the teaching certificate.
b. If an individual does not hold a Louisiana Level 2 or 3 teaching certificate, but does hold an educational leader endorsement, then the renewal date is tied to the renewal date on the educational leader endorsement.
c. If an individual holds neither a Louisiana Level 2 nor Level 3 teaching certificate nor an Educational Leader endorsement, then the renewal time period begins with the date of issue of the Turnaround Specialist Endorsement.

AUTHORITY NOTE: Promulgated in accordance with R.S. 17:6 (A)(10), (11), (15); R.S. 17:7(6); R.S. 17:10; R.S. 17:22(6); R.S. 17:391.1ñ391.10; R.S. 17:411.
HISTORICAL NOTE: Promulgated by the Board of Elementary and Secondary Education, LR 35:645 (April 2009).

Source: Louisiana Department of Education. Bulletin 746—Louisiana Standards for State Certification of School Personnel. Title 28, Part XIII, Louisiana Administrative Code, December 2009. p.64.

Appendix E

90 DAY STRATEGIC PLAN

The Kate Middleton Way (TKM Way)

September 13, 2008

		Timeline			Intended Result	
Area of Focus	Deliverable (What)	30 Days	60 Days	90 Days	(Outcome)	Person Responsible
Examine data for returning and new students	Data wall Interval assessment results Small group lists Spreadsheet	✓	✓	✓	Meaningful students engaged instruction based upon student data	Aretha E. Williams
Conduct data analysis by grade level teachers w/ principal & coach	Data wall Calendar of meeting dates/times Teacher Next Steps Teacher reflections Personal meetings with students Photos Student Achievement Report	✓	✓	✓	Teachers will use data results to plan, progress monitor, provide interventions, and remediate for student improvement	Aretha E. Williams
Create weekly Grade 4 GLE online assessments in ELA and math using EAGLE.	Grade 4 EAGLE ELA and math assessments Assessment Results Data wall	✗	✗	✗	Teachers will use data results to plan, progress monitor, provide interventions, and remediate for student improvement	Aretha E. Williams
Provide focused professional development Book study	**Good To Great** Book Calendar of study dates Study sign in sheet Study agenda with discussion questions School's Next Steps Teacher reflections with successes and challenges Photos	✓	✓	✓	Meaningful planned and executed engaging lessons for all students in PK-5	Aretha E. Williams

		Timeline				
Area of Focus	Deliverable (What)	30 Days	60 Days	90 Days	Intended Result (Outcome)	Person Responsible
Provide focused professional development Book study Require rigor in attire, grooming, speech, writing, attitude, and demeanor.	**Close the Achievement Gap Book** PBS Code of Conduct Calendar of study dates Study sign in sheet Study agenda with discussion questions Teacher Next Steps Teacher reflections with successes and challenges Photos		✓	X	Highly focused students engaged in meaningful planned instruction based upon student data Teachers setting the examples for students in the areas of attire, grooming, speech, writing, attitude, and demeanor.	Aretha E. Williams
Keep the momentum	Photos Monthly celebrations Teacher reflections with successes and challenges	✓	✓	✓	Highly focused students and staff	Aretha E. Williams
Provide appropriate early bird and twilight tutoring for students based upon achievement data	Participating student list based upon current student achievement data Observation sheet VMath and Literacy materials in use iLEAP/LEAP writing rubric, and Non fiction texts for Grades K, 1, 2, 3, 4, & 5 in use Photos	✓	✓	✓	Improved academic achievement on district assessments and statewide testing	Aretha E. Williams

Area of Focus	Deliverable (What)	Timeline 30 Days	Timeline 60 Days	Timeline 90 Days	Intended Result (Outcome)	Person Responsible
Create a safe and orderly environment based upon the PBS data. Create smoother transitions	Data wall tracking transition incidents PBS—TKM Way Code of Conduct Photos	✓	✓	X	Reduction in number of high level offense referrals during transitions (PE, lunch, change of classes)	Aretha E. Williams
Conduct a face to face w/ cafe manager concerning food preparation and service	Plan for better food preparation New plan for faster service Photos Student satisfaction survey	✓	X	z	Children served in a timely fashion	Aretha E. Williams
Improve Campus Appearance	Number of painted classrooms Number of painted student bathrooms Number of classrooms with new ceiling tiles Number of painted classrooms with dry erase boards Campus curb appeal—landscape Photos Security gate Handicap entrance ramp	✓ z	✓ z	✓ z	An attractive environment conducive to learning	Aretha E. Williams
Provide sufficient faculty restroom facilities	Number of new faculty restrooms Photos	z	z	z	Additional faculty restroom facilities	Aretha E. Williams
Determine areas of greatest need for student achievement	Balanced Scorecard (BSC) Data wall Photos	✓	✓	✓	BSC will identify areas of need to benchmark and track improvement	Aretha E. Williams

✓ = Meets Expectations
X = Improving But Needs Attention
z = Not Meeting Expectations

2ND 90-DAY STRATEGIC PLAN

The Kate Middleton Way (TKM Way)

Area of Focus	Deliverable (What)	Timeline 30 Days	Timeline 60 Days	Timeline 90 Days	Intended Result (Outcome)	Person Responsible
Math GLEs in grades 2–5	EAGLE software will be used to help teachers design appropriate test items that focus on precision GLEs Photos Agenda of Training Evaluation from Training	✓	✓	✓	Teachers will be trained on their collaborative planning time. Follow up will occur each week as principal, PDRT, and math facilitators meet to test questions. Successful staff will share their results with others and assist others as needed.	Aretha E. Williams Harriet Hillson
Firm up dates with team and create a more cohesive master calendar	Master Calendar for remainder of 2009 school year Copy of Calendar to all staff Photos	✓	✓	✓	Calendar delivered. All events and sponsors will be documented that have to do with school improvement. Secondary items will be included.	Aretha E. Williams Jessica Radovich Laura Falati
BSC and 2nd Semester 90-day Plan	Increase team to include more teacher leaders that will do weekly monitoring of peers, data and report out at each Tues. 7:15 a.m. meeting. Sign In sheet of all team members. Weekly meetings Meeting Agendas Photos	✓	✓	✓	Teachers will use data results and assist peers in taking ownership of their class data to drive math best practices. Take a closer look at IA results and plan for a new lesson design to teach hard-to-reach students and those that should have passed.	Aretha E. Williams Lisa Savage Ranell Jones Cathy Inch Cherie Johnson
Job-embedded Professional Development in Math	Math Consultant Math Strategist PDRT Principal PBS/United Streaming State Website Master Math Teacher videos Photos	✓	✓	✓	Consultant\Strategist will observe, model, give feedback, have conferences with teachers and principal on a weekly, biweekly basis PDRT, Principal will team teach, model and provide teachers with feedback. Videos and websites will be used to enhance math lessons.	Aretha E. Williams Kathy Ross Joan Albrecht Lynn Williams

Appendix F

ST. HELENA CENTRAL HIGH SCHOOL

Balanced Scorecard for 2007–2008

Mission Statement: The mission of St. Helena Central High School is to provide all students an opportunity to build character and achieve academic excellence.

Vision Statement: St. Helena High School is dedicated to providing the highest quality education with the cornerstone of value learning and self-worth among students and faculty for a productive transition in society at large.

Goals:
Goal 1: Foster Community Collaboration
Goal 2: Fully implement School-Wide Positive Behavior
Goal 3: Improve the quality of instruction for lesson effectiveness
Goal 4: Fully implement School-Wide Positive Behavior
Goal 5: Improve the quality of delivery of instruction

Goals and Strategic Objectives (by goal)		Measures	Baseline (where are we now)	2008	2010 Target	Responsibility
Goal 1: Improve Academic Achievement						
1.1 Increase School Performance Score by at least 7.5 pts.	1.1a	Conduct weekly professional development for continuous use of the LCC (La. Comp. Curr.) as the main source for planning unit plans and lessons	58.7%	65.1%	85.5%	Principal, DE, & Supervisor
1.2 80% of students will reach high standards attaining proficiency or better in reading/language arts and math	1.2a	Organize a tutorial pullout program for students during the regular school day requiring additional practice while addressing these deficiencies	56.8%	65.1%	81.7%	Principal, Guidance Counselor, DE, & Remediation Teachers
1.3 Increase the percentage of students passing iLEAP & GEE (Graduate Exit Exam) by 75%	1.3a	Administer formative assessment (Edusoft Testing) with GEE/iLEAP like rigor at the end of each unit in core subject areas and review/post data on display data board	56.8%	65.1%	81.7%	Teachers & DE
1.4 Increase the school's ACT/SAT Composite score to state average of 20	1.4a	Organize computer Study Skills classes for students seeking acceptance in higher education programs	16%	18%	23%	School Leadership Team
1.5 Decrease the number of students requiring extensive Carnegie credits by 50%	1.5a	Initiate a Credit Recovery Program during after school hours for students lacking Carnegie credits in Alg. 1, Geometry & Biology			100%	Bldg. Administration
1.6 Increase the number of students by 50% participating in technical classes	1.6a	Offer dual enrollment opportunity at no cost to student at Technical College contingent upon ACT or PLAN test scores				Principal & Guidance Counselor
1.7 Increase the number of students completing 4.5 credits during the freshmen year by 95% or more	1.7a	Require 100% of all students in 9th grade to engage in a smaller learning community for greater student success by creating a Freshmen Academy				Building Administration

Goals and Strategic Objectives (by goal)		Measures	Baseline (where are we now)	2008	2010 Target	Responsibility
Goal 2: Improve Student Attendance						
2.1 Increase 9th–12th grade overall attendance	2.1a	Enforce school attendance policy daily by monitoring students' attendance and discussing truancy with parents/guardians	96.2%	98.2%	99.0%	Principal, Guidance Counselor, & Parent Facilitator
	2.1b	Display attendance graphs to show attendance comparison each 9-week period				Dean of Students
	2.1c	Monitor student attendance and absence through a computerized attendance record keeping system track of any unexcused absences daily				Superintendent, Supervisor, Bldg. Administration
	2.1d	Refer students to outside agencies after each 3rd absence				Guidance Counselor
	2.1e	Hold a drawing/special recognition assembly or other special events for good attendance				Dean of Students
Goal 3: Community Collaboration						
3.1 Increase Parental Involvement in sponsored activities by 50%	3.1a	Host parental involvement activities at varied times to solicit greater participation	25.0%	60.0%	100.0%	Bldg. Administration & faculty
	3.1b	Promote activities to solicit parent volunteers throughout the school day	unknown	20 hrs. per mth	50 hrs. per mth	Bldg. Administration, Parent Organization, & Parent Facilitator
	3.1c	Promote a Career Exploration fair to include parent participation during the Fall and Spring semesters	25.0%	60.0%	100.0%	Guidance Counselor, Vocational Counselor, & Parent Facilitator
	3.1d	Organize conferences with parents to review and sign their child's five-year plan	50.0%	90.0%	100.0%	Guidance Counselor
	3.1e	Teachers will plan interactive homework assignments to involve parents across the curriculum	unknown	25.0%	75.0%	Bldg. Administration & faculty
	3.1f	Update school's website for parents to visit with pertinent information of value for parents and the community at large	154,000 (since construction for 3yrs.)	unknown	100% usage	Bldg. Administration & district webmaster

Goals and Strategic Objectives (by goal)		Measures	Baseline (where are we now)	2008	2010 Target	Responsibility
Goal 4: To fully implement School-Wide Positive Behavior Program						
4.1 To decrease student behavioral referrals	4.1a	Percent of behavioral referrals as documented in JPAM's Data System	19.3%	9.65%	4.82%	Bldg. Administration, & faculty
	4.2b	Percent of students eligible for positive behavior rewards	unknown	75%	100%	Bldg. Administration, & faculty
Goal 5: To incorporate varied instructional strategies for lesson effectiveness based upon the components of effective teaching and current research practices						
5.1 To participate in ongoing professional development	5.1a	Percentage of students' time on task (Stallings Snapshot)	25%	75%	100%	DE, Bldg. Administration, & School Leadership Team
	5.2b	Formative and Summative Assessment Results	unknown	16%	100%	DE, Bldg. Administration, & EAG Team
	5.3c	Percentage of teachers using Higher Order Thinking strategies	25%	80%	100%	DE, Supervisor, & Bldg. Administration
	5.5e	VTBS (Virgilio Teacher Behavior Inventory)	25%	75%	100%	DE, Supervisor, & Bldg. Administration
	5.7g	Curriculum Alignment based on state standards, grade level expectations, and benchmarks	50%	100%	100%	DE, Supervisor, & Bldg. Administration
	5.8h	Ruby Payne's Framework for Understanding Poverty (Book study)	25%	100%	100%	DE, Supervisor, & Bldg. Administration

Appendix G

Communications Plan Template for Turnaround Initiative

Responsible Party			
Objective #			
Explanation of objective:			
Targeted Stakeholder(s)	**Strategic Actions**	**Necessary Materials**	**Important Notes**
District Superintendents			
School Boards			
Potential Turnaround Principals			
State Officials			
Foundations or Other Partners			
Other Key Stakeholders			
General Public			

Appendix H

Turnaround Readiness Sequence Template for Program Planning and Execution

Turnaround Readiness Sequence

	Stakeholder		Turnaround Element				
			Selection of Schools	State, District, School MOAs	Incentives	Procedures (paperwork, programs)	Degrees of Freedom
						Other Enabling Conditions:	
Turnaround Partners *supporting* ⬇	State	Governor					
		Dept. of Education					
		Dept. of Higher Education					
		Board of Education					
	University	Business					
		Education					
		Other					
	Other Program Partners	Recruiting					
		Support					
		Delivery					
	Special Interests	Associations					
		Foundations					
Turnaround Professionals *enabling*	School District	School Board					
		Central Office					
		School					
		Parents					
		Community					
	Principals	Experienced					
		Emerging					
		Potential Successors					
	Staff	Assistant Principal					
		Teachers					
Achievement	Readiness Indicators						

References

After Action Review process (AAR): Learning from your actions sooner rather than later. http://www.mindtools.com/pages/article/newPPM_73.htm. Accessed 6-22-10.

American Society for Quality. (2010). "The Baldrige criteria for performance excellence." http://asq.org/learn-about-quality/malcolm-baldrige-award/overview/overview.html. Accessed 10-15-10.

Ansell, D. (2004). *Improving Schools Facing Challenging Circumstances.* Nottingham, England: National College for School Leadership.

Beer, M., and Nohria, N. (2000). "Cracking the code of change." *Harvard Business Review,* 78(3), 133–141.

Bibeault, D.G. (1982). *Corporate turnaround: How managers turn losers into winners.* New York: McGraw Hill.

Blankstein, A.M. (2004). *Failure is not an option: Six principles that guide student achievement in high performing schools.* Thousand Oaks, CA: Corwin Press.

Boyne, G.A. (2004). "A '3Rs' strategy for public service turnaround: Retrenchment, repositioning, and reorganization." *Public Money & Management,* 24(2), 97–103.

Brooks, D. (2009, May 7). "The Harlem miracle." *The New York Times.* http://www.nytimes.com/2009/05/08/opinion/08brooks.html. Accessed 10-3-10.

Bryk, A.S., Sebring, P.B., Allensworth, E., Luppescu, S., and Easton, J.Q. (2009). *Organizing schools for improvement: Lessons from Chicago.* Chicago: Chicago University Press.

Burbach, H., Kelly, D., and West, J. (2005). *Stephen H. Clarke Academy (A).* Darden Business Publishing. UVA-OB-0857.

Burbank, R. (1995). "The classic five-step turnaround process: Case study of Prodigene, Inc." *The Journal of Private Equity, Special Turnaround Management Issue,* Spring 2005, 53–58.

Center for Research on Education Outcomes (CREDO). (2009, June). *Multiple choice: Charter school performance in 16 states.* Palo Alto, CA. http://credo.stanford.edu/reports/MULTIPLE_CHOICE_CREDO.pdf. Accessed 11-10-10.

Chang, C. (2010, September 14). "Pastorek presents plan for eventual return of New Orleans schools; read the plan." *The Times-Picayune.* http://www.nola.com/education/index.ssf/2010/09/pastorek_present_plan_for_retu.html. Accessed 10-2-10.

Chenoweth, K. (2007). *It's being done: Academic success in unexpected schools.* Cambridge, MA: Harvard Education Press.

Chenoweth, K. (2007b, April 11). "It's being done." *Education Week.*

Childress, S., Elmore, R., Grossman, A., and King, C. (2007). *Note on the PELP Coherence Framework.* Public Education Leadership Project at Harvard University. PEL-010.

Chung, J. (2009, April 20). "History's verdict: What 100 days can reveal." *The Wall Street Journal.* http://online.wsj.com/article/SB124096652262466393.html. Accessed 6-25-10.

Collins, J. (2001). *Good to great: Why some companies make the leap and others don't.* New York: HarperCollins.

Collins, J. (2005). *Good to great and the social sectors: A monograph to accompany good to great.* New York: HarperCollins.

Collins, J., and Porras, J.I. (1994). *Built to last: Successful habits of visionary companies.* New York: HarperBusiness.

Committee on Education and Labor. (2009, May 12). "High school dropout crisis threatens U.S. economic growth and competiveness, witnesses tell house panel." Press Release. http://edlabor.house.gov/newsroom/2009/05/high-school-dropout-crisis-thr.shtml. Accessed 5-10-10.

Corcoran, S.P., Schwartz, A.E., and Weinstein, M. (2009, August). *The New York City Aspiring Principals Program: A school-level evaluation.* New York: Institute for Education and Social Policy, New York University.

Council of the Great City Schools (2010). *A call for change: The social and educational factors contributing to the outcomes of Black males in urban schools.* Washington, D.C.: Lews, S., Simon, C., Uzzel, R., Horwitz, A., and Casserly, M.

Crain, R.L., and Strauss, J. (1985). *School desegregation and black occupational attainment: Results from a long-term experiment.* Johns Hopkins University, Washington, D.C.: Center for Social Organization of School for the National Institute of Education.

D'Amico, J.J. (2001). "A closer look at the minority achievement gap." *ERS Spectrum,* Spring 2001, 1–8.

Dillon, S. (2009, June 1). "U.S. effort to reshape schools faces challenges." *The New York Times.* http://www.nytimes.com/2009/06/02/education/02educ.html?pagewanted=1. Accessed 6-25-10.

Douglass-Hall, A., and Chau, M. (2007). *Basic facts about low-income children birth to age 18.* National Center for Children in Poverty, Columbia University Mailman School of Public Health.

Education Commission of the States. (2010). "Charter schools." http://www.ecs.org/html/issue.asp?issueID=20. Accessed 11-15-10.

Education Trust. (2010, January 6). *Gauging the gaps: A deeper look at student achievement.* Washington, D,C,: Rowan, A.H., Hall, D., and Haycock, K. http://

www.edtrust.org/sites/edtrust.org/files/publications/files/NAEP%20Gap_0.pdf. Accessed 6-26-10.

EduLead. (2008). *Louisiana school turnaround specialist program: LSTS communications plan*. Prepared for the Louisiana Department of Education. Richmond, VA: Temple Fairchild, T., DeMary, J., and Shields, T.

EduLead. (2008). *Louisiana school turnaround specialist program: LSTS blueprint. version 2*. Prepared for the Louisiana Department of Education. Richmond, VA: Fairchild, T., DeMary, J., and Shields, T.

EduLead. (2008). *Louisiana school turnaround specialist program: White paper*. Prepared for the Louisiana Department of Education. Richmond, VA: Fairchild, T., DeMary, J., and Shields, T.

Eldridge-Williams, A. (2009). *90-day strategic plan: The Kate Middleton way*. Documents provided by interviewee.

Elmore, R.F. (2004). "Conclusion: The problem of stakes in performance-based accountability systems." Fuhrman, S.H., and Elmore, R.F. (Eds.), *Redesigning accountability systems for education* (274–296). New York: Teachers College Press.

Everyone Graduates Center. (2007). *State summary table: Promoting power*. Baltimore, MD: Johns Hopkins University Everyone Graduates Center.

Fairfax County Public Schools. *School Profiles 2009–2010*. http://schoolprofiles.fcps.edu/schlprfl/f?p=108:13:163087688262752::::P0_CURRENT_SCHOOL_ID:100. Accessed 11-8-10.

Fairlie, R.W. (2005). "Are we really a nation online? Racial and ethnic disparities in access to technology and their consequences." *Report for the Leadership Conference on Civil Rights Education Fund*. Washington, D.C.

Freeman, R.E. (1984). *Strategic management: A stakeholder approach*. Boston, MA: Pitman.

Freeman, R.E., Velamuri, S., and Moriarty, B. (2006). *Company stakeholder responsibility: A new approach to CSR*. Charlottesville, VA: Business Institute for Corporate Ethics.

Fullan, M. (2006). *Turnaround leadership*. San Francisco: Jossey-Bass.

Fuhrman, S. (1993). "The Politics of Coherence." In S. Fuhrman (Ed.) *Designing coherent education policy: Improving the system* (1–34). San Francisco: Jossey-Bass.

Gediman, D., Gregory, J., and Gediman, M. (Eds.). (2009). *Edward R. Murrow's This I Believe: Selections from the 1950s Radio Series*. BookSurge Publishing.

Gibson, E., and Billings, A. (2003). "Best practices at Best Buy: A turnaround strategy." *Journal of Business Strategy* 24(6), 10–16.

Goleman, D., Boyatzis, R., and McKee, A. (2002). *Primal leadership: Realigning the power of emotional intelligence*. Boston: Harvard Business School Press.

Gordon, E.E. (2009, September). "The future of jobs and careers." *Techniques*. ACTE Online. http://www.acteonline.org/techniques.aspx. Accessed 11-10-10.

Halberstam, D. (1993). *The fifties*. New York: Villard Books.

Hargreaves, A, and Fink, D. (2006). *Sustainable leadership*. San Francisco: Jossey-Bass.

Harlem Children's Zone, Inc. (HCZ) *Growth Plan FY 2001–FY 2009*, Updated Fall 2003. http://www.hcz.org/images/stories/pdfs/business_plan.pdf. Accessed 9-22-10.

Hess, F.M. and Petrilli, M.J. (2008, December 23) "Bush the Hall Monitor." *National Review Online*. http://www.nationalreview.com/articles/226594/bush-hall-monitor/frederick-m-hess. Accessed 11-8-10.

High School for Violin and Dance. *New York City Department of Education 2005–2006 Progress Report (Draft): High School for Violin and Dance.*

High School for Violin and Dance. *New York City Department of Education 2008–2009 Progress Report: High School for Violin and Dance.*

High School for Violin and Dance. *School Comparison Report by subject for 2006–2009.*

https://p1pe.doe.virginia.gov/reportcard/report.do?division=29&schoolName=1369. Accessed 6-26-10.

http://www2.ed.gov/programs/racetothetop/index.html. Accessed 6-27-10.

http://www.nasbe.org/leadership/information by state/virginia/state-profile/case-study. Accessed 6-26-10.

http://achievementfirst.org. Accessed 6-26-10.

http://ausl-chicago.org/about.html. Accessed 6-26-10.

http://kipp.org. Accessed 6-26-10.

http://pages.cms.k12.nc.us/gems/eastmeck/SIPAll.pdf. Accessed 6-27-10.

http://projectimplicit.net/nosek. Accessed 6-26-10.

http://schools.nyc.gov/documents/offices/GT/TL/2009_GenEd_Grad_Card_FINAL.pdf. Accessed 11-7-10.

http://schools.nyc.gov/offices/empowerment/default.htm. Accessed 5-28-10.

http://schools.nyc.gov/SchoolPortals/09/X042/AboutUs/Statistics/register.htm. Accessed 6-2-10.

http://schools.nyc.gov/OA/SchoolReports/2008–09/Progress_Report_2009_EMS_X042.pdf. Accessed 8-17-10.

http://www.achievementfirst.org/about-us/history. Accessed 9-20-10.

http://www.archives.gov/research/vietnam-war/casualty-statistics.html. Accessed 9-17-09.

http://www.atlantapublicschools.us/18611010892250280/site/default.asp. Accessed 6-28-10.

http://www.broadprize.org/about/overview.html. Accessed 11-4-10.

http://www.broward.k12.fl.us/ease. Accessed 11-15-10.

http://www.census.gov/mso/www/pres_lib/2003Education/textmostly/slide15.html. Accessed 11-4-10.

http://www.census.gov/prod/2006pubs/p60–231.pdf (20) Accessed 9-17-09.

http://www.edreform.com Accessed 6-25-10.

http://www.emsc.nysed.gov/irts/accountability/highPerform/2009/RI_2008–09.pdf. Accessed 8-17-10.

http://www.emsc.nysed.gov/repcrd2005/information/elementary/guide.shtml. Accessed 6-7-10.

http://www.fwcs.k12.in.us/Home/BSC_DISTRICT_082508.pdf. Accessed 6-24-10.
http://www.greendot.org/news/article/green_dot_helping_schools_make_grade. Accessed 6-26-10.
http://www.greendot.org/about_us/school_model. Accessed 9-17-10.
http://www.greendot.org/green_dot039s_transformation_of_locke_high_school_yields_i-mpessive_retention_and_enrollment_rates. Accessed 9-17-10.
http://www.hcz.org/our-results/by-the-numbers. Accessed 9-22-10.
http://www.imentor.org/about-imentor. Accessed 6-1-10.
http://www.kipp.org/about-kipp/five-pillars. Accessed 9-22-10.
http://www.kipp.org/news/kipp-secures-10-million-in-matching-funds-for-federal-grant. Accessed 9-22-10.
http://www.leadlouisiana.net/index.asp. Accessed 6-27-10.
http://www.leadlouisiana.net/la_state_turnaround_specialist_program.asp. Accessed 6-27-10.
http://www.leadlouisiana.net/la_state_turnaround_specialist_program.asp. Accessed 6-27-10.
http://www.louisianaschools.net/LDE/bese/1081.html. Accessed 3-19-10.
http://nces.ed.gov/nationsreportcard/about/#overview. Accessed 11-4-10.
http://www.ncrel.org/sdrs/areas/issues/students/atrisk/at61k50a.htm. Accessed 6-24-10.
http://www.nlns.org/Foundations.jsp. Accessed 6-27-10.
http://www.nlns.org/Locations_NewOrleans.jsp#results. Accessed 6-27-10.
http://www.nlns.org/Program.jsp Accessed. 9-23-10.
http://www.nlns.org/Results.jsp Accessed. 9-23-10.
http://www.nlns.org/epic.jsp Accessed. 6-27-10.
http://www.nlns.org/epic.jsp#epicknowledge. Accessed 11-4-10.
http://www.npli.org/nsca/overview.html. Accessed 9-25-10.
http://www.nsrfharmony.org. Accessed 6-01-10.
http://www.nsrfharmony.org/protocol/learning_texts.html. Accessed 6-1-10.
http://www.nycleadershipacademy.org/overview/overview. Accessed 11-4-10.
http://www.nycleadershipacademy.org/knowledge/our-work. Accessed 11-3-10.
http://www.pbis.org. Accessed 9-27-10.
http://www.pbs.org/makingschoolswork/dwr/nc/pughsley.html. Interview. Accessed 6-26-10.
http://www.publiccharters.org/aboutschools/benefits. Accessed 11-3-10.
http://www.rsdla.net/InfoGlance/FAQs.aspx. Accessed 10-6-09.
http://www.schoolmatters.com. Accessed 9-10-07.
Hoxby, C.M., Murarka, S. and Kang, J. (2009, September). *How New York City's charter schools affect achievement, August 2009 report.* Second report in series. Cambridge, MA: New York City Charter Schools Evaluation Project.
Jefferson Parish Public School System (JPPSS) Accountability Department. *JPPSS District Composite Report.* (Compiled July 2010).
Joyce, P. (2004). "The role of leadership in the turnaround of a local authority." *Public Money & Management*, 24(4), 235–242.

JPPSS Accountability Department. (2009, February 2). *The Kate Middleton way: Data driven support materials.* Grade 3 iLEAP data, p. 2.
JPPSS Accountability Department. (2010, July 10). *iLEAP/LEAP/GEE Combined Archive Multiyear Summary Report 2005–2009.* Grade 4 iLEAP data.
Kaplan, R.S. and Miyake, D.N. (February 2010). "The balanced scorecard." *The School Administrator,* 67(2), 10–15.
Kaplan, R.S., and Norton, D.P. (1996). *The balanced scorecard: Translating strategy into action.* Boston: Harvard Business School Press.
Kate Middleton Elementary School. (2009). *90-day strategic plan: The Kate Middleton way.*
Kate Middleton Elementary School. (2010). *Dynamic indicators of basic early literacy skills (DIBELS) progress monitoring document.*
Kolderie, T. (1987). "Education that works: The right role for business." *Harvard Business Review* 65(5): 56–62.
Kotter, J.P. (1996). *Leading change.* Cambridge, MA: Harvard Business School Press.
Kotter, J.P. (1995). "Leading change: Why transformation efforts fail." *Harvard Business Review* 73(2): 19–27.
Kowal, J.M. and Hassel, E.A. (2005). *School restructuring options under No Child Left Behind: What works when? Turnarounds with new leaders and new staff.* The Center for Comprehensive School Reform and Improvement. http://www.centerforcsri.org/pubs/restructuring/KnowledgeIssues4Turnaround.pdf. Accessed 9-12-07.
Kozol, J. (1991). *Savage inequalities.* New York: Crown Publishers, Inc.
Kuhn, T. (1970). *The Structure of Scientific Revolutions.* Chicago: University of Chicago Press.
Kuhn, A. (1974). *The Logic of Social Systems.* San Francisco: Jossey-Bass.
Kutash, J., Nico, E., Gorin, E. ,Tallant, K., and Rahmatullah, S. (2010). *School turnarounds: A brief overview of the landscape and key issues.* Boston: FSG Social Impact Advisors. http://www.galeaders.org/site/documents/education_turnaround_brief.pdf. Accessed 9-19-10.
Lehman, I.J. (2004). The genesis of NAEP. In L.V. Jones and I. Olkin (Eds.). *The nation's report card: evolution and perspectives* (25–92). Bloomington, IN: Phi Delta Kappa Educational Foundation.
Lena Vern Dandridge, et al. vs. Jefferson Parish School Board, et al. United States District Court No. 14–801. http://www.jppss.k12.la.us/dandridge-information. Accessed 6-10-10.
Lencioni, P. (2002). *The five dysfunctions of a team: A leadership fable.* San Francisco: Jossey-Bass.
Liedtke, J., Fairchild, T., and Kelly, D. (2005). *J.E.B. Stuart high school.* Darden Case Collection. Charlottesville, VA: Darden Business Publishing. UVA-OB-0853.
Louisiana Department of Education. (2009). *2008–2009 Principal report card: Kate Middleton Elementary School.* Spring 2009 iLEAP Test—Performance by Achievement Level (3).

Louisiana Department of Education. (2009, April). *Bulletin 746. Item 710.* HISTORICAL NOTE: Promulgated by the Board of Elementary and Secondary Education, LR 35:645.

Louisiana Department of Education. *Bulletin 111. The Louisiana School, District and State Accountability System.*

Mann, D. (1987). "Business involvement and public school improvement." *Phi Delta Kappan* 69, 123–128 and 228–232.

Martorell, F., Heaton, P., Gates, S., and Hamilton, L. (2010, February). Preliminary findings from the New Leaders for New Schools Evaluation. (RAND Working Paper WR-739-NLNS.) Santa Monica, CA: RAND Corporation. http://www.rand.org/content/dam/rand/pubs/working_papers/2010/RAND_WR739.pdf. Accessed 3-21-11.

Mass Insight Education and Research Institute. (2007, March). *Considering school turnarounds: Market research and analysis.* Boston, MA.

Mass Insight Education & Research Institute. (2007). *The turnaround challenge: Why America's best opportunity to dramatically improve student achievement lies in our worst-performing schools.* Boston, MA.

Mead, S. (2007, Winter). "The easy way out: 'Restructured' usually means little has changed." *Education Next* 7(1). http://www.hoover.org/publications/ed-next/4612407.html. Accessed 10-30-07.

McKinsey and Company, Social Sector Office. (2009, April). *The economic impact of the achievement gap in America's schools.*

Mirel, J. (2001). *The evolution of New American Schools: From revolution to mainstream.* Thomas B. Fordham Foundation. http://www.edexcellence.net/doc/evolution.pdf. Accessed 6-27-10.

Mordaunt, J., and Cornforth, C. (2004). "The role of boards in the failure and turnaround of nonprofit organizations." *Public Money & Management* 24(4), 227–234.

Moynihan, A. (2002, October 11). "Outsourcing enables owner to focus on core business." *The Business Review* (Albany). http://www.bizjournals.com/albany/stories/2002/10/14/focus10.html. Accessed 6-26-10.

Murphy, J.F., and Meyers, C.V. (2008). *Turning around failing schools: Leadership lessons from the organizational sciences.* Thousand Oaks, CA: Corwin Press.

National Alliance for Public Charter Schools (2009). *Public Charter School Dashboard.* http://www.publiccharters.org/files/publications/DataDashboard.pdf. Accessed 6-28-10.

National Center on Education Statistics. *Enrollment in Postsecondary Institutions, Fall 2008; Graduation Rates, 2002 & 2005 Cohorts; and Financial Statistics, Fiscal Year 2008.* http://nces.ed.gov/pubs2010/2010152rev.pdf. Washington, D.C.: Knapp, L. G., Kelly-Reid, J. E., and Ginder, S. A. Accessed 11-3-10.

National Center on Response to Intervention (RTI). http://www.rti4success.org/index.php?option=com_frontpage&Itemid=1. Accessed 11-7-10.

National Commission on Excellence in Education. (1983). *A nation at risk: The imperative for educational reform: A report to the Nation and the Secretary of Education, United States Department of Education / by the National Commission on Excellence in Education.* The Commission: [Supt. of Docs., U.S. G.P.O. distributor], Washington, D.C. http://www2.ed.gov/pubs/NatAtRisk/index.html. Accessed 9-19-10.

National Governor's Association Center for Best Practices. (2008). *Implementing Graduation Counts; State Progress to Date, 2008.* Washington, D.C.

National Governor's Association Center for Best Practices (2009). *Achieving Graduation for All: A Guide to Dropout Prevention and Recovery.* Washington, D.C.: Princiotta, D. and Reyna, R.

National School Reform Faculty. (n.d.). "Why protocols?" http://www.plcwashington.org/study-groups/protocols/intoduction-to-protocols/why-protocols.pdf. Accessed 6-24-10.

New Leaders for New Schools. (2009). Principal Effectiveness: A New Principalship to Drive Student Achievement, Teacher Effectiveness, and School Turnaround with Key Insights from UEF.™ New York: New Leaders for New Schools.

New York City Department of Education. http://schools.nyc.gov/Accountability/resources/testing/default.htm#CT%20Regents. Accessed 11-4-10.

New York City Independent Budget Office. (2010, February). *Fiscal brief.*

The New York State School Report Card: Accountability and Overview Report 2008–2009. PS 42 Claremont. https://www.nystart.gov/publicweb-rc/2009/1e/AOR-2009–20900010042.pdf. Accessed 8-17-10.

Nolan, Norton, and Co. (1991). *Measuring performance in the organization of the future: A research study.* Lexington, MA. Executive Summary.

Nosek, B.A., and Hansen, J.J. (2008). "Personalizing the Implicit Association Test increases explicit evaluation of the target concepts." *European Journal of Psychological Assessment* 25: 226–236.

Pandit, N.R. (2000). "Some recommendations for improved research on corporate turnarounds." *Management* 3(2): 31–56.

Paton, R., and Mordaunt, J. (2004, August). "What's different about public and non-profit 'turnaround.'" *Public Money & Management* 24(4): 209–216.

Payne, R.K. (2005). *A framework for understanding poverty.* Highlands, TX: aha! Process, Inc.

Pearce, J.A., and Robbins, K.D. (1993). "Toward improved theory and research on business turnaround." *Journal of Management* 19(3): 613–636.

Petersen, J. (2007). "The brave new world of data-informed instruction." *Education Next.* Winter.

Pew Hispanic Center. Data and Resources: Unauthorized Immigrants in the U.S. http://pewhispanic.org/unauthorized-immigration. Accessed 11-8-10.

Pfeffer, J., and Sutton, R.I. (2000). *The knowing-doing gap.* Boston: Harvard Business School Press.

Porter, M.E. (1998). *Creating and sustaining superior performance.* New York: Free Press.

Preece, S. (2005). "The performing arts value chain." *International Journal of Arts Management* 8(1): 21–32.

Prince William County Schools. *Benton Middle School, 2008–2009 School Profile.* http://www.pwcs.edu/Departments/accountability/Profiles/Documents/Benton.pdf. Accessed 6-15-10.

Prince William County Schools. *Fred M. Lynn Middle School 2008–2009 School Profile.* http://www.pwcs.edu/Departments/accountability/Profiles/Documents/FredLynn.pdf. Accessed 6-15-10.

Public Impact. (2008a, June). *School turnaround leaders: Competencies for success. Part of the school turnaround collection from Public Impact.* Public Impact for the Chicago Public Education Fund. Chapel Hill, NC: Steiner, L.M., Hassel, E.A., Hassel, B., and Valsing, E. http://www.publicimpact.com/publications/Turnaround_Leader_Selection_Toolkit.pdf. Accessed 10-15-10.

Public Impact. (2008b, June). *School Turnaround Leaders: Selection toolkit. Part of the school turnaround collection from Public Impact.* Public Impact for the Chicago Public Education Fund. Chapel Hill, NC: Steiner, L.M., Hassel, E.A., and Hassel, B. Valsing, E., and Crittenden, S. http://www.publicimpact.com/publications/Turnaround_Leader_Selection_Toolkit.pdf. Accessed 10-15-10.

P.S. 42—Claremont Community School (2010, March 23). *Standardized test scores and reports for PS 42—Claremont 2000–2009.*

Rainwater Leadership Alliance (2010). *A New Approach to Principal Preparation: Innovative Programs Share Their Practices and Lessons Learned.* Fort Worth, TX: Cheney, G.R., Davis, J., Garrett, K., and Holleran, J.

Rampey, B.D., Dion, G.S., and Donahue, P.L. (2009). *NAEP 2008 Trends in Academic Progress* (NCES 2009–479). National Center for Education Statistics, Institute of Education Sciences, U.S. Department of Education, Washington, D.C.

Recovery School District Legislatively Required Plan. (2006, June 7). http://www.louisianaschools.net/lde/uploads/8932.doc. Accessed 9-20-10.

Reid, Z. (2009, February 2). "School thrives under principal's firm hand" *Richmond Times Dispatch.*

Roberto, M.A., and Levesque, L.C. (2005). "The art of making change initiatives stick." *Sloan Management Review* 46(4), 53–60.

Robbins, K.D., and Pearce, J.A. (1992). "Turnaround: Retrenchment and recovery." *Strategic Management Journal* 13(4): 287–309.

Sarrio, J. (2007, October 29). "Elite groups aid Tennessee schools in trouble: retirees are like a SWAT team of education law." *The Tennessean.* http://tennessean.com/apps/pbcs.dll/article?AID=/20071029. Accessed 10-31-07.

Schwartz, P. (1991). *The art of the long view: paths to the future in an uncertain world.* New York: Currency Doubleday.

Shapiro, T.M. (2004). *The hidden cost of being African-American: How wealth perpetuates inequality.* New York: Oxford University Press.

Slatter, S., Lovett, D., and Barlow, L. (2006). *Leading Corporate Turnarounds: How to Fix Troubled Companies.* San Francisco: Jossey-Bass.

Sluss, M. (2009, July 19). "Black students recount early days of integration." *The Roanoke Times.* http://www.roanoke.com/news/roanoke/wb/212343. Accessed 6-26-10.

Smrekar, C., Guthrie, J., Owens, D., and Sims, P. (2001). *March toward excellence: School success and minority student achievement in Department of Defense schools.* National Institute on Early Childhood Development and Education, Washington, D.C.

South Carolina Department of Education. Education Oversight Committee, Division of Accountability (2001). *Criteria and procedures for palmetto gold and silver program. State Statute 59-18-1100.*

Standard & Poor's. "Narrowing the achievement gap." www.SchoolMatters.com. Accessed 9-10-07.

Standard & Poor's. "Louisiana statewide education highlights 2004 data." www.SchoolMatters.com. Accessed 9-10-07.

Steele, C.M., and Aronson, J. (1995). "Stereotype threat and the intellectual test performance of African Americans." *Journal of Personality and Social Psychology* 69(5): 797.

Sum, A., Khatiwada, I., McLaughlin, J., and Palma, S. (2009). *The consequences of dropping out of high school: Joblessness and jailing for high school dropouts and the high cost for taxpayers.* Boston: Northeastern University. http://www.clms.neu.edu/publication/documents/The_Consequences_of_Dropping_Out_of_High_School.pdf. Accessed 9-19-10.

Tatum, B.D. (2003). *Why are all the black kids sitting together in the cafeteria: A psychologist explains the development of racial identity.* New York: Basic Books.

Tatum, B.D. (2007). *Can we talk about race? And other conversations in an era of school resegregation.* Boston: Beacon Press.

Taylor, D. (2005). "The Kate Middleton Elementary School: Portraits of hope and courage after Katrina." *A Supplement to Scholastic, Inc.* New York: Scholastic, Inc.

Thernstrom, A., and Thernstrom, S. (2003). *No excuses: Closing the racial gap in learning.* New York: Simon & Schuster.

Tough, P. (2008). *Whatever it takes: Geoffrey Canada's quest to change Harlem and America.* Boston: Houghton Mifflin and Company.

Turnaround Management Association. (n.d.). Overview of body of knowledge course content. http://www.turnaround.org/TMAccess/Materials.aspx. Accessed 11-4-10.

Turque, B. (2010, June 3). "D.C. teachers' union ratifies contract, basing pay on results, not seniority." *The Washington Post.* http://www.washingtonpost.com/wp-dyn/content/article/2010/06/02/AR2010060202762.html?sid=ST2010060202812. Accessed 9-22-10.

Tuttle, C.C., Teh, B., Nichols-Barrer, I., Gill, B.P., and Gleason, P. (2010). *Student characteristics and achievement in 22 KIPP middle schools.* Washington, D.C.: Mathematica Policy Research, Inc. http://www.mathematica-mpr.com/publications/pdfs/education/KIPP_fnlrpt.pdf. Accessed 11-8-10.

References

University of Virginia School Turnaround Specialist Program. (2010, March 15). *Annual Report Excerpts (2004–2008)*. http://www.darden.virginia.edu/web/uploadedFiles/Darden/Darden_Curry_PLE/UVA_School_Turnaround/UVASTSP AnnualReport2008_Excerpts.pdf. Accessed 11-3-10.

U.S. Census Bureau. *Zip Code Tabulation Data, 10456, Fact Sheet. Census 2000 Demographic Profile Highlights*. http://factfinder.census.gov/servlet. Accessed 6-3-10.

U.S. Census Bureau, Summary File 1 [SF 1] and Summary File 3 [SF 3] *American FactFinder Fact Sheet: Zip Code Tabulation Area 70053*. Accessed 6-10-10.

U.S. Census Bureau, Summary File 1 [SF 1] and Summary File 3 [SF 3]. *Fact Sheet: Zip Code Tabulation Area 10457*. Accessed 6-10-10.

U.S. Census Bureau, Census 2000 Summary File 1 [SF 1], *Matrix PCT11. QT-P9. Hispanic or Latino by Type: 2000*. Accessed 6-10-10.

U.S. Census Bureau, Summary File 1 [SF1] and Summary File 3 [SF3]. *Zip Code Tabulation Area 22191 and 20112*.

U.S. Dept. of Commerce, Bureau of the Census (2008). *Public education finances 2006*. U.S. Census Bureau. Table 17. http://www2.census.gov/govs/school/06f33pub.pdf. Accessed 11-7-10.

U.S. Department of Education Office of Elementary and Secondary Education. (2010, June). *Guidance on school improvement grants: Under section 1003(g) of the elementary and secondary education act of 1965*. http://www2.ed.gov/programs/sif/sigguidance05242010.pdf. Accessed 11-4-10.

U.S. Department of Education. (2010). "Support for Turning Around Low-Performing Schools." http://www.ed.gov/blog/2010/04/support-for-turning-around-low-performing-schools. Accessed 5-10-10.

U.S. Department of Education. (2010). "Voices from Turnaround Schools." http://www.ed.gov/blog/2010/05/voices-of-reform. Accessed 9-30-10.

U.S. Department of Education. (2010). "What's Possible: Turning Around America's Lowest-Achieving Schools." http://www.ed.gov/blog/2010/03/whats-possible-turning-around-americas-lowest-achieving-schools. Accessed 11-3-10.

U.S. National Center for Education Statistics. *Fast Facts 2007–2008*. http://nces.ed.gov/fastfacts/display.asp?id=84. Accessed 11-8-10.

Viadero, D. (2007, August 15). "Scholars reaching outside education for school fixes," *Education Week* 1: 17.

Viadero, D. (2009, October 2). "Race to the top said to lack key science." *Education Week*, vol. 6, p. 1, 18–19. http://www.edweek.org/ew/articles/2009/10/07/06research_ep.h29.html. Accessed 1-27-10.

Viadero, D. (2010, January 25) "Scholars identify five keys to urban school success." *Education Week*. Accessed 1-27-10.

Virginia Department of Education. *Fred M. Lynn Middle, Prince William County. Virginia Assessment Results for 2006–2007*. Customized Report. http://www.doe.virginia.gov/statistics_reports/school_report_card/index.shtml. Accessed 8-25-10.

Virginia Department of Education. *Fred M. Lynn Middle, Prince William County. School Level Report Card.* http://www.doe.virginia.gov/statistics_reports/school_report_card/index.shtml. Accessed 8-20-10.

von Bertalanffy, L. (1968). *General system theory: Foundations, developments, applications.* New York: Braziller.

Walshe, K., Harvey, G., Hyde, P., and Pandit, N. (2004). "Organizational failure and turnaround: Lessons for public services from the for-profit sector." *Public Money & Management* 24(4): 201–208.

Watkins, M. (2003). *The first 90 days.* Boston: Harvard Business Press.

Wheatley, M. (1992). *Leadership and the new science: Discovering order in a chaotic world.* First Edition. San Francisco, CA: Berrett-Koehler Publishers, Inc.

Zuckerman, E. (2010, January 27). School reform still evolving in New Haven. *Yale Daily News.* http://www.yaledailynews.com/news/city-news/2010/01/27/school-reform-still-evolving-new-haven. Accessed 11-10-10.

Index

Academy for Urban School Leadership (AUSL): turnaround model, 29, 33–35
accountability, 42, 49, 204; drop-out rate, 9–11, 15–16, 206; growth testing, 9; interim assessments, 29, 54, 93, 100, 117; metrics, 105–6, 217; technology and, 8–10; turnaround results, 138, 157–58, 174–76, 179. *See also* case studies
Achievement First, 27, 28–29, 34, 68
achievement gap, 8–12, 214–15; economic consequences of, 11–12, 16; McKinsey Report, 11–12; moral imperative, 4, 6, 12, 75
American Recovery and Reinvestment Act (ARRA), 11, 21, 23; approaches to turnaround, 22–23

balanced scorecard, 101, 111–14, 116, 136, 175; project management, 76, 107, 110, 112–14; sample, 242
Baldridge Performance Excellence Program, Quality Award, 107
Broad Foundation, Eli and Edythe, 34, 41; Broad Center, 34; Broad Prize, 41; Broad Superintendents Academy, 218
Broward County Public Schools, 71, 107; Enterprise Accountability System, 71
business/education interactions, 40–43

charter schools, 26–29, 34, 42, 68, 83, 213; definition, 26; Hoxby Study, 68
Chicago Public Education Fund, 34, 44, 85
coaching/mentoring support, 30–32, 102; case examples, 130–32, 154, 193
Coleman, J. Harrison, 56, 73, 84, 90, 95, 202, 213. *See also* Fred M. Lynn Middle School
communications plan, 101, 114–16; sample, 249
Council of Chief State School Officers, 10, 112
Council of the Great City Schools, 214, 222

data-informed decision making, 28, 92–93; case examples, 136, 152, 158, 167, 173, 188, 193

demand for turnaround, 21, 22, 99, 223; lack of supply, 22, 94, 99
district, role of, 64, 83–89
drop-out: factories, 9, 10, 205; rates, 9–11, 15–16, 206

Eldridge-Williams, Aretha, 73, 89, 109, 201, 213. *See also* Kate Middleton Elementary School
emerging leaders, 95
enabling conditions: autonomy/degrees of freedom, 86–87, 148, 152, 165, 191; incentives, 35, 88, 177, 191, 203, 208; Memorandum of Understanding (MOU), 85–87; more time, 27, 28, 50–51; resource realignment, 16, 83, 166; sample, 231
executive development programs, 32–34, 85, 94, 96–99, 209–11
expectations, role of, 14, 16, 27, 28, 31, 221, 223

Fred M. Lynn Middle School, 163–80; DASH-BYEs, 179; demographics, 163; developing the executive, 167–70; district support, 177; focusing on execution, 170–79; home-and-school connection, 170; preparing the environment, 165–67; results, 174–76, 179; sustainability, 179–80; Virginia School Turnaround Specialist Program, 164, 169; "Walking in J's Shoes," 168; "The Wrap," 173

Gates Foundation, Bill and Melinda, 41
Green Dot Public Schools, 27–28

Harlem Children's Zone, xi, 25–26; Canada, Geoffrey, xi, 25; Neighborhood Promise Grant program, 26; Promise Academy, 26
high performing, high poverty schools, 42, 57
High School for Violin and Dance, 181–97; demographics, 183–84; developing the executive, 186–88; empowerment school, 191, 193; focusing on execution, 188–97; National Academy for Excellent Teaching, 186; New York Leadership Academy, 182, 197; parent engagement, 191; preparing the environment, 184–86; protocols, 192; results, 194–95; student empowerment, 196; "The 3Ps," 188–89; "The 3Ss," 192–94; succession planning, 194–97; 37½ Minutes, 190

incentives. *See* enabling conditions

John, Tanya, 92, 202. *See also* High School for Violin and Dance

Kate Middleton Elementary School, 125–40; 90-day plan, 136, 138, 139; Dandridge Consent Decree, 139, 213; developing the executive, 130–32, 138; DIBELS, 136, 139; district shepherd, 135, 139; focus on execution, 132–40; Hurricane Katrina, 127–28; Louisiana School Turnaround Specialist Program, 135; parent and community involvement, 133–35; preparing the environment, 126–30; results, 138; "The Kate Middleton Way," 129–30; vision and mission, 129
Knowledge is Power Program (KIPP), 27, 34, 97, 213, 218; Mathematica Policy Research, Inc., 213

lessons learned, 220–22
Louisiana: Board of Elementary and Secondary Education (BESE), 24–25, 209–10; Board of Regents, 210, 218; Pastorek, Paul, 25, 210; Recovery School District (RSD), 24–25, 209
Louisiana School Turnaround Specialist Program, 33, 88, 95, 135, 209–10, 237

Mass Insight (MERI), 17, 21, 48, 55, 89, 212, 218, 222; turnaround zone, 25, 34, 51, 87, 103
Memorandum of Understanding (MOU). *See* enabling conditions
Microsoft Partners in Learning Program, xii, 32, 265

National Assessment of Educational Progress (NAEP), 4, 6–8, 11, 59
A Nation at Risk, 4, 6, 16, 40, 204, 227, 228
New Leaders for New Schools, 30–31, 84, 95, 209, 212, 217–18; Effective Practices Incentive Community, 31, 217
New Schools Venture Fund, 21, 29, 34, 35, 222
New York City Leadership Academy, 29–30, 34, 84, 95, 182, 197, 212, 218; Aspiring Principals Program, 30; Leadership Performance Planning Worksheet, 30, 218
90-day plan, 82, 99, 101, 108–10, 112, 221; sample, 244
No Child Left Behind, 6, 11, 16, 21, 204–5, 208, 219

Obama Administration, 14, 208; Race to the Top, 23, 50, 69, 208; Investing in Innovation (i3) grants, 27, 208

poverty, 11–12, 56–58, 125, 144, 163, 184, 215. *See also* race
project management. *See* balanced scorecard
P.S. 42–Claremont Community School, 143; demographics, 144; "design your own" status, 152; developing the executive, 151–53, 159; focusing on execution, 153–61; New York Leadership Academy, 146, 148, 161; parent support, 147–48; preparing the environment, 145–51; protocols, 151–52; results, 157–58; sense of urgency, 143; special education needs, 154–56; sustainability, 159; team-building for change, 146–47, 160–61
Public Education Leadership Project (PELP), Harvard's, 33, 96, 207
public impact, 32, 44, 84
public policy, 203; accelerators, 206–7; Federal, 4–6, 11, 21–24, 205–6, 215–20; recommendations, 215–19; school turnarounds, 205–6

race, 3, 58–61; desegregation, 5, 21, 211–14; implicit bias, 16, 60, 223; poverty, 59, 215; role of, 223; role of racial history, 4–6, 20–21, 92, 215, 224. *See also* achievement gap
Race to the Top. *See* Obama Administration
Rainwater Leadership Alliance, 218
recovery school district. *See* Louisiana
resources on school turnarounds, 43, 229
Riddile, Mel, 50–51, 211; Stuart High School, 51, 211

scaling up, 29, 215–20

school and community circumstances: community milieu, 91; community support, 73, 133; school setting, 90
school district. *See* district
selection criteria, 94; schools, 83; turnaround leaders, 84–85, 94–95
staff morale, 13, 91
stakeholders: communications, 48, 115–16; company stakeholder responsibility, 77; engagement, 51, 54, 74–76; internal and external, 54, 109, 112; primary and secondary, 78
state, role of, 83–89, 209–11
strategic support, 103–4; community stakeholders, 104–5; shepherds, 89, 97
succession planning, 55, 96, 222, 223; dual-track program, 98; successors, 95–96
sustainability, 44, 54–56, 223. *See also* case studies
systems, 69–73; change, 17, 51, 69; influences, 69–70; theory, 71–72

Taylor, Rosalind, 212, 213; Woodville Elementary School, 212
Teach for America, 34, 149, 152, 159, 222
teacher contracts, 208–9; union, 14, 41, 66, 78, 208. *See also* stakeholders
3Es framework, 81–106; developing the executive, 93–99; focusing on execution, 99–106; preparing the environment, 82–93
TIMMS, 4
triage: diagnosis, 45, 49–50; quick wins, 13, 82, 90, 99, 101; sense of urgency, 15–16, 31, 78, 113
turnaround credential, 32

turnaround leadership endorsement, 33, 87, 99; Louisiana's turnaround specialist endorsement, 88, 210, 237–38
Turnaround Management Association (TMA), 43–44, 53, 219; "Body of Knowledge," 44, 53; Certified Turnaround Professionals (CTP), 43, 219
turnaround professionals, 17, 33, 97, 104–5, 207; network, 32, 102, 211
Turnaround Readiness Sequence, 207; sample, 251
turnaround value chain, 115, 117–21, 221; influencers, 119–20; influences, 117–18
turnaround zone. *See* Mass Insight
2-S model for approaching turnarounds, 65–79. *See also* stakeholders; systems
typology of turnaround approaches, 23–35; human capital, 29–35; structural, 24–29

University of Virginia Darden/Curry Partnership for Leaders in Education, 32–34
urgency. *See* triage

Virginia School Turnaround Specialist Program, xi–xii, 32–33, 84, 88, 90, 112, 169, 212
vision, 70; case examples, 129, 146, 153, 171, 194

Wallace Foundation, xii, 34, 94, 218, 222; Executive Leadership Program, 33, 34
Wallin, Camille, 90, 201. *See also* P.S. 42–Claremont Community School
Warner, Mark, ix–x, 32, 88, 208

About the Authors

TIERNEY TEMPLE FAIRCHILD, PhD

Dr. Tierney Temple Fairchild is a consultant and writer specializing in executive leadership and policy issues in education, race and equity, and turnarounds. As president of Fairchild Partners, Inc., Tierney consults with national and regional organizations, state agencies, private foundations, and leading nonprofits.

Dr. Fairchild has over ten years of private sector experience in human resources, executive development, corporate contributions, and community relations. Her cross-sector work began at United Technologies, where she designed and implemented a strategic K-12 education reform initiative for the CEO and Board of Directors. Dr. Fairchild has extensive media experience, and her writing has been published in leading newspapers.

She was the founding executive director of the Darden/Curry Partnership for Leaders in Education at the University of Virginia and has been a visiting lecturer at both Darden and Curry, where she taught and published articles and business case studies. Tierney has designed and delivered a portfolio of executive development experiences for districts, school boards, and principals that focus on building leadership capacity to improve and sustain student achievement. She also led the development of Governor Warner's Virginia School Turnaround Specialist Program and, with the Commonwealth, was awarded a $3 million grant from Microsoft Partners in Learning to scale the program nationally.

Tierney earned her PhD in education leadership and policy studies at the Curry School, University of Virginia; her MBA from the Darden School, University of Virginia; and her BA in English at the University of Pennsylvania. She lives in Charlottesville, Virginia, with her husband, Greg, and three children, Naia, Cole, and Jude.

JO LYNNE DeMARY, EdD

Dr. Jo Lynne DeMary currently serves as professor of Education and Director of the Center for School Improvement at Virginia Commonwealth University (VCU). Through this center, she seeks to partner with states, districts, and schools to bring best practices into the classroom. Through a partnership between VCU and the University of Richmond, she and Dr. Tom Shields founded and serve as codirectors of EduLead, which provides a continuum of supports for aspiring and early career principals.

Dr. DeMary has over forty years of experience in public education as a teacher, assistant principal, principal, elementary school supervisor, director of special education, and assistant superintendent of instruction. She has the distinction of being the first woman to serve as state superintendent. She was appointed to the position by then-Governor Jim Gilmore in 2000 and reappointed to a four-year term by Governor Mark Warner in 2002.

Jo Lynne was honored by the United Negro College Fund as a 2007 Flame Bearer of Education. In 2006, she received the YWCA's Outstanding Woman's Award in Education. VCU has honored her with the Alumni Star Award, and Dr. DeMary has received the outstanding educational leadership alumni award from the William and Mary School of Education, an award that has subsequently been renamed in her honor.

Dr. DeMary earned her bachelor's degree and her doctorate from the College of William and Mary. She received her master's degree from VCU. Dr. DeMary resides in Midlothian, VA. She is the proud mother of son John DeMary and daughter Stephanie Hicks and blessed to be the grandmother of Dylan and Jason Hicks.